The History of Austria

Crafted by Skriuwer

At **Skriuwer**, we're more than just a team—we're a global community of people who love books. In Frisian, "Skriuwer" means "writer," and that's at the heart of what we do: creating and sharing books with readers worldwide. Wherever you are in the world, **Skriuwer** is here to inspire learning.

Frisian is one of the oldest languages in Europe, closely related to English and Dutch, and is spoken by about **500,000 people** in the province of **Friesland** (Fryslân), located in the northern Netherlands. It's the second official language of the Netherlands, but like many minority languages, Frisian faces the challenge of survival in a modern, globalized world.

We're using the money we earn to promote the Frisian language.

For more information, contact : **kontakt@skriuwer.com** (www.skriuwer.com)

Disclaimer:
The images in this book are creative reinterpretations of historical scenes. While every effort was made to accurately capture the essence of the periods depicted, some illustrations may include artistic embellishments or approximations. They are intended to evoke the atmosphere and spirit of the times rather than serve as precise historical records.

TABLE OF CONTENTS

Chapter 1: Early Settlements And Prehistoric Austria

- *Origins in Paleolithic and Mesolithic sites*
- *Transition to agriculture during the Neolithic*
- *Rise of Bronze and Iron Age cultures (Hallstatt)*
- *Archaeological insights and legacy*

Chapter 2: The Influence Of The Celts And The Arrival Of The Romans

- *Celtic expansions and oppida settlements*
- *Integration into Roman provinces like Noricum*
- *Roman infrastructure: roads, cities, fortified frontiers*
- *Cultural blending and enduring Roman legacy*

Chapter 3: The Early Middle Ages And The Rise Of Bavarian Rule

- *Post-Roman migrations: Germanic and Slavic groups*
- *Bavarian influence and the establishment of local duchies*
- *Christianization and monastic foundations*
- *Seeds of later dynastic power*

Chapter 4: The Babenberg Dynasty And The Formation Of A March

- *Imperial appointment of margraves*
- *Borders, fortifications, and settlement growth*
- *Economic and social structures under Babenbergs*
- *Cultural ties and emergence of "Ostarrîchi"*

Chapter 5: Expansion Under The Later Babenbergs

- *Capture of King Richard the Lionheart and impact of the ransom*
- *Territorial gains in Styria and beyond*
- *Court culture, religious patronage, and urban development*
- *Growing tension with neighboring powers*

Chapter 6: The Emergence Of The Habsburg Dynasty

- *Defeat of Bohemia and the rise of Rudolph I*
- *Securing Austrian core lands*
- *Administrative and dynastic consolidation*
- *Foundations of Habsburg prestige in Europe*

Chapter 7: Austria Under The Late Middle Ages

- *Interplay of feudalism and emerging central authority*
- *Impact of the Black Death on society and economy*
- *Dynastic and local power struggles*
- *Origins of a strong court culture*

Chapter 8: The Early Modern Period And Religious Turmoil

- *Reformation challenges and Counter-Reformation efforts*
- *Rise of Protestant estates and Catholic response*
- *Consolidation of Habsburg rule through military conflicts*
- *Economic and cultural developments under shifting alliances*

Chapter 9: The Ottoman Wars And Territorial Adjustments

- *Long Turkish War and defense of Austrian frontiers*
- *Key battles at Vienna and later Great Turkish War*
- *Treaty of Karlowitz and Habsburg expansion*
- *Cultural impact of border tensions*

Chapter 10: The Baroque Era And Rise Of Imperial Culture

- *Grand architectural projects and courtly life*
- *Religious fervor and Baroque spirituality*
- *Growing artistic achievements in music and fine arts*
- *Patronage networks and centralized governance*

Chapter 11: The Age Of Maria Theresa And Enlightenment Reforms

- War of the Austrian Succession and preservation of Habsburg lands
- Administrative centralization and social legislation
- Religious conservatism versus Enlightenment ideas
- Foundations for further transformations under her successors

Chapter 12: Joseph II And The Quest For Modernization

- Radical Enlightened Absolutism
- Religious toleration edicts and monastic suppressions
- Administrative unification and serf reforms
- Resistance and partial rollback of Josephinist policies

Chapter 13: The Napoleonic Era & The Reshaping Of Europe

- Defeats at Austerlitz and Wagram
- Dissolution of the Holy Roman Empire (1806)
- Creation of the Austrian Empire under Francis I
- War fatigue and eventual role in Napoleon's downfall

Chapter 14: The Metternich System & The Austrian Empire

- Congress of Vienna and conservative restoration
- Concert of Europe and intervention policies
- Suppression of national movements through Carlsbad Decrees
- Rise of liberalism and brewing internal tensions

Chapter 15: The Revolutions Of 1848 And Their Aftermath

- Metternich's fall and Vienna's upheaval
- National revolutions in Bohemia, Hungary, and Italy
- Military suppression and neoabsolutist restoration
- Seeds of future constitutional developments

Chapter 16: Austria-Hungary And The Dual Monarchy

- *Consequences of defeats in Italy and Germany*
- *The Ausgleich (Compromise of 1867) establishing dual structure*
- *Separate parliaments, shared ministries, and economic union*
- *Unresolved national issues and evolving political landscape*

Chapter 17: The Late 19th Century And Growth Of National Tensions

- *Industrialization, social transformations, and urban growth*
- *National rivalries intensify in Bohemia, Galicia, and the South Slavs*
- *Moderate reforms vs. persistent ethnic demands*
- *Austria-Hungary's focus on Balkan ambitions*

Chapter 18: The Road To World War I

- *Alliance with Germany and rivalry with Serbia*
- *Annexation of Bosnia-Herzegovina (1908) and crises*
- *Rising nationalism, labor unrest, and leadership changes*
- *Assassination at Sarajevo triggering global conflict*

Chapter 19: Austria During World War I

- *Initial campaigns vs. Serbia and on the Eastern Front*
- *Mounting hardships on the home front and national frictions*
- *Losses on the Italian Front and reliance on German support*
- *Death of Emperor Franz Joseph and Karl I's final attempts*

Chapter 20: Conclusion And Overview Of Post-War Shifts

- *Collapse of the monarchy and emergence of successor states*
- *Treaty of Saint-Germain defining Austria's new borders*
- *Legacy of Habsburg rule and the new Austrian Republic*
- *Reflections on centuries of Austrian history leading to 1918*

CHAPTER 1: EARLY SETTLEMENTS AND PREHISTORIC AUSTRIA

Introduction

Austria's history goes back thousands of years, long before written records. The land that now forms Austria sits in Central Europe. With its mountains, valleys, and rivers, it offered early humans both challenges and opportunities. In this chapter, we will explore the earliest settlements, the environment these communities encountered, and the ways they adapted to survive. We will also examine the sources we use to study these prehistoric societies, including archaeological findings, cave art, and the remnants of their tools.

1.1 The Geographic Setting

Austria is located in the eastern part of the Alps. This mountainous region has many valleys, lakes, and rivers. The Danube River is one of the most important waterways, flowing from west to east across a portion of what is now Austria. The landscape varies widely: in the west and southwest, the mountains soar to high peaks, while the eastern parts open into plains and rolling hills. This diverse geography allowed different types of prehistoric communities to develop, from mountain hunters to valley farmers.

During the last Ice Age, much of the region was covered by glaciers or was too cold for widespread settlement. However, as the climate warmed, glaciers receded, and more land became available for human habitation. This new environment supported various forms of wildlife, including deer, wild boar, and other animals that served as sources of food.

1.2 Paleolithic Presence

The earliest evidence of human activity in the region of Austria dates to the Paleolithic period, or Old Stone Age. During this time, humans were nomadic hunter-gatherers. They followed herds of animals, searching for favorable conditions. Caves and rock shelters in the mountainous areas might have served as temporary homes. Archaeologists have discovered stone tools, such as scrapers and spear points, that show these groups hunted animals and processed their skins and meat.

One notable site is the Repolust Cave in Styria, which reveals traces of human use from tens of thousands of years ago. Remnants like stone flakes and animal bones tell us that early humans had adapted to a cool climate and made use of whatever resources they could find. Because they moved frequently, they left only scattered artifacts. As a result, our picture of life in Paleolithic Austria is incomplete but still very meaningful.

1.3 Mesolithic Adaptations

After the last Ice Age ended, around 10,000 BCE, the climate became milder, and the environment changed. This period is known as the Mesolithic, or Middle Stone Age. Forests spread, and game like deer and wild boar thrived. People in this period still hunted and gathered, but they might have shifted to smaller territories because local resources were now richer. The Mesolithic inhabitants probably fished in lakes and rivers and collected fruits, nuts, and other plants in the forests.

Archaeologists have found microliths, which are small stone tools, characteristic of this era. These were often used as tips for arrows or barbs for fishing spears. In some regions, evidence of pit houses or semi-permanent camps suggests that groups might have stayed in one place for longer periods. However, we still do not see large, permanent settlements in Austria at this time.

1.4 Neolithic Revolution and Agricultural Beginnings

A major change happened during the Neolithic period, starting around 5,500 BCE in Central Europe. People began to domesticate plants and animals, giving rise to farming communities. This shift, often called the Neolithic Revolution, allowed for more stable food supplies. As a result, populations grew, and permanent settlements started to appear. The Danube corridor was an important route for the spread of new ideas, such as crop cultivation and animal husbandry, from regions further east.

In Austria, archaeological sites from this period show the presence of the Linear Pottery Culture, named after their distinctive pottery decorations. These farming communities grew cereals like wheat and barley and kept domesticated animals such as cattle, sheep, and goats. Over time, settlements expanded in the fertile valleys. Houses were typically built of wood and mud, with thatched roofs. Such communities often had storage pits for grains and possibly communal areas for gatherings and rituals.

1.5 Tools and Pottery

During the Neolithic, tool technology advanced. Stone axes, adzes, and chisels became more refined, allowing farmers to clear forests for fields. Pottery making became a key skill, serving for cooking, storing, and trading. Some of this pottery is decorated with simple linear or geometric designs. These artifacts help us understand social connections, as similar pottery styles suggest cultural links between different groups.

These new farming and crafting skills changed social structures. There might have been specialized roles, like potters, stone workers, or those who oversaw communal storage. With stable food supplies, communities could support more complex social organization. Surplus produce could be exchanged with neighboring villages, leading to early trade networks.

1.6 Megaliths and Ritual Practices

Although Austria is not as famous for megalithic monuments as other parts of Europe, there are some stone structures and burial mounds that point to collective rituals and community practices. The burial traditions from this period show varying degrees of complexity. Some communities buried their dead in single graves, while others used collective burial sites. Grave goods, like pottery and stone tools, indicate belief systems that recognized some form of afterlife or spiritual realm.

By studying these sites, archaeologists gain insight into the social hierarchies of the time. Burials with more elaborate goods might suggest that certain families or individuals held higher status. However, the full extent of social stratification in Neolithic Austria remains a matter of ongoing research.

1.7 Chalcolithic Transition

As the Neolithic progressed, metalworking started to emerge, marking the transition to the Chalcolithic, or Copper Age. Copper was initially rare and mainly used for ornaments or prestige items rather than tools. Wooden or stone tools were still more practical for everyday tasks. Yet the introduction of metal shaped new trade routes. The Alps contained mineral resources, including salt and some metal ores, which became valuable commodities.

Communities along the Salzach and Inn rivers, for example, might have engaged in early salt mining or trading. Salt was vital, serving as a preservative for food and as an important resource for trade and economic exchange. These developments laid the groundwork for later Bronze Age cultures.

1.8 The Bronze Age in Early Austria

The Bronze Age began around 2,300 BCE in Central Europe. People learned to alloy copper with tin, making a stronger metal. Bronze tools and weapons became widespread. This led to improvements in agriculture, crafts, and warfare. In Austria, the Bronze Age is often associated with hillforts and fortified settlements, as well as burial mounds. These settlements were sometimes located on hilltops for defense. Archaeological evidence shows that communities engaged in metalworking and long-distance trade, possibly exchanging amber and other valuable goods with distant regions.

One key site from the Early Bronze Age is in the area of Lower Austria. Grave goods, including pottery and bronze artifacts, show that these people valued metal items. The existence of more elaborate metal objects, such as swords and decorative pins, points to a society with some degree of social ranking. Some individuals or families had the means to acquire or produce expensive metal goods, indicating emerging elites.

1.9 Salzberg and the Importance of Salt

In the heart of the Austrian Alps, places like Hallstatt in Upper Austria rose to prominence during the Bronze and Early Iron Ages. The name "Hallstatt" itself has become synonymous with a key cultural phase. Hallstatt had rich salt mines, which provided valuable trade goods. Salt was critical for preserving meats, fish, and other foods in a time before refrigeration. This gave communities near salt deposits an economic advantage. The surplus they gained from salt trade might have fueled the growth of more hierarchical societies.

As trade networks expanded, people in Austria had increased contact with regions like the Mediterranean and the Balkans. Artifacts from distant lands—fine pottery, jewelry, and weapons—have been found in Austrian grave sites from this period. These items underscore the importance of Austria as a crossroads for trade routes stretching across Europe.

1.10 Early Iron Age and the Hallstatt Culture

Around 800 BCE, the use of iron became more common in Central Europe, ushering in what is often referred to as the Early Iron Age. The Hallstatt Culture (about 800–500 BCE) is one of the most important cultural complexes in prehistoric Europe. It covered a broad area, but the discovery of significant burial sites in the Hallstatt region gave the culture its name.

These burial sites include both simple cremation burials and elaborate inhumation graves with grave goods of iron swords, spears, and even wagons. Some of the burials show that these communities had contact with the Mediterranean world, as indicated by imported luxury items, such as Greek pottery. The presence of chieftain-like figures is suggested by richly furnished graves, including gold and bronze ornaments. This points to a structured society with tribal leaders or kings who held considerable power.

1.11 Economic and Social Structures

During the Hallstatt period, society in what is now Austria seems to have become more complex. Farming continued to be the backbone of life, but iron tools made agricultural tasks easier, allowing for larger harvests. Increased production could support larger populations and more specialized craftspeople. Iron smelting required knowledge of ores, charcoal, and furnace construction. This specialized knowledge likely contributed to new social stratifications. Skilled metalworkers were important to the community, as they produced weapons and tools that gave certain groups military and economic advantages.

Trade routes expanded further during this period. Amber from the Baltic, tin from distant regions, and luxury goods from the Mediterranean made their way through the Alpine passes. Powerful local leaders possibly controlled these routes, collecting tribute or taxes from merchants passing through. This role as a trade intermediary would remain significant for Austria's location in Europe throughout its later history.

1.12 Religion and Ritual Life

It is challenging to reconstruct the exact religious beliefs of these prehistoric communities, as they left no written records. However, burial rites and the goods found in graves suggest a strong focus on ancestor veneration and possibly a polytheistic set of beliefs. Some archaeological sites have been interpreted as sanctuaries where people might have offered animals or valuable items to deities associated with nature, fertility, or warfare. Artifacts such as figurines might have represented gods, spirits, or revered ancestors.

Ritual feasting could have also played a role. Large communal gatherings for feasts or celebrations might have served both religious and social functions, reinforcing community ties and the authority of local leaders. The building of burial mounds or the placement of precious goods in graves could have been part of attempts to secure the favor of the gods or spirits, ensuring the health of crops and the continuation of community prosperity.

1.13 Shifts Toward the Late Iron Age

By around 500 BCE, new cultural influences were spreading across the region. The La Tène Culture, associated with the Celts, began to overlap and, in some areas, replace the Hallstatt Culture. The Celts would play a major role in shaping the future of Austria, as we will explore in the next chapter. However, the foundation for that transformation was laid in the prehistoric societies we have just described. They had established agriculture, trade routes, social hierarchies, and certain religious and cultural practices that would continue to evolve.

1.14 The Role of Warfare

Warfare was likely a reality for prehistoric communities, particularly as competition for resources grew. The building of hillforts suggests the need for defense, and the presence of weapons in graves points to warrior elites. Control of valuable resources, such as salt or metal ores, might have led to conflicts. Warriors who excelled in battle could rise to influential positions, further shaping the social structure.

Yet, conflict was not the only source of change. Alliances and trade agreements also played key roles in shaping regional politics. Over time, local chieftains could amass larger networks of alliances, possibly leading to the formation of tribal confederations. These would set the stage for the Celtic expansions that follow in the coming centuries.

1.15 Cultural Continuity and Change

While archaeology provides snapshots of different time periods, it is important to note the continuity in material culture, settlement patterns, and traditions. Some practices, such as burying the dead in mounds or using certain styles of pottery, continued for generations, although they might be adapted to new influences. Each generation inherited skills and beliefs from their ancestors, even as they adopted new ideas through trade and contact with neighboring regions.

These prehistoric societies built the roots of Austria's cultural identity long before there was any concept of an "Austrian" people. Their interactions with the environment, the establishment of trade networks, and the formation of social hierarchies all contributed to a landscape ready for the transformations that would come with the Celts and, later, the Romans.

1.16 Legacy of Prehistoric Austria

The sites left by prehistoric communities form an important part of Austria's cultural heritage. Many archaeological finds are displayed in museums, where they provide insight into daily life thousands of years ago. Some of the locations, such as Hallstatt, are UNESCO World Heritage Sites, recognized for their outstanding cultural value. These sites attract researchers from around the world, eager to piece together the story of prehistoric Austria.

The significance of salt mining at Hallstatt, for example, goes beyond economics. It tells a story of how a resource could shape an entire community's prosperity, social structure, and external relations. The region's importance for trade would carry on into later historical periods, confirming that prehistoric developments had lasting impacts.

CHAPTER 2: THE INFLUENCE OF THE CELTS AND THE ARRIVAL OF THE ROMANS

By the 5th century BCE, Austria's prehistoric societies were undergoing significant changes. The Celts, a group of tribal societies that spread across much of Europe, began to dominate the cultural landscape. Their ironworking skills, social organization, and warfare tactics left a strong mark on Central Europe. Over the next several centuries, Celtic tribes came to inhabit vast areas of what is now Austria, influencing language, trade, and daily life. This chapter will explore how Celtic culture shaped the region, leading up to the arrival of the Romans in the 1st century BCE. We will see how the Alpine lands became part of the Roman Empire, introducing roads, cities, and a new administrative system that would last for hundreds of years.

2.1 The Expansion of the Celts

The Celts were not a single kingdom or nation but rather a collection of tribes bound by similar languages, art styles, and cultural practices. Originating in Central Europe, the Celts expanded in multiple directions. Their La Tène Culture, which developed around 500 BCE, showed advances in ironworking, pottery, and artistic expression. Austria, with its resources and strategic positions along trade routes, attracted these tribes.

Several Celtic groups settled in different parts of the region. They established hillforts and oppida—large fortified settlements that sometimes served as regional centers. These oppida could hold thousands of inhabitants and often featured workshops, storage facilities, and areas for trade. The Celtic presence led to the decline of some earlier cultural practices, yet there was also continuity as the Celts adopted certain local traditions.

2.2 Celtic Society and Economy

Celtic society was hierarchical but varied from tribe to tribe. A warrior aristocracy often controlled land and resources. Skilled craftsmen produced iron tools, weapons, jewelry, and decorative items that displayed a distinctive curvilinear art style. Trade played a big role in Celtic life. They exported items like salt, copper, and iron, receiving in return luxury goods from distant regions.

Agriculture remained essential. The Celts grew cereals, raised livestock, and exploited resources like wood from the dense forests. Land ownership was typically tied to elite families, and competition for resources could lead to inter-tribal conflicts. Over time, some Celtic chieftains became very powerful, possibly controlling several oppida and forging alliances that extended far beyond one valley or region.

2.3 Religion and Rituals among the Celts

The Celts practiced a polytheistic religion, with gods linked to natural elements—rivers, trees, and mountains. Certain sites were deemed sacred, and Druids played a vital role as religious leaders, judges, and keepers of cultural lore. However, what we know about the Druids mainly comes from Roman and later sources, which can be biased.

Ritual offerings included weapons, jewelry, and even the remains of animals or, in rare cases, humans. These offerings were made in rivers, lakes, or specially designated sanctuaries. Seasonal festivals might have been observed to mark planting and harvesting or to celebrate important events in the community's cycle of life. The cultural emphasis on warrior status also influenced religious practices, with some rituals possibly focused on gaining the favor of war deities.

2.4 The Noricum Kingdom

One of the most influential Celtic confederations in the area of present-day Austria was Noricum. The Kingdom of Noricum encompassed parts of Austria and beyond, serving as a major center for iron production. The high quality of Noric steel was well-known throughout the ancient world. Noric swords were prized by many, including the Romans.

The Kingdom of Noricum traded extensively with neighboring regions. They formed political alliances and maintained relatively stable societies that featured oppida, such as the one at Magdalensberg in Carinthia. Over time, Noricum established closer relations with the Roman Republic, which was expanding northward. These ties led to an exchange of goods, culture, and technology, paving the way for a more peaceful Roman takeover later on.

2.5 Rome's Northern Push

While the Celts maintained dominance in the region for centuries, the power dynamics began to shift as the Roman Republic grew. By the 2nd century BCE, Roman armies had expanded into southern Gaul (modern-day France) and were eyeing the Alps. Rome's interest in the region was not purely military. They recognized the wealth in metals, salt, and other resources. Additionally, controlling the Alpine passes would give them easier access to lands further north and east.

One of Rome's strategies was to build roads to facilitate trade and military movement. They also sometimes formed treaties or alliances with local Celtic rulers. In many cases, these local leaders found it advantageous to cooperate with the Romans, as it brought trade benefits and security against rival tribes.

2.6 The Incorporation of Noricum into the Roman World

Noricum became a Roman client state in the 1st century BCE. The kingdom still had local rulers, but they acknowledged Roman supremacy. This arrangement proved beneficial for both sides: Rome gained access to Noric iron and other resources, while Noricum gained protection and a ready market for its goods. Over time, this partnership grew, and by 16 BCE, Noricum was formally incorporated into the Roman Empire under Emperor Augustus, becoming a province.

The transition was relatively peaceful compared to other conquests. Roman legions moved in to establish garrisons, but large-scale conflicts seemed minimal, possibly due to existing alliances. Under Roman rule, Noricum enjoyed a degree of autonomy in local governance, as long as taxes were paid and Roman interests were safeguarded.

2.7 Roman Provinces in the Alpine Region

Besides Noricum, other Roman provinces emerged in the Alpine region, such as Raetia and Pannonia. Parts of present-day Austria fell into these administrative units. The boundaries changed over time as Rome reorganized its provinces. Each province was governed by a Roman official (either a governor or prefect) who reported to the Emperor. The Roman administration introduced a new legal system, taxation, and infrastructure projects, including roads, bridges, and aqueducts.

Cities grew around Roman military camps and trade centers. Places like Vindobona (the site of modern Vienna) began as Roman fortresses, strategically located near the Danube River. The Romans recognized the Danube as a frontier against tribes to the north, so they fortified it, establishing the Limes—a system of forts and watchtowers along the river.

2.8 Roman Infrastructure and Urban Life

One of the most lasting influences of Roman rule was the development of urban centers. Roads, often paved with stone, connected major cities. This allowed for faster military deployment but also boosted trade and cultural exchange. The Romans built public buildings, baths, amphitheaters, and temples. Local elites often adopted Roman customs, wearing togas and speaking Latin in official contexts. Over time, a Romanized culture merged with local traditions.

Vindobona, Carnuntum (near present-day Petronell-Carnuntum), and other settlements became lively hubs of commerce and governance. At Carnuntum, archaeologists have uncovered remains of a significant city complete with a forum, public baths, and a gladiator school. The spread of Roman law and administrative practices made these cities centers of activity, drawing in merchants, artisans, and farmers from surrounding rural areas.

2.9 Economic Transformations under Rome

Roman incorporation brought new trade opportunities. The empire was vast, stretching from Britain to Egypt. Goods from across this expanse could be found in Austrian cities. Wine from Italy, olive oil from the Mediterranean, spices from the East, and pottery from Africa arrived via well-established routes. Local products such as metalwork, grain, and livestock were exported in return.

Roman coinage replaced barter and earlier forms of currency, further integrating the region into the empire's economy. Mines in the Alpine regions produced not only iron but also lead, copper, and even gold in some areas. Salt continued to be a major export. With strong infrastructure and relative peace, many towns thrived, though taxation and military duties could be burdensome for some communities.

2.10 Cultural and Religious Changes

As Roman power grew, local Celtic gods and customs blended with Roman deities and festivals. Many Celtic deities were equated with Roman gods. Religious syncretism was common throughout the empire. Temples that combined Celtic and Roman elements are found across the provinces. The Roman pantheon of Jupiter, Mars, and Minerva merged with native gods associated with local springs, forests, or mountain peaks.

Latin became the official language for administration, though local dialects and Celtic languages persisted, especially in rural areas. Over time, a Gallo-Roman culture emerged in many parts of the province. Monuments, inscriptions, and works of art show this cultural blend. Some local nobility sought Roman citizenship to gain privileges. This process contributed to the gradual Romanization of the region.

2.11 Military Presence and Border Defense

The presence of the Roman legions in Austria was significant. The Danube formed a major segment of Rome's frontier, requiring fortifications to defend against Germanic tribes. Places like Carnuntum served as legionary bases, hosting thousands of soldiers. These soldiers influenced local life: they demanded supplies, provided security, and sometimes settled in the area after retirement.

Veteran settlements often sprang up around legionary camps. Retired soldiers received land grants as a reward for service. These settlements promoted the spread of Roman culture and loyalty to the empire. A stable military presence also boosted the local economy, as merchants catered to the needs of the legions.

2.12 Daily Life in Roman Austria

Archaeological discoveries—such as pottery, household items, and inscriptions—give us glimpses of daily life under Roman rule. People lived in stone or wooden houses, depending on their status and means. Villas, or country estates, existed in rural areas, complete with heated floors (hypocaust systems) and private baths. In the cities, public baths were social centers, where people of various backgrounds mingled.

Markets sold grain, vegetables, meat, and wine, reflecting both local produce and imports from the wider empire. Local artisans might have specialized in pottery, metalwork, or textile production. Roads teemed with travelers: merchants, government officials, and soldiers. Inns and way stations appeared along major routes, catering to these travelers.

2.13 Roman Administration and Law

Roman administration brought a structured legal system to the provinces. Laws covered property rights, contracts, crimes, and the status of individuals. Free men could be Roman citizens, Latin-rights holders, or non-citizens, each with different privileges. Slavery was also part of the social fabric. Many slaves worked in agriculture or as household servants, although some skilled slaves served as teachers, artisans, or managers.

Local magistrates often worked alongside Roman officials, creating a blend of local traditions and Roman legal codes. Over time, as more locals gained Roman citizenship, they could hold offices in the imperial administration. This created a path for upward mobility, especially if they had wealth or connections.

2.14 Later Challenges and Barbarian Pressures

By the 3rd century CE, the Roman Empire faced mounting pressures on its borders. Germanic tribes such as the Alemanni, Goths, and later the Lombards began probing Roman defenses. The Danube frontier became a hotspot for incursions. The empire's military resources were stretched thin as threats also rose in the east. This period saw the construction of stronger fortifications, reorganization of military units, and occasional withdrawals from less defensible areas.

Despite these challenges, the region that is now Austria remained a core part of the frontier for some time. Cities like Carnuntum and Vindobona adapted to the changing security situation. Emperors would sometimes visit to oversee military campaigns or to negotiate treaties with Germanic chieftains. The local population might have suffered from raids, disruptions to trade, and higher taxes to fund defense efforts.

2.15 The Spread of Christianity

Christianity began to spread within the Roman Empire, including the Alpine provinces, during the 2nd and 3rd centuries CE. Initially persecuted, Christians gradually gained acceptance, especially after Emperor Constantine's Edict of Milan in 313 CE. Churches and Christian communities appeared in many towns. Early Christian graves and inscriptions provide evidence of this new faith taking root.

However, the Christianization of Austria would be a slow process, extending well beyond the Roman period. In rural areas, pagan traditions persisted much longer. Still, the Roman framework of roads, cities, and administration helped Christianity spread more easily, setting the stage for the religion's major influence in the Middle Ages.

2.16 Decline of Roman Authority

By the late 4th and early 5th centuries, Rome's grip on its western provinces weakened. Waves of Germanic migrations and invasions swept across Europe.

Some tribes were pushed westward by the Huns, while others seized opportunities as Roman defenses collapsed. The Western Roman Empire faced internal power struggles and economic crises, diminishing its ability to hold the frontiers.

In the provinces that covered modern Austria, Roman officials gradually lost control. Germanic groups, like the Bavarians and Lombards, moved into the region. The Roman administrative structure started to dissolve. Local elites either fled or made arrangements with the new rulers. Cities that had once been centers of Roman life declined or were abandoned.

2.17 The End of Roman Rule in Austria

Historians usually date the fall of the Western Roman Empire to 476 CE, when the last emperor in Italy was deposed. However, in the provinces, the process of disintegration was gradual. Some Roman legions were recalled to fight elsewhere, and local garrisons could not hold off invaders indefinitely. The transition to early medieval rule took different forms in different areas.

In Austria, some communities may have continued certain Roman practices for a time, living under the authority of Germanic kings who recognized the value of Roman infrastructure. In other places, Roman roads fell into disrepair, and villa estates were abandoned. Christian communities survived, passing on not just religious beliefs but also certain elements of Roman literacy and law.

2.18 Lasting Impact of Rome on Austria

Although Roman power in Austria ended, the influence of Roman civilization did not vanish. Road networks, place names, legal concepts, and cultural practices endured. The introduction of urban life had a deep impact, even if many Roman towns shrank or were destroyed. Future rulers recognized the strategic significance of the Danube frontier, following patterns set by the Romans.

Latin also influenced the local languages, though Germanic dialects took root after the migrations. Christianity, which had spread under Roman rule, continued to grow, eventually becoming the dominant faith in the region. In later centuries, as new political entities formed, they often built their legitimacy on Roman precedents, calling upon Roman law and heritage to cement their authority.

2.19 Transition to the Early Middle Ages

With the collapse of Roman administration, the door opened for new powers. The Bavarians, Avars, and Slavs all played roles in reshaping the political landscape. In the next chapters, we will examine how these groups established their presence and how the foundations laid by Rome influenced later medieval states. The Roman provinces gave way to smaller, often competing, territories that laid the groundwork for the medieval principalities.

The Celts, once dominant, had by now been absorbed into the Roman world and, later, into the new Germanic realms. Their language survived in some pockets, but Latin-based and Germanic languages came to dominate. Nonetheless, traces of Celtic heritage remained in local folklore, place names, and archaeological sites.

CHAPTER 3: THE EARLY MIDDLE AGES AND RISE OF BAVARIAN RULE

When the Western Roman Empire fell apart in the 5th century CE, new groups began to settle in the lands that would later become Austria. Rome had withdrawn its legions and administrators, leaving behind roads, forts, and cities that soon found themselves in need of new leadership. The Early Middle Ages in Austria were shaped by waves of Germanic and Slavic migration, the formation of local power centers, and the influences of larger political entities, such as the Franks. This period laid the groundwork for future developments, including the rise of Bavarian rule, which would leave a lasting mark on the region's political, social, and cultural landscape.

This chapter explores the collapse of Roman authority, the arrival of Germanic tribes, the formation of the Duchy of Bavaria, and the relationships between local communities and outside powers. We will see how shifting alliances, religious changes, and ongoing conflicts shaped Austria's transition from a Roman province to a cluster of early medieval principalities.

3.1 After the Romans: A Changing Landscape

By the late 4th and early 5th centuries CE, the Roman Empire was under constant pressure from various external threats. In the Danube region, Germanic and other tribal groups sought new lands, sometimes through peaceful settlements and sometimes by force. As Roman troops pulled back to defend the core of the empire or to respond to crises elsewhere, frontier regions like Noricum, Raetia, and parts of Pannonia became vulnerable.

Local Romanized Celtic populations, along with any remaining Roman officials, had limited resources to maintain roads, forts, and towns. Some towns were abandoned, while others adapted to the new situation by seeking alliances with incoming groups. Archaeological evidence shows some forts reused as local strongholds, but many were not maintained. Over time, the local population dwindled in certain areas as trade networks collapsed.

Despite these setbacks, some Roman legacies persisted. People continued to use segments of Roman roads, and Christianity, introduced during Roman rule, took hold in certain pockets. Latin-based legal customs also influenced local governance when new rulers appeared. Even if Roman authority had faded, the memory of Roman urban life and administrative practices did not disappear completely.

3.2 Germanic and Slavic Migrations

Several groups moved into or through the territory of modern Austria during the Early Middle Ages. Two of the most significant were the Germanic Bavarians (also referred to as Baiuvarii) and various Slavic peoples, joined later by the Avars who swept in from the east.

- **The Bavarians**: They emerged as a distinct group around the 6th century, possibly forming from remnants of earlier Germanic tribes in southern Germany and Austria, including the Alemanni and remaining Romanized populations. The Bavarians gradually expanded their control over areas north of the Alps and in parts of what is now Upper Austria and Salzburg. They established a loose network of leadership under local dukes, often traced back to the powerful Agilolfing dynasty.
- **The Slavs**: Pushed westward by other migrating peoples, Slavic groups began to settle in the eastern Alpine regions around the 6th and 7th centuries. They founded small communities in valleys and near rivers. Over time, these Slavs would become part of the larger cultural mix that shaped early medieval Austria. In some areas, they mixed with existing Celtic and Romanized populations.
- **The Avars**: Arriving from the Eurasian steppe, the Avars established a powerful khaganate in the Pannonian Basin (roughly present-day Hungary and parts of eastern Austria) during the late 6th century. Their presence influenced political dynamics in Austria's eastern regions. They extracted tribute from local populations and carried out raids to assert their power.

These groups often fought one another or formed alliances depending on circumstances. Over the centuries, the land saw ongoing change as different tribes gained or lost power. Local populations adapted to each new overlord, forging new identities in the process.

3.3 Christianization and Monastic Foundations

Christianity continued to spread throughout the Early Middle Ages, even as pagan groups settled in Austria. Missionaries from the Roman Church and later from Irish-Scottish missions arrived to convert local Germanic and Slavic leaders, seeing the sponsorship of noble families as a key strategy to win broader populations.

Monastic communities began to take root, aided by missionaries and local rulers who donated land for the building of monasteries. These monasteries served as centers of learning and culture. Monks preserved and copied manuscripts, including biblical texts and classical works, helping to keep literacy alive in a largely illiterate society. Monasteries also played roles in agriculture, clearing forests and introducing new farming methods, thus boosting local economies.

Important monastic foundations in Bavaria and its neighboring areas acted as bridgeheads for Christian influence. Some of these communities were located just north of the Alps, but they had contacts that reached into what is now Austrian territory. Over time, missionary efforts produced converts among Bavarian, Slavic, and even Avar populations, although the success rate varied and conflicts arose when local rulers saw Christianity as a threat to their traditional authority.

3.4 The Emergence of the Bavarian Duchy

By the 7th and 8th centuries, the Bavarians were coalescing into a more structured polity under ducal leadership. While their power center lay in what is now southern Germany, it extended into parts of modern Austria. The dukes of Bavaria recognized the potential of controlling strategic trade routes through the Alps, as well as fertile lands for agriculture.

Key features of Bavarian rule included:

- **Ducal Authority**: A duke, often from the Agilolfing dynasty, held a form of regional power. He was expected to defend his lands, maintain alliances, and resolve disputes among local nobles.
- **Landholding Nobility**: Bavarian society rested on a network of noble families who owned land and owed military service to the duke. In turn, the duke provided protection and opportunities for these nobles to increase their wealth through conquest or marriage alliances.

- **Integration of Christian Structures**: Bishops and abbots sometimes played roles in governance. The duke might grant lands to church institutions, ensuring religious support for his rule. Monasteries and bishoprics became significant landowners, adding another layer to the social hierarchy.

Control was not absolute. Many areas remained under the sway of local lords who only nominally acknowledged Bavarian authority. Smaller Slavic territories might pay tribute or align with the Bavarians to fend off threats from the Avars. Over time, Bavaria's influence grew, but it also faced challenges from the expanding Frankish Kingdom to the west.

3.5 The Frankish Expansion under the Merovingians and Carolingians

To understand the next phase of Austrian history, we must look at the Franks. Initially ruled by the Merovingian dynasty, the Franks controlled large parts of what is now France, western Germany, and the Low Countries. By the 8th century, power shifted to the Carolingians—famously led by Charles Martel, Pepin the Short, and Charlemagne (also known as Karl der Große).

- **Charles Martel (early 8th century)**: Known for halting the Islamic expansion into Frankish lands at the Battle of Tours (732), he also turned his attention to the east, forging alliances or subjugating nearby Germanic peoples.
- **Pepin the Short**: Charles Martel's son, crowned King of the Franks in 751, continued consolidating Frankish territory.
- **Charlemagne (r. 768–814)**: The most famous Carolingian ruler expanded the Frankish realm into a vast empire, eventually crowned Emperor by the Pope in 800. He waged multiple campaigns, including those against the Lombards in Italy, Saxons in the north, and Avars in the east.

The Bavarian dukes found themselves caught between asserting independence and maintaining a delicate relationship with the Franks. Sometimes they allied with the Frankish kings; at other times, they resisted. This power struggle greatly affected the region of Austria, which was geographically positioned between the Bavarian heartland and the lands of other Germanic and Slavic groups.

3.6 The Bavarian-Frankish Conflict and Integration

Under the Merovingians, the Bavarians had a semi-independent status, occasionally paying tribute. However, this relationship changed dramatically under Charlemagne. When Duke Tassilo III of Bavaria tried to assert full independence, Charlemagne intervened militarily.

- **Campaign against Tassilo III (late 8th century)**: Charlemagne accused Tassilo of breaking his oaths and refusing to assist in the Frankish campaigns. In 788, Charlemagne deposed Tassilo and took direct control of Bavaria. Tassilo was forced into a monastery, marking the end of the Agilolfing dynasty's rule.

Once Bavaria was under Carolingian control, Charlemagne reorganized the region's administration. This reorganization impacted what is now Austrian territory:

1. **Appointment of Counts and Bishops**: Charlemagne placed loyal Frankish nobles and clerics in positions of power. They oversaw local governance, collected taxes, and enforced royal decrees.
2. **Development of Frontier Marches**: To defend against external threats, especially from the Avars, Charlemagne established border regions called marches. These marches had military governors who were responsible for protecting the frontier and organizing defenses.

Though the old Bavarian structures did not vanish overnight, the Carolingian system imposed new layers of control. Local lords who cooperated with the Franks often gained titles and lands, while those who resisted faced confiscations or exile.

3.7 The Defeat of the Avars and the Opening of the East

One of Charlemagne's major achievements in Central Europe was the defeat of the Avars, who had long been a threat to the eastern borders. Beginning in the late 8th century, Carolingian armies launched a series of campaigns into the Pannonian Basin:

- **Frankish-Avar Wars**: These wars resulted in the destruction or subjugation of the Avar Khaganate by the early 9th century. The Avars, weakened by internal strife and repeated military losses, were unable to withstand the Carolingian forces, especially when some Slavic groups joined the Franks.
- **Establishment of Avar Marches**: After the Avar defeat, Charlemagne created frontier districts that included parts of present-day Lower Austria and beyond. These areas would eventually be reorganized into regions known as marches, meant to serve as buffer zones against further eastern incursions.

With Avar power broken, the Frankish Empire extended deeper into southeastern Europe. This expansion would later shape the conditions for the formation of the Eastern March (Ostmark), which in time became the core territory of the Babenbergs and, much later, the Habsburgs. For now, though, local governance rested in the hands of Frankish counts and bishops who implemented Carolingian policies.

3.8 Cultural Changes under Frankish Rule

Frankish rule brought several cultural and administrative shifts:

1. **Feudal System**: While the Bavarians had their own version of landholding and loyalty, the Carolingians introduced a broader feudal framework. Land was granted in fief to nobles who pledged military service. This system tied the region more closely to the empire's political structures.
2. **Christianization**: The Frankish kings strongly supported the Church, seeing it as a unifying force. Monasteries received patronage, and missionary activities increased among remaining pagan groups. Churches dedicated to saints popular in the Frankish realm, such as St. Martin or St. Remigius, started appearing in Austrian lands.
3. **Latin Literacy**: The Carolingian Renaissance, promoted by Charlemagne, encouraged the copying of manuscripts and the establishment of schools in monasteries and cathedrals. Latin learning spread among the clergy, some of whom came from or settled in Austrian regions. Though still limited to a small elite, literacy gradually increased.

In daily life, most people were still peasants or small-scale farmers, living in scattered villages and working for local lords. The broader political changes may have been less noticeable to them, but the introduction of new churches, monasteries, and the presence of Frankish soldiers would have reminded them of the empire that now claimed their land.

3.9 The Division of the Carolingian Empire

Charlemagne's empire did not remain unified for long after his death in 814. His son, Louis the Pious, struggled to keep control, and the empire was eventually divided among Louis's sons. This process culminated in the **Treaty of Verdun (843)**, which split the Carolingian realms into three main parts:

- **West Francia** (roughly modern France)
- **East Francia** (roughly modern Germany, Austria, and beyond)
- **Lotharingia** (a middle kingdom stretching from the North Sea to northern Italy)

Austria's regions fell under East Francia, ruled by Louis the German. Over time, East Francia evolved into the Holy Roman Empire. However, the division and subsequent struggles for power weakened central authority, allowing local dukes and counts more freedom.

3.10 Rise of Local Powers and the Role of Bavaria

In East Francia, Bavaria once again emerged as a significant entity. By the late 9th and early 10th centuries, new dynasties took root. The **Luitpoldings** became important in Bavaria, and their influence extended into eastern regions. They governed through a network of counts who held smaller districts (Gaue) within the duchy.

During this period, Magyar raiders from the Hungarian plains started attacking East Francia, including Bavaria. The Magyars replaced the Avars as the primary eastern threat, leading to new defensive measures. Some local leaders tried to fortify their lands, constructing small castles or refurbishing old Roman fortresses. Despite these efforts, Magyar raids were destructive, forcing the East Frankish kings and Bavarian dukes to cooperate for defense.

3.11 The Early Dukes and Struggle for Autonomy

By the 10th century, we see dukes of Bavaria acting almost like independent monarchs, although they nominally recognized the king of East Francia (who was often also crowned as King of Germany). The relationship between the Bavarian dukes and the East Frankish or German kings was complicated:

1. **Military Cooperation**: The king needed the duke's support to repel external threats, especially the Magyars.
2. **Internal Rivalries**: Kings, such as Henry the Fowler (r. 919–936) and Otto the Great (r. 936–973), sought to centralize power, while Bavarian dukes fought to maintain their autonomy.
3. **Church Support**: Both sides tried to control church appointments, using bishops to strengthen their authority.

These tensions would lead to periodic conflicts and shifting alliances, all influencing the eastern frontier in what is now Austria. If Bavaria was strong, it might exert direct control over Austrian regions. If Bavaria was weak or in revolt against the king, the frontier might see more chaos and local power struggles.

3.12 The Magyar Threat and the Battle of Lechfeld (955)

One of the defining moments in the 10th century was the **Battle of Lechfeld in 955**, near Augsburg. King Otto I (the future Holy Roman Emperor Otto the Great) led a combined German force—including Bavarian contingents—to a decisive victory against the Magyars. This ended the era of major Magyar raids into East Francia, providing a measure of stability to Bavaria and the surrounding regions.

For Austria, this victory mattered greatly. With the Magyar threat reduced, local leaders could focus on development rather than constant defense. It also boosted Otto's prestige, enabling him to further strengthen the monarchy's power. The dukes of Bavaria still held sway over Austrian territories, but they now operated within an empire led by a more assertive king.

3.13 Foundations of the Marches

Following the Battle of Lechfeld, Otto I and his successors worked to secure the eastern frontier. They reorganized territories into **marches**—military buffer zones that could respond quickly to external threats. One of the most important was the **Marchia orientalis** (Eastern March), a predecessor to what would become the Duchy of Austria under the Babenbergs.

At first, these marches were small and directly governed by appointees loyal to the king or emperor. Their main job was defense, but they also oversaw local administration, justice, and the collection of royal revenues. The role of **Margrave** (or Markgraf) was crucial. A margrave held more military authority than a normal count, reflecting the importance of securing the frontier.

In the second half of the 10th century, the region that is now Lower Austria began to take shape as a distinct political unit under these margraves. Over time, the families who held these positions would gain influence, setting the stage for the Babenbergs' eventual rise to prominence in the late 10th and early 11th centuries.

3.14 The Church as a Stabilizing Force

Throughout the Early Middle Ages, the Christian Church served as an important stabilizing force. Bishops and abbots often worked to limit violence and establish norms of behavior, such as the **Peace of God** and **Truce of God** movements in later centuries. Although these movements took stronger hold in the High Middle Ages, their roots can be seen in earlier attempts by church leaders to mediate conflicts.

Monasteries continued to be centers of learning and literacy. While the region was still mostly rural and agrarian, monasteries helped expand agriculture by clearing land and improving farming techniques. The Church, supported by royal and ducal donations, also provided spiritual legitimacy to rulers, performing coronations and blessing military campaigns against pagans and other "outsiders."

In many Bavarian-held Austrian lands, bishoprics were established or expanded. Dioceses, such as Salzburg (which traces its roots to the ancient Roman city of Iuvavum), began to wield considerable influence. Salzburg's archbishops, in particular, would become major landowners and political players, shaping the course of Austrian history in the centuries ahead.

3.15 Daily Life in Early Medieval Austria

For most people, life revolved around farming, herding, and local community ties:

- **Villages and Manors**: Small villages scattered across valleys and near rivers were home to peasants who worked the land. Noble or ecclesiastical estates (manors) provided structure, with peasants owing labor or rent to their lord.
- **Trade and Markets**: Trade was limited, but some market towns existed along important travel routes. Salt, iron, and agricultural products were main goods. Surplus could be traded locally or sent to ducal courts.
- **Defense and Fortifications**: Local lords might maintain simple wooden forts or refurbish old Roman walls for protection. Peasants were often required to help in fortification work or to serve in local militias when threats arose.
- **Religion and Rituals**: The local church calendar shaped the rhythms of the year. Feast days, fasts, and pilgrimages to nearby shrines provided spiritual structure. In more remote areas, older pagan customs sometimes blended with Christian practices.

While the nobility and church were dominant forces, small-scale alliances or feuds between lords were common. These could disrupt life for peasants, leading to destruction of fields or the seizure of livestock. Over time, stronger ducal or royal authority tried to curb such disputes, but success varied widely.

3.16 Transition from the Early to High Middle Ages

By the late 10th century, the stage was set for new developments. The Carolingian line had ended, replaced by the Saxon (Ottonian) dynasty and then by the Salian dynasty. Bavaria and the frontier marches had adapted to the shifting landscape of power. The Magyars were now settled in the Hungarian plains, gradually converting to Christianity and becoming part of the European political fabric.

In Austria, the newly formed **Eastern March** was growing in importance. Dukes and margraves appointed by the king gained local loyalty and started to shape the region's future. It was during this transitional phase that the **Babenberg** family rose to prominence. They would soon become the primary rulers of the march, forging the beginnings of a lasting Austrian state.

3.17 The Legacy of Bavarian Rule

Bavarian influence in Austria was profound. It introduced administrative structures and cultural elements that persisted even after Austria became more autonomous. The Bavarian dialects played a major role in shaping the German language in Austrian regions, and Bavarian nobility continued to hold extensive lands on both sides of the modern German-Austrian border.

Religious life, closely tied to Bavarian sees like Salzburg, contributed to a shared ecclesiastical culture. The monastic networks that expanded from Bavaria into Austria helped tie the region into the broader Christian world. Even after the Babenbergs established their own power, the ties to Bavaria remained culturally significant, influencing everything from legal traditions to folk customs.

CHAPTER 4: THE BABENBERG DYNASTY AND THE FORMATION OF A MARCH

With the Magyar threat reduced after the Battle of Lechfeld (955), the eastern frontier of the German kingdom—sometimes called East Francia—took on new importance. The region that would soon become the heartland of Austria was organized into marches, governed by margraves whose job was to secure and develop these borderlands. It was in this context that the **Babenberg** family emerged as the leading power in the Eastern March (Ostmark). Over the course of the 10th to 12th centuries, they transformed a relatively small frontier district into a stable political entity, laying the groundwork for what we now recognize as Austria.

This chapter explores how the Babenbergs gained authority, the challenges they faced, and the key steps in building up the march. We will look at alliances, conflicts, religious foundations, and economic developments that propelled the Babenbergs from minor lords on the frontier to influential figures in the German kingdom.

4.1 Origins of the Babenbergs

The family's earliest documented ancestors can be traced back to the Franconian nobility in the 9th and 10th centuries. Known in some sources as the **Popponids** or **Babenbergs**, they first gained prominence around the Main River region in what is now Germany. Their name is linked to the castle of Babenberg on the River Main. Over time, they became involved in court politics, sometimes aligning with the reigning kings or emperors, and at other times facing conflicts.

Their fortunes improved when the Ottonian kings (especially Otto I and Otto II) sought trustworthy nobles to govern border regions. As the Eastern March needed strong leadership to ward off Magyar incursions, the Babenbergs found an opportunity to prove their loyalty and their military capabilities.

4.2 The Appointment of Leopold I

The real turning point for the Babenbergs came with the **appointment of Leopold I (also called Luitpold)** as Margrave of the Eastern March around 976. This followed a period of upheaval during which the Duke of Bavaria rebelled against Emperor Otto II. To weaken Bavarian influence, the emperor separated certain border areas from the Duchy of Bavaria and appointed new margraves who were directly loyal to the imperial throne.

Leopold I set about organizing and defending his territory. Though sources on his early reign are sparse, we know he established some form of administrative structure, dividing the march into counties or districts. He also encouraged settlement, bringing in people to work the land, rebuild fortifications, and revitalize trade routes. The early Babenberg margraves faced continual threats from remaining Magyar raiders, as well as from potential conflicts with neighboring lords.

4.3 Defining the Eastern March

Under the Babenbergs, the Eastern March began to take shape as a recognizable political unit. This march covered much of what is now Lower Austria and parts of Upper Austria, though exact boundaries shifted over time due to wars, alliances, and imperial decisions. The Babenbergs worked to:

1. **Establish a Capital or Administrative Center**: Initial centers included Melk and Gars am Kamp, located in the Danube region. Vienna was not yet the main seat of power, though it would grow in importance in later generations.

2. **Develop Fortified Sites**: Castles or fortresses were built or strengthened at strategic points along rivers and mountain passes. These served as bases of military power and administration.

3. **Support the Church**: Grants of land to monasteries and bishoprics helped secure ecclesiastical support. Monks also played a role in cultivating land and Christianizing local populations.

Through these efforts, the Eastern March steadily gained a sense of identity under the Babenberg leadership. Key families aligned themselves with the margrave, hoping to benefit from land grants, titles, or marriage alliances.

4.4 Margrave Henry I and the Growth of Power

Leopold I was succeeded by his son Henry I (also called Heinrich I), who ruled as Margrave from 994 to 1018. Henry continued his father's policies, working to expand Babenberg influence and fortify the region against any renewed threats. Under Henry, we see clearer signs of the Eastern March functioning as a defined territory within the wider Holy Roman Empire.

- **Territorial Administration**: Henry appointed loyal counts to oversee different parts of the march. By placing trusted individuals in key positions, the margrave could collect taxes, enforce laws, and raise troops more effectively.

- **Relations with Bavaria**: The Babenbergs still had to navigate the fact that Bavaria was a neighboring power with claims over eastern lands. At times, tensions arose, but alliances through marriage or imperial intervention usually resolved them.

- **Support from the Emperor**: As long as the Babenbergs remained loyal to the emperor, they could count on receiving privileges and titles. Henry worked closely with Emperor Henry II (r. 1002–1024), ensuring that the Eastern March was part of broader imperial plans.

Henry I's reign saw a gradual increase in internal stability. More Christian communities took root, and trade along the Danube resumed, connecting the march with larger markets to the west and south.

4.5 Economic Foundations and Settlement

During the late 10th and early 11th centuries, the Babenbergs encouraged settlement to boost the region's population and productivity. Much of the land was forested or lightly populated, requiring significant work to clear fields and establish villages. The margraves granted privileges to settlers, including temporary exemptions from certain taxes, to attract farmers and artisans.

Key developments included:

- **Agricultural Growth**: Clearing forested land expanded the area under cultivation. Cereal crops, vineyards, and livestock farming increased.

- **River Trade**: The Danube was a major artery for transporting goods. Riverboats carried grain, salt, and other products downstream and brought in items like cloth and wine from other parts of the empire.

- **Market Towns**: Small settlements near fortified castles evolved into market towns. These towns held periodic fairs, drawing merchants and peasants from surrounding areas. Over time, some of these towns would become important urban centers.

The Babenbergs used revenues from trade and agriculture to build stronger fortifications, fund local churches, and maintain a small retinue of knights or armed men. Economic growth went hand in hand with the consolidation of political power.

4.6 Religious Institutions and Cultural Identity

From the beginning, the Babenbergs tied their rule closely to the Church. They founded and endowed several monasteries, which became spiritual and cultural landmarks. One example is the **monastery at Melk**, which later rose to great prominence. Though initially a fortification, Melk evolved into a Benedictine monastery, receiving Babenberg patronage that helped it flourish.

Why were monasteries so important?

1. **Spiritual Legitimacy**: A pious ruler who supported monks, built churches, and sponsored pilgrimages could claim moral authority.

2. **Literacy and Record-Keeping**: Monasteries housed scribes who could keep records, copy texts, and thus provide administrative support.

3. **Christianization**: Monks and priests spread Christian teachings among the rural populace, which helped unify the march under a single faith and set of moral guidelines.

These religious institutions contributed to a growing cultural identity in the Eastern March, blending older Bavarian traditions with new influences from the empire and the Church. The Babenbergs supported the creation of religious art, the building of Romanesque churches, and the sponsorship of liturgical ceremonies that highlighted their role as God-appointed guardians of the land.

4.7 Margrave Adalbert "the Victorious" and Regional Ambitions

After Henry I, the title passed to other Babenberg margraves, among them **Adalbert "the Victorious" (r. 1018–1055)**. Under Adalbert, the Babenbergs continued to assert themselves as key players on the eastern frontier. Some notable aspects of his rule include:

- **Military Campaigns**: While major Magyar raids had ended, smaller conflicts with neighboring lords or rebellious vassals still occurred. Adalbert used military action to expand or defend Babenberg influence.

- **Dynastic Marriages**: He arranged strategic marriages to connect the Babenberg family with other powerful noble houses. This extended the family's network of alliances and secured support in times of conflict.

- **Church Relations**: Adalbert worked with the local bishops and abbots, granting them lands in return for loyalty and moral backing. The relationship between secular and ecclesiastical authorities remained important for keeping order.

Adalbert's nickname "the Victorious" suggests success on the battlefield, but he also consolidated Babenberg authority through diplomacy. His rule solidified the Eastern March's position within the Holy Roman Empire, making it a recognized entity that was no longer just a backwater frontier.

4.8 The March Becomes Known as Austria

It is around this time, in the mid-11th century, that we begin seeing the name **"Ostarrîchi"** (which later evolved into "Österreich," the German name for Austria) in documents. One of the earliest references dates to 996, in a document where Emperor Otto III granted land in the region to a Bavarian monastery. The use of "Ostarrîchi" indicates that the Eastern March had developed a distinct identity separate from Bavaria, even if it was still closely connected.

Language and cultural distinctions grew over time. While the Bavarian dialect formed the basis of the local German language, the region started to show signs of a self-contained administrative framework, with its own sets of laws, customs, and alliances. The Babenbergs, by providing stable government and defending the territory, played a large role in fostering this emerging identity.

4.9 Conflicts with the Emperor and Internal Challenges

Despite their loyalty to the Holy Roman Emperors, the Babenbergs were not immune to conflicts with the imperial throne. Power struggles arose when emperors tried to curb the independence of major lords, or when margraves sought to increase their autonomy:

- **Investiture Controversy (late 11th–early 12th century)**: This wide-ranging conflict between the Emperor and the Pope over the right to invest bishops also affected the Babenbergs. Depending on the margrave's stance, they might side with the Emperor or try to maintain neutrality. Their choices shaped relationships with the Church and local bishops.

- **Rival Nobles**: Some lesser nobles resented Babenberg authority. They might ally with the emperor or with neighboring rulers against the margraves. Rebellions, though not frequent, did occur when local counts felt the Babenbergs overstepped their rights.

Generally, the Babenbergs tried to balance imperial loyalty with regional autonomy, carefully navigating each new political crisis. Their continued success in managing these challenges gradually strengthened their hold on the march.

4.10 Leopold II and Leopold III: Consolidation and Expansion

Two key figures in the 11th and early 12th centuries were **Leopold II (r. 1075–1095)** and **Leopold III (r. 1095–1136)**, often referred to in Austrian history:

1. **Leopold II**: Faced the turmoil of the Investiture Controversy. At times, he opposed Emperor Henry IV, who was locked in conflict with Pope Gregory VII. Leopold II supported the papal side, which led to tensions. However, he

managed to keep the march intact, even gaining new lands when Henry IV lost influence in certain areas.

2. **Leopold III ("the Saint")**: Canonized later for his pious life, Leopold III is remembered for founding **Klosterneuburg Monastery** in 1114. He also married Agnes, the sister of Emperor Henry V, strengthening ties to the imperial family. Leopold III oversaw a period of relative peace and expansion, acquiring new territories through inheritance and donations.

Under their leadership, the Eastern March grew in both size and reputation. Monasteries, churches, and towns received endowments, weaving the Babenberg name into the religious and cultural fabric of the land.

4.11 Economic and Cultural Development in the 12th Century

By the 12th century, the Babenbergs' dominion was no longer just a sparse borderland. Towns emerged, trade routes flourished, and agriculture became more productive:

- **Town Charters**: The margraves began granting charters to certain settlements, giving them rights to hold markets, collect tolls, and govern themselves to some extent. This encouraged merchants and artisans to settle, stimulating urban growth.

- **Mining and Resources**: Parts of the Alpine region had mineral resources (iron, salt, etc.). While large-scale mining was still in its early stages, the Babenbergs recognized the potential and encouraged exploration. Revenue from resource extraction supplemented agricultural income.

- **Cultural Exchange**: The Danube corridor made it easier for pilgrims, scholars, and traders to pass through. This connectivity allowed the region to benefit from ideas circulating within the empire and beyond. Romanesque architecture spread, and literary works found an audience among educated clergy and nobles.

These economic and cultural advances formed the basis for even greater growth in later centuries. The Babenberg court, especially under the later margraves (who became dukes), sponsored poets, chroniclers, and religious scholars, reflecting a slow but steady move toward a more sophisticated court culture.

4.12 From Margraviate to Duchy

A pivotal change came when the Babenbergs' territory was elevated from a mere march to a **duchy**. The exact timeline and details vary in historical records, but the event signaled the empire's recognition of the Babenbergs as more than just border lords. By the mid-12th century, they held the ducal title, which placed them on a par with other major nobles of the realm, like the Dukes of Bavaria or Swabia.

The step up to dukedom boosted the region's prestige and the Babenbergs' influence. This change was codified in key documents like the **Privilegium Minus (1156)**, issued by Emperor Frederick Barbarossa. The Privilegium Minus granted the new Duchy of Austria special rights, including hereditary succession through the female line, which was unusual for that time. It was a turning point, setting Austria on a distinct path within the empire.

4.13 Rivalries with Bavaria and Bohemia

Even after becoming a duchy, the Babenbergs found themselves surrounded by powerful neighbors: Bavaria to the west and Bohemia to the north. Conflicts arose over border regions, trade tolls, and alliances with the emperor. Some of the friction points included:

1. **Border Disputes**: Rivers and mountain ranges formed natural frontiers, but overlapping claims led to skirmishes. Occasionally, the Babenbergs allied with Bohemia against Bavaria, or vice versa, depending on shifting political winds.

2. **Marriage Diplomacy**: To ease tensions, marriage alliances were frequently arranged. This could lead to temporary peace, but also gave in-laws a say in internal affairs.

3. **Imperial Mediation**: The emperor often stepped in to resolve disputes, using the threat of military intervention or the promise of titles and privileges.

Through it all, the Babenbergs generally managed to keep their territory intact and even added small expansions over time. Their skillful diplomacy and the support of monastic and episcopal allies played key roles.

4.14 The Role of the Church under the Babenbergs

As Austria's rulers, the Babenbergs maintained a close relationship with the Church, reflecting a common trend in medieval Europe:

- **Foundations and Donations**: New monasteries like Klosterneuburg (founded by Leopold III) and Heiligenkreuz (founded by Leopold III's son, Leopold IV) became spiritual and cultural centers.

- **Bishops and Political Influence**: Bishops controlled large tracts of land and could field knights if needed. This made their allegiance crucial in times of conflict. The Babenbergs used their position to influence ecclesiastical appointments, though they often had to balance their own preferences with papal directives.

- **Relics and Pilgrimages**: The Babenbergs collected religious relics, which attracted pilgrims. Pilgrimages boosted local economies and elevated the spiritual standing of the duchy.

These religious policies were not just pious acts. They were strategic moves that helped the Babenbergs solidify power by uniting secular and ecclesiastical interests under their leadership.

4.15 Court Culture and the Beginnings of Austrian Identity

The Babenbergs' court, especially in the 12th century, was a microcosm of medieval aristocratic life. They hosted traveling minstrels, poets, and knights, showcasing the knightly culture that was spreading across Europe. Tournaments, feasts, and hunts became markers of status and prestige. Some margraves and dukes took part in imperial campaigns or even crusades, further aligning themselves with the broader chivalric ideals of the age.

Over time, a sense of distinct identity grew around the Babenberg court. This was not a modern national identity, but rather an awareness that the land called "Ostarrîchi," or Austria, had its own traditions, ruling family, and place in the empire. Chronicles written by clergy sometimes praised the margraves and dukes for their defense of Christian lands, hinting at the pride local elites felt in their leaders.

4.16 The Influence of Surrounding Regions

Although the Babenbergs focused on local development, they did not exist in a vacuum. Neighboring regions like Bavaria, Bohemia, and Hungary each had an impact:

- **Bavaria**: Continued to provide cultural and linguistic influences. Marital ties remained strong, and Bavarian markets were important trade partners.

- **Bohemia**: Ruled by the Přemyslid dynasty, Bohemia was both a rival and ally at different times. The two realms sometimes cooperated against common foes or competed for influence in border areas.

- **Hungary**: After the Christianization of the Magyars, Hungary became a stable kingdom. Marriages between Hungarian and Austrian nobles were common, leading to cultural exchanges and alliances.

By mediating these relationships, the Babenbergs ensured that Austria retained a degree of independence while still being part of the complex web of Central European politics.

4.17 Challenges at the Turn of the 12th–13th Centuries

As the 12th century moved toward its close, the Holy Roman Empire entered a new phase. The **Hohenstaufen dynasty** came to the throne, leading to fresh conflicts with the papacy. For the Babenbergs, this meant potential instability, as siding with the emperor or the pope could result in either rewards or penalties.

Additionally, internal family struggles sometimes arose over succession. The Privilegium Minus allowed succession through the female line, but that did not eliminate disputes among male relatives or distant cousins who felt entitled to inherit. Securing a smooth transition of power was crucial to maintaining the duchy's standing.

4.18 Leopold V and Leopold VI: Height of Babenberg Power

Two notable dukes in the late Babenberg period were **Leopold V (r. 1177–1194)** and **Leopold VI (r. 1194–1230)**, who significantly increased the family's prestige:

1. **Leopold V**: He gained notoriety when he captured King Richard the Lionheart of England on his return from the Third Crusade in 1192. Richard had offended Leopold during the crusade, and the duke saw an opportunity for a ransom. This act brought a large sum of money into Austria, funding major construction projects.

2. **Leopold VI ("the Glorious")**: Under his rule, Vienna rose to new prominence as a commercial hub, and the duchy expanded its boundaries to include areas like Styria. Leopold VI also supported the arts and founded many religious institutions, contributing to a mini-renaissance in Austrian culture.

These dukes represented the peak of Babenberg influence, forging ties with royal houses across Europe and overseeing a duchy that was growing wealthy through trade, agriculture, and resource extraction.

4.19 Lasting Babenberg Legacies

By establishing a strong political center and fostering economic growth, the Babenbergs set many of the foundations that future dynasties, including the Habsburgs, would build upon. Their policies in agriculture, trade, and religious patronage had long-term consequences:

- **Administrative Framework**: They showed how to govern a frontier region effectively, turning it into a recognized duchy. This included the development of local offices, taxation systems, and courts.

- **Cultural Flourishing**: Through monasteries and courtly life, they nurtured a tradition of learning, arts, and architecture that shaped medieval Austrian culture.

- **Stronger Urban Centers**: Towns like Vienna, Melk, and others would continue to grow, eventually playing major roles in European trade and politics.

- **Dynastic Ties**: Their marriages extended across Europe, weaving Austria into the fabric of high medieval aristocracy.

Despite their many achievements, the Babenberg line would come to an end in the mid-13th century, leaving a power vacuum that the Habsburgs would later fill. Still, the centuries of Babenberg rule laid the cornerstone of Austria's medieval identity.

CHAPTER 5: EXPANSION UNDER THE LATER BABENBERGS

By the late 12th century, the Babenberg family had firmly established itself as the ruling dynasty of Austria. Under margraves who later became dukes, Austria evolved from a frontier march to a recognized duchy. The Babenbergs oversaw economic growth, built strong ties with the Church, and developed the region's cultural identity. In this chapter, we will focus on the later phase of Babenberg rule, where leaders such as Leopold V and Leopold VI expanded both the territory and the influence of Austria. We will also examine the final Babenberg duke, Frederick II, whose death in 1246 led to a major crisis. That crisis paved the way for outside powers—especially Bohemia—to assert claims over Austrian lands, setting the stage for the rise of the Habsburgs.

5.1 Setting the Stage: Austria as a Duchy

When the Privilegium Minus was granted in 1156 by Emperor Frederick Barbarossa, Austria moved from being a mere border march into the rank of a duchy. The Babenberg rulers gained special rights:

1. **Hereditary Rule**: The Babenbergs could pass down their lands, not only through male heirs but also through the female line—unusual at that time.
2. **Greater Autonomy**: The duke held more freedom from the authority of the Dukes of Bavaria, who had historically overshadowed Austrian rulers.
3. **Territorial Definition**: While boundaries were still flexible, Austria now had clearer recognition as a separate duchy within the Holy Roman Empire.

By the late 12th century, towns like Vienna and regions like the Danube Valley were flourishing under Babenberg oversight. New fortifications, churches, and monastic houses demonstrated that the duchy was no longer simply a rugged frontier zone. Trade along the Danube linked Austria to Hungary and Bavaria, allowing local markets to prosper. This set the background for the achievements of the "later Babenbergs."

5.2 Leopold V ("The Virtuous"): Early Ambitions

Leopold V (r. 1177–1194) was a key figure who took the Austrian duchy to new levels of influence. He inherited a duchy that had been stabilized by the efforts of his father, Henry II Jasomirgott (the first to hold the ducal title). Leopold built on this foundation by:

- **Strengthening the Military**: Austria's army was not as large as that of major powers like the Kingdom of France or the Holy Roman Emperor, but Leopold aimed to create a disciplined force that could protect trade routes and fortresses against external threats.
- **Promoting Trade and Urban Growth**: During his rule, he encouraged more settlement in areas still covered by forests, and supported the establishment of market towns to foster economic expansion.
- **Engagement in Imperial Politics**: Like most major nobles of the empire, Leopold had to navigate the shifting alliances of the Holy Roman Empire. He maintained ties with Emperor Frederick Barbarossa, gaining favor by offering troops for imperial campaigns when needed.

These measures laid the groundwork for Austria's future prosperity. Yet Leopold V is most famously remembered for an event that would bring both conflict and unexpected wealth.

5.3 The Capture of King Richard the Lionheart

One of the most dramatic episodes in Leopold V's career involved England's King Richard I, known as Richard the Lionheart. Richard had taken part in the Third Crusade (1189–1192) alongside other European rulers, including Emperor Frederick Barbarossa. During the crusade, tensions arose between Richard and Leopold. Various accounts mention disagreements over the distribution of captured territories and the display of flags in the Holy Land. These conflicts left Leopold feeling slighted.

5.3.1 Circumstances of the Capture

On his return journey from the Holy Land in late 1192, Richard traveled through Central Europe in disguise, hoping to avoid his political enemies. Despite his precautions, he was recognized near Vienna (some stories say in Erdberg, others near a small village) and taken prisoner by Leopold V's men. Leopold saw an opportunity to gain both prestige and wealth from ransoming a well-known monarch.

5.3.2 Negotiating the Ransom

The capture of Richard caused international uproar. The Pope condemned Leopold for imprisoning a crusader, but that did not stop the Austrian duke from demanding a large ransom. Eventually, the sum agreed upon was enormous for the time—reportedly 150,000 marks of silver. This ransom was to be shared between Leopold and Emperor Henry VI, but Austria's portion was still vast. It is said that this windfall funded large-scale construction projects, including fortifications and perhaps the rebuilding of city walls.

5.3.3 Consequences for Austria

Leopold V's action boosted Austria's treasury and underlined the duchy's importance in European affairs. However, it also led to strained relations with England and some disapproval within the empire. The Pope excommunicated Leopold for violating the sanctity of a crusader, though the excommunication was eventually lifted. Nonetheless, the ransom money was a major source of funds that would later help expand the Babenbergs' projects, giving the duchy a sudden injection of wealth at a time when money was essential for building authority.

5.4 Leopold V's Later Years and Crusader Ties

Before his death in 1194, Leopold V also joined in the efforts of Emperor Henry VI, who carried on the imperial project in Italy and sought to bring the Kingdom of Sicily under his rule. Leopold V died from injuries sustained during a siege in 1194, and his territories were passed down to his sons. The short remainder of his rule after capturing Richard was marked by attempts to balance local governance with these imperial responsibilities. While not all of his campaigns were successful, his ambition had already left a strong imprint on Austria's fortunes.

5.5 Leopold VI ("The Glorious")

Leopold VI (r. 1194–1230), known as "the Glorious," inherited the duchy from his father. His reign is seen as the golden age of the Babenberg period in Austria. He expanded Austrian control into neighboring territories, engaged actively in the political life of the Holy Roman Empire, and fostered a rich cultural environment at his court.

5.5.1 Territorial Acquisitions

During Leopold VI's reign, Austria grew beyond its original borders:

1. **Annexation of Styria**: Through familial ties and strategic marriages, Leopold VI acquired Styria (Steiermark) after the death of its ruling duke. Styria was a valuable addition because of its mines, forests, and farmlands, making it a natural economic partner to Lower Austria.
2. **Influence in Carniola and Carinthia**: Although Leopold VI did not fully incorporate these regions, he gained influence through alliances and occasional military actions. This showed the Babenbergs' rising ambitions south of the Alps.
3. **Management of Bohemian Relations**: To the north, the Kingdom of Bohemia was also expanding. Leopold sought to maintain peace or alliances whenever possible, though tensions would flare up if border disputes arose.

By bringing Styria into the fold, Leopold VI added considerable resources to the duchy, enhancing Austria's standing among the German princes.

5.5.2 Courtly Culture and Architecture

Leopold VI's reign was also notable for cultural growth:

- **Patronage of the Arts**: Minstrels, poets, and chroniclers found Leopold's court to be welcoming. Troubadours from France and minnesingers from German regions visited or served in Austria, leaving behind works that praised chivalry, courtly love, and heroic deeds.
- **Religious Foundations**: Leopold VI continued the Babenberg tradition of founding and supporting monasteries. Notable examples include the Cistercian abbey at Lilienfeld. These institutions were centers of learning, agricultural improvements, and spiritual life.
- **Architectural Projects**: Building on the resources gained from the ransom of King Richard and from Styria's wealth, Leopold VI sponsored the construction of churches in the Romanesque and emerging Gothic styles. Vienna, in particular, saw the development of new structures and fortifications.

This cultural flowering contributed to a sense of identity and pride among the local nobility and urban residents, helping to tie the diverse territories more closely under Babenberg rule.

5.6 Ties with the Papacy and the Empire

Leopold VI navigated the complex politics of the Holy Roman Empire during a time when emperors and popes often clashed. He typically aligned himself with the empire while also maintaining good relations with the Church. At times, he joined crusading efforts—though not always successfully—in part to reinforce his image as a pious ruler. These crusades also offered a chance to forge new alliances and gain prestige.

Nonetheless, church-state relations could be tricky. Leopold VI had to balance local bishops' ambitions, papal directives, and imperial demands. Striking a careful middle ground, he avoided the worst of the conflicts that plagued other German princes during this era.

5.7 Frederick II "The Quarrelsome"

Leopold VI's son, Frederick II (r. 1230–1246), would be the last male Babenberg to rule Austria. Nicknamed "the Quarrelsome," Frederick II faced constant disputes with both the emperor and neighboring rulers.

5.7.1 Personality and Early Challenges

Frederick II's aggressive approach earned him a reputation. He did not shy away from conflict. From the start of his reign, he clashed with Emperor Frederick II (of the Hohenstaufen dynasty, who, confusingly, shared the same name), as well as with the Duke of Bavaria and the King of Bohemia. His combative nature sometimes achieved short-term goals, like securing territories or forcing rivals to back down, but it also isolated Austria diplomatically.

5.7.2 Loss of Prestige and Internal Struggles

Under Frederick II's rule, Austria did not continue the steady territorial expansion seen under Leopold VI. Instead, Frederick II lost ground in important ways:

1. **Conflicts with the Emperor**: Disputes arose over the extent of ducal rights in Austria versus imperial authority. Frederick II's refusal to support certain imperial campaigns angered Emperor Frederick II (Hohenstaufen). This led to a temporary imperial ban against him, weakening his position.
2. **Rebellions and Factionalism**: Within Austria and Styria, some nobles felt Frederick II was too harsh or too focused on his personal feuds. Local rebellions flared up, draining the ducal treasury and military resources.
3. **Diplomatic Isolation**: While Leopold VI had balanced alliances skillfully, Frederick II's brash decisions and frequent disputes made it difficult to sustain long-term partnerships. Bohemia, in particular, began looking for opportunities to push into Austrian affairs.

Despite these issues, Frederick II managed to maintain some control, primarily because of the Babenbergs' existing structures and the loyalty of certain noble families. However, his reign was far from stable.

5.8 The Battle of the Leitha River and Frederick II's Death

The decisive end to Frederick II's rule came with a conflict against King Béla IV of Hungary. Tensions with Hungary had been ongoing, fueled by border disputes and Frederick II's attempts to assert dominance. In 1246, at the **Battle of the Leitha River**, Frederick II was killed. His death was a turning point for Austria:

1. **No Direct Male Heir**: With Frederick II's passing, the male line of the Babenbergs ended. He had not produced a son who could inherit the duchy, leaving a power vacuum.
2. **Immediate Succession Crisis**: Neighboring rulers, including the King of Bohemia, the Duke of Bavaria, and the King of Hungary, eyed Austrian lands. They each had potential claims through marriage ties or earlier agreements.
3. **Local Nobles in Uncertainty**: The Austrian nobility worried about the next ruler's identity. Some supported a Babenberg female heir, while others favored powerful foreign princes. This division led to a period of instability known as the "Interregnum" in Austrian history.

Frederick II's death marked the end of an era. The Babenbergs had governed Austria for nearly three centuries, transforming it from a frontier march into a wealthy duchy. But now, the duchy's future hung in the balance.

5.9 The Disputed Succession and Austria's Fate

With no immediate male Babenberg heir, the question arose: Who would govern Austria and Styria? Several claimants appeared:

- **Gertrude of Babenberg**: Frederick II's niece. She had a legitimate claim but lacked the military backing to enforce it.
- **Margaret of Babenberg**: Frederick II's sister. She was older and had been married before, but she also claimed rights to the duchy.
- **Foreign Princes**: King Ottokar II of Bohemia, among others, saw an opportunity to extend influence. Marriages were proposed as a way to gain control.

While the Holy Roman Emperor should have played a major role in resolving this, the empire itself was in a politically weakened state. The emperor at the time, Frederick II (Hohenstaufen), was facing his own challenges in Italy and elsewhere. As a result, Austrian affairs became a tug-of-war among neighboring powers.

5.10 Bohemian Intervention: Ottokar II's Rise

Among the various contenders, **Ottokar II of Bohemia** stood out. He was the son of King Wenceslaus I of Bohemia and, after some internal Bohemian struggles, became King of Bohemia in 1253. Seeking to strengthen his kingdom, he turned to Austria:

1. **Marriage to a Babenberg Heiress**: Ottokar married Margaret of Babenberg in 1252, despite the notable age difference. Through this marriage, he claimed the rights to Austria and Styria.
2. **Military and Political Pressure**: Ottokar was not content with a mere paper claim. He used his army to occupy significant parts of Austria, facing limited resistance due to the confusion after Frederick II's death.

3. **Coronation as Ruler of Austria**: By 1253–1254, Ottokar managed to be recognized as Duke of Austria, although this status was not universally accepted. He also acquired Styria, further consolidating his hold.

Ottokar's takeover signaled a sharp break from centuries of Babenberg rule. Though he was not a Babenberg himself, he tried to maintain stability by respecting local customs and privileges—at least initially. For a time, it seemed Bohemia might successfully incorporate Austria into a larger realm in Central Europe.

5.11 The Brief Return of Stability

During the early years of Ottokar II's reign in Austria, some stability returned:

- **Reopening Trade**: With a single ruler over both Bohemia and Austria, trade routes between Prague and Vienna flourished. Merchants benefited from fewer border tolls and safer roads.
- **Urban Growth**: Vienna continued to develop as a key city along the Danube, with investments in walls, markets, and places of worship.
- **Legal Continuity**: Ottokar allowed Austrian nobles to keep many of their local rights, preventing immediate unrest.

However, this new order was not destined to last. Ottokar's ambitions reached beyond Austria and Styria—he sought control of Carinthia, Carniola, and even claims in the empire's politics. This brought him into conflict with the rising Habsburg family, who would soon gain imperial favor.

5.12 Seeds of Conflict with the Habsburgs

While the Babenberg story ended with Frederick II's death, the future story of Austria lay with a new dynasty—the Habsburgs. They were initially a Swiss-based noble family with estates in what is now northern Switzerland and southwestern Germany. A key moment came in 1273, when **Rudolph of Habsburg** was elected King of the Romans (effectively the Holy Roman Emperor-elect). This changed the power balance:

1. **Ottokar's Rivalry**: Ottokar had hoped to be chosen as emperor, or at least to see someone elected who would not threaten his expansions. Rudolph's election disrupted Ottokar's plans.
2. **Imperial Demands**: Rudolph demanded that all imperial lands illegally seized be returned to the empire. He claimed that Ottokar's acquisitions of Austria, Styria, and other regions needed proper imperial approval, which Ottokar had never formally obtained.
3. **Path to War**: Ottokar refused, and tensions rose. The stage was set for a direct confrontation that would determine the fate of Austria.

By the mid-1270s, the conflict between Ottokar II and Rudolph of Habsburg escalated. Armies gathered, alliances were made or broken, and Austria was at the center of a pivotal struggle in Central Europe.

5.13 The Battle of Marchfeld

A key turning point came with the **Battle of Marchfeld** (also called the Battle on the March River), fought on August 26, 1278, near Dürnkrut in Lower Austria. The clash pitted Ottokar II's Bohemian-Austrian forces against the army of Rudolph of Habsburg, who had allied with Hungarian troops led by King Ladislaus IV:

- **Strategic Maneuvers**: Ottokar's forces were strong but lacked the crucial alliance with Hungary. Rudolph secured the Hungarian cavalry, giving him a decisive edge.
- **Outcome**: Ottokar II was killed in the battle, and his army was defeated. This victory allowed Rudolph of Habsburg to take direct control of Austria and Styria, confiscating them as imperial fiefs.
- **Consequences**: The death of Ottokar ended Bohemia's brief dominance over Austria. The local nobility, disoriented by the last decades of shifting rulers, found a new overlord in the Habsburg king.

The Battle of Marchfeld stands as one of the most significant moments in Austrian medieval history, marking the start of Habsburg rule that would last for centuries.

5.14 The End of the Babenberg Legacy

Although the Babenbergs had not ruled Austria for over three decades by the time of the Battle of Marchfeld, their legacy was still present in the duchy's institutions, churches, and cultural traditions. They had created a stable administrative framework that Ottokar II utilized and expanded. Now the Habsburgs would inherit those structures, building on them to forge a long-lasting monarchy.

In many ways, the Babenbergs had laid the groundwork for a strong, centralized authority in Austria. Their policies in land clearing, urban development, and church patronage shaped a duchy that was viable, economically and socially, even under foreign rule. Once the Habsburgs arrived, they found a region capable of supporting their ambitions—thanks, in part, to the accomplishments of the Babenbergs.

5.15 Remembering the Babenbergs

For centuries after their extinction, the Babenbergs were remembered in Austrian chronicles and legends:

- **Historical Chronicles**: Medieval chroniclers often praised their piety, their support for the Church, and their role in defending the eastern frontier of the empire.
- **Religious Foundations**: Monasteries like Melk and Klosterneuburg kept records of donations and endowments from Babenberg dukes, thus preserving the family's memory.
- **Cultural Myths**: The story of Leopold V capturing Richard the Lionheart became a popular tale, told in various forms. While criticized for its moral implications, it highlighted Austria's emerging role in European politics.

The Babenbergs left an enduring cultural imprint, evident in place names, family tombs, and historical writings. Even though the dynasty came to a dramatic end, their achievements provided the springboard for Austria's next ruling family.

CHAPTER 6: THE EMERGENCE OF THE HABSBURG DYNASTY

When Rudolph of Habsburg defeated King Ottokar II of Bohemia at the Battle of Marchfeld in 1278, a major shift in Central European power occurred. That moment not only ended Bohemia's brief rule over Austria but also set the stage for the Habsburg family to become the new ruling dynasty in the region. Initially, few could have guessed how central the Habsburgs would become to European politics. Over the centuries, they would transform Austria into the core of an expansive realm. But in the late 13th century, they were still relative newcomers to Austrian lands, with everything to prove.

In this chapter, we will explore the early rise of the Habsburgs, focusing on how they consolidated their hold on Austria after defeating Ottokar II. We will also look at the challenges they faced, the methods they employed to unite the local nobility, and the role of the Holy Roman Empire in shaping their fortunes. By tracing the dynasty's first steps in Austria, we gain insight into how they laid long-lasting foundations for governance, cultural development, and dynastic growth.

6.1 The Habsburg Family: Origins and Reputation

The Habsburgs originated from what is now northern Switzerland. Their ancestral seat was the **Habichtsburg** (Hawk's Castle), from which the family name was derived. By the 13th century, they had accumulated moderate estates in the regions around the Rhine and in parts of southwestern Germany. They were not considered among the most powerful princely families of the Holy Roman Empire at that time—those were houses like the Wittelsbachs of Bavaria or the Přemyslids of Bohemia.

However, the Habsburgs had a reputation for:

1. **Political Pragmatism**: They were skilled at forming alliances and making cautious but firm moves in imperial politics.
2. **Close Ties to the Church**: Like many noble families, they donated lands to monasteries and supported ecclesiastical institutions, which helped secure Church backing.

3. **Loyalty to the Empire**: When the imperial throne needed support, the Habsburgs often provided it, gaining favor over time.

Rudolph's election as King of the Romans in 1273 was a turning point for the family. Suddenly, a relatively lesser-known nobleman found himself at the pinnacle of imperial power. He used this position to challenge King Ottokar II's claim over Austria and Styria, setting events in motion that reshaped the region.

6.2 Rudolph I's Confrontation with Ottokar II

Rudolph I's immediate concern after his election was to restore imperial authority over lands that had slipped from the empire's direct control. Ottokar II had taken Austria, Styria, Carinthia, and Carniola without formal imperial approval. Rudolph demanded that Ottokar return these territories, offering to reinvest him if he agreed to pay homage. Ottokar refused, likely because he felt more powerful at the time. The ensuing conflict culminated in the Battle of Marchfeld (1278), where Ottokar died and Rudolph emerged victorious.

6.2.1 Seizure of Austrian Lands

Following the battle, Rudolph moved quickly to secure Austria and Styria:

- **Imperial Confiscation**: He declared that these duchies, once held by Ottokar, reverted to the empire.
- **Habsburg Enfeoffment**: Then he claimed the right, as King of the Romans, to grant them to whomever he chose. Unsurprisingly, he granted them to his own family—his sons, **Albert I** and **Rudolph II**.

This bold step placed the Habsburg dynasty at the head of Austrian rule. However, it also caused friction with local Austrian nobles who were wary of yet another foreign power claiming dominion. Rudolph had to tread carefully to win their acceptance.

6.2.2 Negotiations and Local Resistance

While many Austrian nobles recognized that resisting Rudolph would be difficult, some tested his resolve. A few had backed Ottokar, enjoying privileges under his administration. They worried about losing status or influence under a new regime. To address these concerns, Rudolph:

- **Issued Charters and Guarantees**: He confirmed local liberties, privileges of towns, and the rights of monasteries.
- **Made Strategic Marriages**: The Habsburgs pursued marital alliances with influential noble families, tying them into the new order.
- **Granted Land and Titles**: Loyal supporters could gain grants of land, ensuring their ongoing service to the dynasty.

By the time Rudolph died in 1291, he had laid the foundation for Habsburg rule in Austria and Styria. Still, these lands were not firmly united under a single ruler just yet. His sons divided the territories between them, continuing a tradition of shared family rule.

6.3 Albert I

Upon Rudolph's death, his son Albert I (r. 1298–1308) emerged as the key figure for Habsburg authority in the region. Initially, the empire's electors did not choose Albert as King of the Romans, selecting Adolf of Nassau instead. This setback forced Albert to solidify his base in the Austrian duchies before challenging Adolf.

6.3.1 Conflict with Adolf of Nassau

Adolf of Nassau tried to reduce Albert's influence. Disputes flared over whether the Habsburgs had too much power in Austria. In 1298, tensions boiled over into open conflict. Albert defeated Adolf at the **Battle of Göllheim** (1298). Adolf was killed, and Albert secured his own election as King of the Romans shortly after.

This victory cemented the Habsburgs' dual roles: they now held both the royal (imperial) title and control over the Austrian territories. Yet ruling Austria was not straightforward, as local governance required careful handling of noble interests, urban autonomy, and Church privileges.

6.3.2 Centralizing the Austrian Lands

As King of the Romans and Duke of Austria, Albert I aimed to increase central control:

1. **Administrative Reforms**: He introduced officials known as **Landeshauptleute** (provincial governors) to represent ducal authority in various regions. This reduced the power of independent counts and lesser nobles.

2. **Financial Organization**: Improved tax collection helped fund Albert's policies, including fortifications and the maintenance of an army loyal to the duke.
3. **Legal Oversight**: Albert worked to standardize legal practices, although local customs remained strong. In towns, existing rights were often respected to keep the peace.

Even with these reforms, the Habsburg grasp was still not absolute. Feudal ties and the scattered nature of nobility made full centralization impossible. But Albert's efforts set a pattern for future Habsburg rulers, who would continue to balance local autonomy with a push for dynastic unity.

6.4 Clashes with Swiss Confederates

While Austria became the Habsburg heartland, the family did not abandon their ancestral lands in what is now Switzerland. Albert I tried to reinforce Habsburg authority over Swiss valleys and towns, many of which sought greater independence. This tension contributed to the formation of the **Swiss Confederation**, as local communities allied to resist Habsburg control. Early battles, like the **Battle of Morgarten** (1315, occurring after Albert's reign but tied to Habsburg ambitions), reflected the difficulty the Habsburgs faced in subduing these fiercely independent regions.

Although the Swiss challenges did not immediately threaten Austria, they diverted Habsburg resources and attention, illustrating how the dynasty's scattered possessions could be a burden as well as an asset.

6.5 The Next Generation of Habsburg Rulers

Albert I was assassinated in 1308 by a disaffected relative, leaving a complex situation. Different branches of the Habsburg family took on segments of their holdings. For a time, dynastic unity was lacking, with multiple cousins ruling different parts of the Austrian lands. In broad terms, though, two main lines emerged:

1. **Albertine Line**: Descended from Albert I, they generally held Austria (both Lower and Upper Austria) and maintained a focus on the duchy's core regions.
2. **Leopoldine Line**: Descended from Albert's brother Leopold, they often controlled the Inner Austrian provinces such as Styria, Carinthia, and Carniola, as well as Tyrol in some instances.

This internal division could create confusion, but the Habsburgs maintained a sense of overarching family unity through marriages, treaties, and shared interests. Their collective goal was to keep Austria and its neighboring territories within the family, resisting any external attempts to seize them.

6.6 Focus on Austria

Despite political complexities, the Habsburg rulers recognized that Austria's prosperity was key to their overall influence. They encouraged agricultural expansion, trade along the Danube, and the development of new mines in Styria. Towns such as Vienna, Linz, and Graz benefited from renewed stability and the patronage of the ducal court.

6.6.1 Vienna as a Ducal Capital

Vienna grew in status as the central city of the Habsburg dukes:

- **Fortifications and Urban Charters**: The city's walls were improved, and privileges for merchants were expanded. This attracted trade from the east (Hungary) and west (Bavaria), as well as from Italy via the Alps.
- **Cultural Institutions**: Although not yet the grand metropolis it would become in later centuries, Vienna saw the growth of schools attached to religious institutions, fostering basic literacy and clerical training.
- **Court Life**: The ducal court, while modest compared to later centuries, supported local artisans, scribes, and occasional visiting minstrels. Over time, a unique Austrian court culture began to form, blending German influences with elements from Bohemia, Hungary, and beyond.

6.6.2 Mining in Styria and Carinthia

The mountainous regions of Styria and Carinthia contained valuable ore deposits, including iron and, in some areas, silver. The Habsburgs encouraged mining operations by granting special privileges to miners and inviting skilled workers from other regions. This policy boosted the ducal income, as taxes and fees from mining provided a steady revenue stream.

6.7 The Struggle with Bavaria and Bohemia

The Habsburgs inherited old rivalries from the Babenbergs. Neighboring powers still eyed Austrian lands:

- **Bavaria**: Now ruled by the Wittelsbach family, Bavaria had common borders with Austria. Conflicts over trade tolls, river rights, and land claims persisted. Sometimes these disputes led to small-scale wars or skirmishes.
- **Bohemia**: After the death of Ottokar II, Bohemia had its own succession issues. The Luxembourg dynasty came to power, notably with King John of Bohemia and later his son, Emperor Charles IV. Tensions with the Habsburgs remained, though alliances were formed occasionally to counter bigger threats.

These ongoing rivalries forced the Habsburgs to remain vigilant. They built new fortresses along strategic routes and used diplomatic marriages to reduce tensions. In some cases, they even cooperated with neighboring princes against common enemies like rebellious nobles or external invaders.

6.8 The Mongol Threat and Eastern Relations

Though the Mongol invasions had begun earlier in the 13th century (ravaging parts of Hungary and other regions in Eastern Europe), the Habsburgs in Austria had minimal direct confrontation with Mongol armies. However, the memory of these incursions shaped alliances. Austria sought to maintain cordial ties with Hungary to avoid the region falling again into chaos. This also influenced the approach to trade routes heading eastward, as secure borders were essential for stable commerce.

6.9 Dynastic Marriages: A Strategic Tool

One of the key reasons the Habsburgs expanded their influence so effectively was their use of **dynastic marriages**. They married into many royal and ducal families across Europe. Over time, this strategy would become famously summarized as, "Let others wage war; you, happy Austria, marry." But even in the early period, this policy was apparent:

- **Connections to Hungarian Royalty**: By marrying daughters or sisters to Hungarian princes, the Habsburgs created pacts that helped ensure Hungary would not threaten Austrian borders.
- **Bohemian and Polish Ties**: Though tensions existed, marriages sometimes eased conflicts.
- **Bavaria**: A close neighbor with cultural similarities, Bavaria was also frequently tied by marital arrangements, reducing the likelihood of constant warfare.

These marriages did not guarantee peace, but they often improved the Habsburg position, giving them claims or influence far beyond Austrian borders.

6.10 Internal Governance and the Emergence of Estates

Under the Babenbergs, local lords and towns had enjoyed certain privileges. The Habsburgs continued and sometimes expanded these traditions. Gradually, a system of **Estates** (assemblies of nobles, clergy, and representatives from towns) began taking shape in the Austrian lands. While still far from a democratic parliament, these Estates served as advisory bodies, approving taxes and discussing local concerns. The dukes found it prudent to consult them, especially when funds were needed for military campaigns.

This system provided a form of balance, as powerful nobles and wealthy towns had to be involved in decision-making. Though the dukes retained strong control, the Estates could become a platform for resistance if the ruling family pushed unpopular policies too far.

6.11 The Rise of the "Inner Austrian" Territories

By the early 14th century, Habsburg holdings included not only Lower and Upper Austria but also Styria, Carinthia, and Carniola in certain periods. Collectively, these latter provinces were sometimes referred to as **Inner Austria** because they lay south of the Alps. Managing such geographically diverse lands tested the dynasty's ability to delegate authority:

- **Separate Administrations**: Each province maintained its local customs, diets (Estates), and officials.
- **Occasional Unions**: When one Habsburg ruler held multiple provinces, a measure of unity was achieved, but if the lands were divided among different family branches, they could drift apart.
- **Shared Interests**: All provinces benefited from stable trade routes, shared defense measures, and the overall prestige of the Habsburg name.

This patchwork would persist for centuries, becoming a hallmark of Habsburg governance: multiple territories under one dynasty, each retaining distinct laws and privileges.

6.12 The Challenge of the Imperial Crown

The Habsburg focus on Austria did not mean they ignored the imperial crown. After Albert I, future Habsburgs often aspired to secure election as King of the Romans (and thus Emperor). But the imperial throne was not hereditary; it depended on the votes of the prince-electors. These electors could be swayed by bribes, promises, or strategic alliances, making each imperial election unpredictable.

- **Loss and Regain**: The Habsburgs did not always hold the crown. Other families, like the Luxembourgs (with Emperor Charles IV) and later the Wittelsbachs, also took a turn.
- **Diplomatic Efforts**: Even when they did not wear the imperial crown, the Habsburgs cultivated relationships at the imperial court. Their solid Austrian base gave them resources to remain major players.
- **Long-Term Goal**: Securing the emperorship repeatedly would eventually allow the Habsburgs to dominate imperial politics. But in the 14th century, this was still a work in progress.

6.13 Urban Life and Social Changes

While ducal politics occupied the top of society, everyday life in Austrian towns and villages continued to evolve. Under the Habsburgs:

1. **Towns Expanded**: Freedoms and charters granted by earlier rulers were maintained and sometimes enlarged. Vienna, in particular, grew with the influx of merchants, artisans, and scholars.
2. **Guilds Strengthened**: Craft and merchant guilds regulated trade, upheld quality standards, and protected their members' economic interests. Over time, these guilds formed a backbone of urban social structure.
3. **Rise of a Burgher Class**: A prosperous middle class of merchants and skilled tradespeople emerged in major towns. They supported the Habsburgs when the dukes provided stability and reliable law enforcement, but they could protest if taxes became too heavy.

In rural areas, peasants lived under feudal obligations to local lords, though the specifics varied region by region. Some peasants in mountain valleys enjoyed more freedoms if they provided specialized labor, such as mining or herding. Others faced heavier burdens.

6.14 Cultural Developments under Early Habsburg Rule

The Habsburgs continued the tradition of sponsoring churches, monasteries, and, to a lesser extent, arts at court. Although the real flowering of Austrian culture would come in later centuries, the foundation was laid in this period:

- **Architecture**: Early Gothic styles began to replace Romanesque buildings in some areas. St. Stephen's Church (later Cathedral) in Vienna saw early phases of construction and remodeling.
- **Literary Works**: Chronicles and annals recorded the new dynasty's deeds. Some poems and religious writings circulated in monastic scriptoria.
- **Courtly Traditions**: Tournaments and feasts became more frequent, reflecting the knightly culture that spread across Europe. Although not as opulent as later courts, the Habsburg environment encouraged a growing sense of chivalric values.

6.15 Foreign Policy and Defensive Measures

Securing Austrian borders required vigilance. The Habsburgs faced possible incursions from:

- **Hungary**: While relations were often secured by marriage, tensions could flare if Hungarian rulers felt threatened or if border disputes arose.
- **Venetian Interests**: In Carniola and Carinthia, the Habsburgs sometimes competed with Venice for influence, especially regarding trade routes over the Alps to the Adriatic Sea.
- **French and Imperial Politics**: If the Habsburgs vied for the imperial crown, they had to manage a broad range of alliances. France, the Papacy, and Italian city-states all played roles in imperial contests.

The Habsburg approach combined fortification building, strategic alliances, and, where necessary, military interventions. Although they did not dominate all these fronts, they managed to hold their ground, letting Austria develop in relative security.

6.16 Crises and Family Disputes

Like any ruling dynasty, the Habsburgs were not immune to internal strife. Disagreements over inheritance sometimes boiled over:

1. **Partition Treaties**: To prevent open conflict, Habsburg family members often negotiated partition treaties. These deals divided territories among brothers or cousins but sometimes resulted in fragmented holdings.
2. **Power Struggles**: A strong figure, such as Albert I, could keep the family in line. But when leadership was weak, rival branches might fight for the best lands or alliances.
3. **Imperial Intervention**: If a dispute threatened stability, the emperor (Habsburg or otherwise) could step in to arbitrate. However, such interventions were often guided by political expediency more than fairness.

These disputes did not tear the dynasty apart, but they did complicate governance. By the mid-14th century, the Habsburgs had grown accustomed to juggling multiple provinces, ensuring they stayed united enough to defend their common heritage.

6.17 The Gradual Emergence of a Habsburg "Center"

Even with scattered lands, Austria remained the core of Habsburg power. The family recognized that maintaining strong authority in Vienna and the surrounding regions was critical to their prestige and future ambitions. Over time, Vienna became not just a regional capital but also a symbol of Habsburg legitimacy. Nobles from distant provinces were summoned there for councils, and foreign envoys visited to negotiate treaties. This helped cement a sense of unity.

6.18 Broader European Context

During the 14th century, Europe faced numerous challenges, including:

- **The Great Famine (1315–1317)**: Poor harvests led to widespread hunger in many regions, though Austria was less affected due to its varied agriculture and trade links.
- **The Black Death (mid-14th century)**: This plague ravaged populations across the continent. Austria, like everywhere else, lost a significant percentage of its population, causing social and economic disruptions.
- **The Hundred Years' War (1337–1453)**: Primarily between England and France, it did not directly affect Austria but redirected attention away from the empire, giving the Habsburgs a freer hand in Central Europe.

While these crises often meant hardship, they also allowed the Habsburgs to focus on local consolidation when other powers were distracted. As long as they could keep their internal affairs stable, they had opportunities to grow stronger.

6.19 Steps Toward a Lasting Dynasty

By the latter half of the 14th century, the outlines of a durable Habsburg power base in Austria were clear:

1. **Administrative Systems**: Provincial governors and local Estates created a framework that balanced central authority with regional interests.

2. **Economic Foundations**: Trade and mining provided revenues that supported the ducal household, military ventures, and architectural projects.
3. **Marital Alliances**: The Habsburgs secured ties with neighboring and distant royal houses, setting the stage for future inheritances.
4. **Dynastic Memory**: Chronicles began to depict the Habsburgs as legitimate successors to the Babenbergs, weaving them into the historical narrative of Austria.

These foundations would prove essential when the dynasty faced future trials, including internal disputes and external invasions. The Habsburg model of governance—uniting multiple territories under a single family—would become a defining feature of Central Europe for centuries.

CHAPTER 7: AUSTRIA UNDER THE LATE MIDDLE AGES

7.1 Introduction

By the early to mid-14th century, the Habsburgs had become the rulers of Austria, including core regions like Lower Austria, Upper Austria, Styria, and parts of Carinthia and Carniola. Although they still faced challenges to their authority—both from within the family and from neighboring realms—their control over Austrian lands was gradually solidifying. This period, often termed the **Late Middle Ages** (roughly 1300–1500), saw Austria navigating through dynastic divisions, external conflicts, economic developments, the devastation of plague, and the rise of new cultural institutions.

In this chapter, we will examine the major events and trends that shaped Austria between the 14th and early 16th centuries. This includes internal Habsburg feuds, expansions and losses, the social and economic impact of the Black Death, the founding of the University of Vienna, and the evolving role of Vienna as a political and cultural center. We will also look at the role of the Church during this time, especially in relation to the monarchy, as well as how Austria interacted with its neighbors—Bohemia, Hungary, and Bavaria.

7.2 The Divided Habsburg Lands

During much of the 14th century, the Habsburg family did not rule their territories with a single leader at the top. Instead, different family members held separate parts of the Austrian realms. This division was guided by inheritance treaties that aimed to prevent open war among the Habsburgs. Yet, these "peaceful" arrangements could still lead to tension:

1. **Albertine vs. Leopoldine Lines**
   - **Albertine Line**: Descended from Duke Albert I, they often held Austria proper (Lower and Upper Austria).

- **Leopoldine Line**: Descended from Albert's brother, Duke Leopold, they usually governed the "Inner Austrian" lands, such as Styria, Carinthia, and Carniola, as well as Tyrol in certain periods.
2. **Separate Courts**
   Each line maintained its own court, administration, and seat of government. For example, Vienna typically served as the stronghold for the Albertine branch, while the Leopoldine branch used towns like Graz or Innsbruck.
3. **Coordination Challenges**
   With different dukes ruling different parts of Austria, coordination of policies—especially military or fiscal strategies—could be difficult. If one branch faced a threat, the other might not always provide swift assistance unless certain conditions were met.

Despite these internal complexities, the Habsburg name carried weight in the Holy Roman Empire. Both lines recognized the importance of presenting a united family front when dealing with outside powers or the imperial throne. Over time, the lines would merge again, but the era of divided rule had a lasting impact on local governance and identities within Austria.

7.3 Rise of Vienna as a Key City

Even with the divided lands, **Vienna** continued to develop as the principal city of Lower Austria and, increasingly, as the symbolic heart of the Habsburg dominion. Several factors made Vienna stand out:

- **Strategic Location**: Situated on the Danube River, Vienna was a hub for riverine trade linking the German lands with Hungary and regions further east. The city's markets benefited from the movement of goods, travelers, and pilgrims passing through.
- **Fortifications and Urban Growth**: Through the 14th century, city walls were improved, and new gates and towers were built to protect against raids or sieges. The presence of these defenses provided stability, allowing merchants and craftsmen to invest in urban life.
- **Courtly Activity**: When the duke (especially an Albertine ruler) resided in Vienna, the city benefited from court patronage. Noble families might keep townhouses there, creating demand for luxury goods and fueling cultural activities like feasts and tournaments.

By the late 14th century, Vienna's population had grown to become one of the larger urban centers in the region. It had thriving markets, guilds of artisans, and a community of educated clerics, which set the stage for further cultural and intellectual developments.

7.4 The Black Death and Its Consequences

Like the rest of Europe, Austria was struck by the **Black Death** in the mid-14th century (around 1348–1350). This devastating plague caused widespread mortality, with some regions losing a significant portion of their population. The impact on Austria included:

1. **Population Decline**
   Farms were left untended, and entire villages were sometimes abandoned. Labor shortages forced surviving peasants to negotiate for better terms, occasionally reducing the power of local nobles.
2. **Economic Shifts**
   With fewer workers available, wages rose in towns for skilled craftsmen. Landowners had to offer more favorable conditions to keep peasants on their estates, leading to a slight improvement in living standards for some rural folk. However, trade also slowed due to fear of contagion, harming certain markets.
3. **Religious and Social Responses**
   Many Austrians turned to the Church, seeking spiritual explanations for the plague. Flagellant movements, in which groups traveled from town to town performing public penance, appeared briefly. There were also cases of persecution: Jewish communities, in particular, faced false accusations of well-poisoning, leading to violent attacks and expulsions.

In the aftermath, the Austrian nobility and the Habsburg dukes tried to restore stability. They promoted the resettlement of abandoned lands and offered incentives to attract new farmers or craftsmen. Despite the initial disaster, this period of post-plague rebuilding set the stage for a restructured labor market and re-energized urban growth later in the century.

7.5 Duke Rudolph IV and His Legacy

One of the most notable Austrian rulers of the late 14th century was **Duke Rudolph IV**, often called **"the Founder"** (German: "der Stifter"). He reigned from 1358 until his death in 1365. Although his rule was short, his actions had a long-lasting impact:

1. **Creation of the University of Vienna (1365)**
   Rudolph IV founded the University of Vienna, modeled partly on the University of Paris. It became the first university in the Austrian lands and a vital center of learning in Central Europe. The faculty taught theology, law, medicine, and the liberal arts. Its establishment was a statement of cultural ambition: Rudolph wanted Vienna to match the prestige of other major European cities.

2. **Development of St. Stephen's Church**
   Rudolph championed the expansion and reconstruction of **St. Stephen's Church** in Vienna. He wanted it to reflect the new Gothic style, emphasizing verticality and grandeur. This project would continue well beyond his reign, eventually making St. Stephen's Cathedral a symbol of Vienna's spiritual and cultural life.

3. **The "Privilegium Maius"**
   Rudolph IV is famous for crafting a document known as the *Privilegium Maius*, which claimed special rights and titles for the Austrian dukes—such as the archducal title—allegedly based on ancient privileges. The Holy Roman Emperor at the time, Charles IV of Luxembourg, rejected these claims as forgeries. However, later Habsburg rulers revived the *Privilegium Maius*, using it to assert their elevated status in the empire.

4. **Efforts to Strengthen Central Authority**
   Despite the divided nature of Habsburg lands, Rudolph IV tried to strengthen the sense of unity. He traveled frequently to the Inner Austrian provinces, reaffirmed ducal rights, and sought recognition of Austria's importance within the empire.

Although Rudolph IV died at a young age (around 26), his initiatives, particularly the University of Vienna, left a permanent mark. Future Habsburgs drew upon his legacy to claim higher prestige and to cultivate Vienna as a scholarly center.

7.6 Internal Struggles After Rudolph IV

Rudolph IV's early death created a vacuum that other family members attempted to fill. Since Rudolph left no surviving sons, leadership reverted to his brothers—Albert III and Leopold III—who divided the Habsburg lands again through the **Treaty of Neuberg (1379)**:

- **Albert III**: Took control of Lower Austria (including Vienna) and part of Upper Austria.
- **Leopold III**: Retained the Inner Austrian lands—Styria, Carinthia, and Carniola—as well as Tyrol.

This arrangement mirrored earlier divisions between Albertine and Leopoldine lines. It also set a precedent for repeated subdivisions in subsequent generations. These splitting processes often weakened the overall Habsburg position, forcing them to defend multiple frontiers and keep multiple courts funded. Still, despite the challenges, the family's diverse domains continued to grow in population and productivity over the long run.

7.7 Economic and Social Developments in Towns

By the late 14th and early 15th centuries, Austria's towns were recovering from the plague and seeing renewed commerce. Some factors that shaped urban life included:

1. **Guild Organization**
   Artisans—such as blacksmiths, weavers, and bakers—joined guilds that regulated quality, wages, and the training of apprentices. While guilds protected members from outside competition, they also limited innovation by restricting who could practice certain trades.
2. **Merchants and Long-Distance Trade**
   Merchant families in Vienna and other towns traded goods like salt, iron, textiles, and wine. They established connections with Venice, Bavaria, and Bohemia, among others. Overland routes through the Alps became crucial for carrying goods from northern Italy into the empire.
3. **Town Charters and Privileges**
   Many Austrian towns had charters that granted them the right to hold markets or fairs, collect tolls, and self-govern through town councils. The dukes typically respected these charters, as they needed the towns' economic vitality and tax revenues.

4. **Emerging Middle Class**
   A "burgher" class, made up of wealthier merchants and guild masters, began to hold more influence in local politics. They could serve on councils or even advise the duke on economic matters. This group was not noble, but it gained social standing through wealth and civic responsibility.

Towns thus became small centers of prosperity and relative freedom, providing a counterbalance to the feudal power of rural lords. The dukes, seeking stable income and goods, recognized that supporting urban growth was in their best interest.

7.8 Relations with Neighboring Powers

7.8.1 Conflicts with Bohemia

The **Luxembourg** dynasty in Bohemia was a major rival or sometimes ally of the Habsburgs. The Holy Roman Emperor Charles IV (of the Luxembourg family) had his capital in Prague, which for a time overshadowed Vienna in cultural and imperial affairs. Tensions flared:

- Over boundary issues in regions like Moravia, which lay close to Austrian borders.
- Due to competition for influence in the empire, especially if both families wanted the imperial crown.

At times, marriages and treaties temporarily eased hostilities, but both families remained wary of each other's power.

7.8.2 Austrian-Hungarian Relations

Hungary became a formidable kingdom under leaders like Louis the Great (r. 1342–1382) and later Sigismund of Luxembourg (r. 1387–1437). The Hungarian crown frequently had claims or interests in Austrian lands, especially along the Danube. Austria, in turn, wanted peaceful relations because Hungarian invasions could threaten Vienna. Strategic marriages were again employed:

- The Habsburgs married their daughters to Hungarian princes or kings.
- Hungarian rulers sometimes supported one Habsburg branch over another in internal family disputes, hoping to gain concessions.

7.8.3 Bavaria

Bavaria, ruled by the **Wittelsbach** family, shared language and cultural similarities with Austria, but also had overlapping territorial claims. Disputes along the Inn River or in the Alpine passes were not uncommon. Nonetheless, trade and intermarriages often bound Bavarian and Austrian nobles together. Skirmishes might break out, but they rarely escalated into prolonged wars because both sides valued commerce and recognized that protracted conflict would be too costly.

7.9 Duke Ernest and Frederick III

Within the Leopoldine branch of the Habsburgs, two figures stand out who helped shape Austria's fortunes in the early 15th century: **Duke Ernest "the Iron"** (r. 1402–1424 in parts of Inner Austria) and his son, **Frederick III** (r. 1457–1493 in all Austrian lands, but Holy Roman Emperor from 1452 onward).

1. **Duke Ernest "the Iron"**
   - Gained his nickname from his determined rule and strong will.
   - Tried to keep the Inner Austrian territories cohesive.
   - Engaged in minor conflicts over Carinthian and Carniolan borders.
   - Strengthened alliances through marriages, setting the path for future consolidation.
2. **Frederick III**
   - Inherited a patchwork of lands but later became the undisputed Habsburg head when the Albertine line died out in certain branches.
   - Elected King of the Romans and eventually crowned Holy Roman Emperor in Rome (1452).
   - Famously used the motto **A.E.I.O.U.** which he inscribed on buildings and coins. The meaning is debated, but one interpretation is *"Alles Erdreich ist Österreich untertan"* ("All the world is subject to Austria"), reflecting Frederick's ambition.
   - Focused on centralizing administration and ensuring the Habsburg family's position in the empire.

Under Frederick III, Austria gradually moved toward being a more unified realm, despite ongoing local resistance and the complexities of multiple provinces. His lengthy rule (until 1493) allowed him to navigate numerous challenges, from the Hussite wars in Bohemia to the threat of the expanding Ottoman Empire in the southeast.

7.10 The Hussite Wars and Border Tensions

A major religious and political upheaval emerged in Bohemia in the early 15th century, sparked by the teachings of **Jan Hus** and the broader call for Church reform. After Hus was executed at the Council of Constance in 1415, his followers in Bohemia revolted, leading to the **Hussite Wars** (1419–1434). Although most of the fighting took place in Bohemia, Austria felt the effects:

- **Border Raids**: Hussite forces sometimes conducted raids into Austrian territories, seizing supplies and testing the defenses of local lords.
- **Refugees and Conflict**: Some Austrian nobles supported the Hussites or adopted moderate reform ideas, creating internal tensions with staunch Catholic leaders.
- **Habsburg Response**: Duke Albert V (of the Albertine line) and others participated in imperial campaigns against the Hussites, hoping to contain what they saw as a dangerous heretical movement.

Ultimately, the Hussite Wars ended with a compromise in Bohemia, but they left a legacy of religious strife and sharpened awareness of reformist ideas. Austria's rulers, aligned with the Catholic Church, became increasingly cautious about any religious dissent within their lands.

7.11 Threat from the Ottoman Empire

While the late 14th century saw the Ottoman Turks establishing footholds in the Balkans, it was in the 15th century that their expansion became a pressing concern for Austria. The fall of Constantinople in 1453 underscored the Ottoman Empire's growing might. Though direct Ottoman campaigns into Austrian territory would intensify only in the 16th century, the seeds of conflict were already sown:

- **Hungary as a Buffer**: Much of the Ottoman pressure was felt first in the Kingdom of Hungary. As long as Hungary could resist, Austria had some measure of protection. However, the Habsburgs recognized that a weakened Hungary would expose Austria to invasions.
- **Diplomatic Maneuvers**: Frederick III and later Habsburg rulers occasionally considered alliances or truces with the Ottomans if it would buy peace or protect trade routes. Such negotiations were delicate, as open friendship with the Ottomans could anger the Pope and other Christian monarchs.

- **Fortifications and Military Readiness**: Austrian border towns in Styria and Carinthia slowly began fortifying. Nobles also started training more heavily armed cavalry. The looming Ottoman threat would influence Austria's military priorities for centuries.

7.12 Cultural and Intellectual Life in the Late Middle Ages

Austria's cultural landscape continued to flourish, despite wars and political fragmentation. The **University of Vienna**, firmly established by the mid-15th century, attracted scholars from across the empire. It became known for studies in theology, canon law, and the liberal arts. Monasteries, especially Benedictine and Cistercian ones, remained important centers for manuscript production and learning.

Literary works in Middle High German found an audience in the Austrian courts. Chronicles documenting the lives of dukes, saints, and local heroes circulated among the nobility. Minstrels performed songs that idealized chivalric virtues. Artwork, particularly Gothic altarpieces and sculptures, adorned churches, reflecting both local craftsmanship and influences from neighboring regions like Bohemia and southern Germany.

7.13 Social Hierarchy and the Estates

By the 15th century, Austria had a more defined **Estates system**, comprising:

1. **High Nobility** (princes, counts, major lords)
2. **Lesser Nobility** (knights, smaller landholders)
3. **Clergy** (bishops, abbots, and influential abbesses)
4. **Burghers** (representatives from cities and towns)

These groups met in **Landtage** (provincial diets) to discuss taxes, military levies, and local laws. While ultimate authority lay with the duke, these assemblies could delay or obstruct unpopular measures. Many times, a duke needed the Estates' consent to collect extraordinary taxes or go to war. This system, though not democratic, gave the upper tiers of society some voice and helped the dukes maintain order by sharing limited power.

7.14 Emperor Frederick III and the Consolidation of Power

A turning point in the late 15th century was the personal reign of **Frederick III**, who, after various family disputes, managed to gather the main Austrian territories under his control. His long life (1415–1493) and methodical approach allowed him to outlive many rivals. Significant aspects of his reign include:

- **Imperial Coronation**: In 1452, he became the last Holy Roman Emperor crowned in Rome by the Pope. His imperial status elevated the Habsburg position in Europe.
- **Defensive Wars and Diplomacy**: Frederick often preferred negotiation to open warfare. He believed in strengthening the monarchy through marriage alliances—a strategy that would define Habsburg policy for generations.
- **Challenges from the Nobility**: Some Austrian nobles saw Frederick as too passive, especially regarding threats like the Hussites or the Ottomans. They criticized him for not waging more proactive campaigns, but Frederick's cautious style helped preserve his resources.

Though Frederick's rule was not filled with major military victories, he set a foundation for the Habsburgs to expand their influence through strategic politics. He famously said, "Let others wage war; thou, happy Austria, marry." This phrase, though more commonly associated with the next century, captures the essence of Habsburg expansion by dynastic union.

7.15 The End of the Middle Ages: Maximilian I's Rise

When Frederick III died in 1493, his son **Maximilian I** inherited the Austrian lands and soon became Holy Roman Emperor (officially crowned in 1508, though recognized as Emperor before then). While Maximilian's major reforms and expansions are often discussed as part of the transitional period between the Middle Ages and the Renaissance, his succession effectively closes the purely "medieval" chapter of Austrian history.

Maximilian's rule marked a new era: he reorganized the empire, introduced important administrative reforms, and sought to expand Habsburg power through both warfare and marriage alliances. But the seeds for his achievements had been planted during the Late Middle Ages under Frederick III, Rudolph IV, and other Habsburg predecessors who shaped Austria's institutions, cultural life, and sense of identity.

7.16 Everyday Life for the Common People

Although much of our narrative focuses on dukes, nobles, and major events, it is essential to understand that the majority of Austria's population were peasants or townspeople who led simpler lives:

- **Peasant Duties**: Many peasants owed labor or rents to local lords. Some lived on **Bauernhöfe** (farmsteads) that had been in the same family for generations. In some mountain areas, freer forms of peasant tenure existed, especially where lords needed specialized labor, such as mining.
- **Rural Communities**: Villages often had communal pastures, shared ovens, and local courts for minor disputes. Church life centered on the parish, providing spiritual guidance and social gatherings.
- **Urban Realities**: In towns, most households consisted of an extended family plus apprentices or servants. Narrow streets, wooden buildings, and the risk of fire were daily concerns. Markets were vibrant but could be disrupted by wars or harsh winters.
- **Festivals and Customs**: Religious feast days, harvest celebrations, and small fairs punctuated the calendar. These events offered moments of joy and communal bonding in a society otherwise governed by demanding labor.

Despite hardships—plagues, wars, and feudal obligations—late medieval Austrian society was gradually evolving. Over time, increased trade, urban privileges, and the slow rise of a more monetized economy would set the stage for changes in the coming centuries.

7.17 Prelude to the Early Modern Era

As the 15th century ended, Austria was on the threshold of what historians call the **Early Modern** period. Several developments signaled this transition:

1. **Printing Press**: The spread of printing presses across Europe, including Austrian cities, revolutionized the dissemination of knowledge. Though not yet widespread by 1500, it foreshadowed an era of rapid communication of ideas.
2. **Humanist Thought**: Intellectual movements from Italy began to influence Austrian scholars. Humanism slowly found its way into the University of Vienna, challenging older scholastic methods.
3. **Dynastic Ambitions**: The Habsburgs, under Maximilian I, began forging alliances that would lead to expanded territories. This included connections to Spain (through the marriage of Maximilian's son Philip to Joanna of Castile) and to the Burgundian Netherlands.

All these factors would come together in the 16th century, forever altering Austria's religious, cultural, and political landscape. But to appreciate that era, we must first understand the late medieval context—a time of dynamic growth, division, and re-consolidation that gave Austria a solid foundation on which to build.

CHAPTER 8: THE EARLY MODERN PERIOD AND RELIGIOUS TURMOIL

8.1 Introduction

By the late 15th and early 16th centuries, Austria entered what is commonly referred to as the **Early Modern period**. Under the Habsburg dynasty, the Austrian lands found themselves at the crossroads of significant changes. The Renaissance began influencing culture and scholarship, but perhaps the greatest upheaval came from the **Protestant Reformation**, which started in 1517 when Martin Luther publicized his Ninety-Five Theses. This religious schism would create deep divisions across Europe, including within Austria.

At the same time, the Ottoman Empire continued its expansion into the heart of southeastern Europe. The fall of Constantinople in 1453 had been a warning sign, and by the early to mid-16th century, Ottoman armies were challenging Habsburg rule in Hungary and threatening Vienna itself. This chapter will cover these pivotal developments: the rise of Maximilian I, the transformations introduced by the Reformation, the political adjustments made by the Habsburgs, and the influence of ongoing conflicts with the Ottomans. We will see how Austria balanced an ambitious dynasty's push for power with the internal fractures caused by new religious ideas.

8.2 Emperor Maximilian I

When **Emperor Frederick III** died in 1493, his son **Maximilian I** inherited the Austrian lands and, shortly after, became the new Holy Roman Emperor (though he was never crowned by the Pope in Rome, he assumed the imperial title in 1508 with papal approval). Maximilian's reign set the tone for many developments that would define Austria in the 16th century.

8.2.1 Administrative Reforms

Maximilian recognized the unwieldy nature of the Holy Roman Empire, composed of hundreds of smaller states. He introduced reforms aimed at creating more centralized structures:

- **Imperial Diet**: He sought to regularize the Diet (Reichstag) of the empire, encouraging more frequent assemblies that included princes, ecclesiastical leaders, and city representatives.
- **Imperial Court (Reichskammergericht)**: This supreme court was intended to reduce feuds by providing a legal framework for disputes, though its effectiveness varied.
- **Local Governance**: Within Austria, Maximilian strengthened the role of provincial Estates, but expected them to contribute troops and funds when needed.

8.2.2 Dynastic Marriages and Territorial Gains

Maximilian famously married Mary of Burgundy in 1477, before becoming Emperor, obtaining the wealthy Burgundian Netherlands (today's Belgium and parts of the Netherlands) for the Habsburgs. Through clever marriages and treaties, he also paved the way for Habsburg inheritances in Spain, Bohemia, and Hungary. His motto of forging alliances by marriage rather than war guided future Habsburg policy:

- **Spain**: The marriage of Maximilian's son Philip to Joanna of Castile led to the future creation of a vast Habsburg empire under their son, Charles V.
- **Bohemia and Hungary**: Arrangements eventually allowed the Habsburgs to press claims to these crowns when their ruling dynasties failed.

These unions made Austria the core of a sprawling network of Habsburg territories, though not all lands would be directly governed from Vienna.

8.2.3 Cultural Patronage

Maximilian I was a Renaissance prince in many respects:

- **Patron of Arts**: He supported notable artists like Albrecht Dürer, commissioning works that celebrated his rule and lineage.
- **Humanist Influence**: Scholars who promoted humanist ideas found a place at his court. Latin and the study of classical texts gained status, complementing the older scholastic traditions at the University of Vienna.
- **Chivalric Revival**: Maximilian fostered a romantic image of knighthood and tournaments. He wrote or sponsored works extolling the virtues of knighthood and the history of the Habsburgs.

By the time of his death in 1519, Maximilian had greatly expanded Habsburg prestige, but he also left behind unresolved tensions: the empire was still diverse and fractious, the Ottoman threat loomed, and new religious currents were emerging that would soon transform Austria and Europe.

8.3 The Reformation Reaches Austria

8.3.1 Martin Luther and the Spread of Protestantism

In 1517, Martin Luther, a German monk, sparked fierce debates by questioning certain practices of the Catholic Church, such as the sale of indulgences. His writings quickly spread thanks to the printing press, which allowed pamphlets to circulate widely in the German-speaking lands.

Austrian territories, sharing language and cultural ties with many German states, could not remain isolated from these ideas. Townspeople, knights, and some members of the clergy found Luther's calls for reform appealing. They also appreciated the emphasis on vernacular scripture, allowing ordinary believers to read the Bible in German.

8.3.2 Early Protestant Communities

During the 1520s and 1530s, Protestant beliefs began to take root in specific Austrian regions:

- **Urban Centers**: Merchants and burghers in cities like Vienna and Linz were intrigued by reform ideas. They attended secret gatherings or hosted traveling preachers who shared Lutheran doctrines.
- **Nobility**: Certain nobles saw in Protestantism a chance to challenge the power of the Catholic Church and the Habsburg monarchy. If they embraced Lutheran teaching, they might claim church lands or avoid taxes traditionally owed to ecclesiastical institutions.

Despite these trends, the Habsburg rulers—staunchly Catholic—resisted the spread of Protestantism. They feared that religious diversity would weaken their authority and disrupt alliances with the Pope and other Catholic powers.

8.4 Charles V and the Austrian Branch of the Habsburgs

When Maximilian I died in 1519, the imperial title passed to his grandson **Charles V**, son of Philip the Handsome (Philip I of Castile) and Joanna of Castile. Charles V inherited an enormous realm: Spain, the Spanish New World colonies, the Burgundian Netherlands, and the Habsburg lands in Austria (though day-to-day rule in Austria would often be delegated). This accumulation of territory made him one of the most powerful European monarchs of his era.

However, Charles V also faced multiple challenges:

1. **Wars with France**: The French monarchy contested his Burgundian and Italian holdings.
2. **Ottoman Threat**: The Ottomans expanded into Hungary and reached the gates of Vienna (as we will discuss in detail soon).
3. **Protestantism in Germany**: As Holy Roman Emperor, Charles sought to maintain religious unity but soon discovered that many German princes supported Luther, either out of genuine conviction or for political reasons.

Given Charles's extensive empire, he could not always be physically present in Austria. He thus relied on regents or on his brother, **Ferdinand I**, to manage the Austrian hereditary lands. This situation laid the groundwork for a separate "Austrian Habsburg" line that would later be led by Ferdinand and his descendants.

8.5 The Ottoman Siege of Vienna

One of the most dramatic moments in early modern Austrian history was the **first Ottoman Siege of Vienna** in 1529. After the **Battle of Mohács (1526)**, where the Kingdom of Hungary suffered a crushing defeat and King Louis II died, the Ottoman Empire under Sultan Suleiman the Magnificent pressed onward. Hungary was partly occupied, and the path to Austria lay open.

- **Approach to Vienna**: In 1529, Suleiman's forces, possibly numbering over 100,000 troops, advanced on the city. Vienna's defenders included a small imperial garrison, local militias, and volunteers from the surrounding region.
- **Fortifications**: Vienna's medieval walls were not fully modern, but they had been hastily reinforced. The defenders resisted the Ottoman assaults, which were hampered by muddy conditions and the logistical challenges of a lengthy campaign.

- **Outcome**: After weeks of skirmishes and attempts to breach the walls, Suleiman withdrew. The early onset of winter and supply issues also played a role in his decision. Though the Ottomans retreated, the siege was a stark warning: the Ottoman Empire was capable of reaching deep into Habsburg lands.

This siege left a psychological impact on Austria. The monarchy recognized that defending Vienna was key to protecting the rest of the empire. Efforts to modernize fortifications, improve roads for troop movements, and maintain alliances with other Christian states became top priorities.

8.6 Ferdinand I and the Consolidation of Austrian Rule

While Charles V juggled his vast empire, his brother **Ferdinand I** increasingly took charge of Austria. In 1521, Charles granted Ferdinand control over the Austrian hereditary lands. Ferdinand also married Anna of Bohemia and Hungary, giving him a claim to those thrones after the death of King Louis II at Mohács.

8.6.1 Challenges in Bohemia and Hungary

- **Bohemia**: The local Estates elected Ferdinand king in 1526, but significant Hussite and Protestant influences persisted. Ferdinand had to balance Catholic loyalty with the religious convictions of powerful noble families.
- **Royal Hungary**: Hungary was split. The Ottomans occupied central and southern parts, while Ferdinand claimed the north and west (often called "Royal Hungary"). A rival claimant, John Zápolya, held the eastern region of Transylvania. This division sparked long-running disputes and conflicts.

8.6.2 Religious Policy in Austria

Ferdinand, a devout Catholic, tried to curb Protestant growth:

- **Pressure on Protestant Nobles**: He demanded that nobles remain loyal to Catholicism or risk losing titles and privileges. In practice, many nobles quietly supported Luther's teachings or protected Protestant preachers on their lands.
- **Urban Crackdowns**: In certain cities, Ferdinand placed Catholic governors or bishops who clamped down on Protestant books and gatherings. Still, local authorities sometimes resisted, believing that the Reformation offered a sense of civic independence from the Habsburgs.

- **Limited Tolerance**: Despite his tough stance, Ferdinand occasionally made compromises. With Ottoman threats looming, he needed the support and resources of Protestant lords. Complete suppression would have caused open revolt.

By balancing repression with selective tolerance, Ferdinand aimed to keep Austria intact under Habsburg Catholic rule. However, these tensions only grew as Protestant ideas spread among both nobles and commoners.

8.7 The Council of Trent and the Counter-Reformation

In response to the Protestant Reformation, the Catholic Church convened the **Council of Trent (1545–1563)**, which launched the **Counter-Reformation**. This movement aimed to reform abuses within the Catholic Church while reaffirming core doctrines. It had significant repercussions in Austria:

1. **Jesuit Influence**
   The Jesuit order, established in 1540, played a key role in education and re-Catholicizing regions that had gone Protestant. Jesuits founded schools and colleges in major Austrian towns, teaching Catholic doctrine alongside humanist subjects.
2. **Support from Habsburg Rulers**
   Ferdinand I and his successors backed Counter-Reformation policies. They encouraged or mandated Catholic practices, rebuilt churches, and financed missions to convert or reconvert Protestant areas.
3. **Tensions with Protestant Estates**
   Many Austrian nobles had adopted Lutheran beliefs by the mid-16th century, resenting the idea of forced Catholic uniformity. The Estates occasionally used their bargaining power—especially financial contributions for defense—to press for religious concessions. This push-and-pull between the monarchy's Catholic stance and the Estates' Protestant leanings would define much of Austrian politics in the latter half of the 16th century.

8.8 Socioeconomic Changes in the 16th Century

While religious conflicts dominated headlines, daily life and the economy in Austria were also changing:

- **Population Growth**: After the late medieval plagues, population levels gradually recovered, spurring agricultural expansion. New villages or renewed settlements appeared in areas previously abandoned.
- **Agrarian Shifts**: Some large estates introduced improved farming techniques, such as crop rotation and selective breeding of livestock. Landlords often demanded higher rents or labor dues, sparking peasant unrest in certain regions.
- **Mining and Metallurgy**: The Inner Austrian provinces (Styria, Carinthia, Tyrol) continued developing their iron, silver, and copper mines. These metals were crucial for minting coins, making weapons, and fueling trade.
- **Urban Growth**: Cities like Vienna, Graz, and Innsbruck expanded. Guilds remained important, but some larger businesses emerged, run by wealthy families who could finance mining operations or commercial ventures.
- **Inflation ("Price Revolution")**: Silver from the New World, controlled by the Spanish branch of the Habsburgs, flooded European markets. This contributed to a general increase in prices, affecting peasants who struggled with higher costs of living.

These economic shifts sometimes exacerbated class tensions, as nobles and urban elites profited more quickly than peasants. The monarchy relied on revenues from trade and mining to fund defense against the Ottomans, perpetuating a cycle of taxation that could provoke unrest if pushed too far.

8.9 Maximilian II and Growing Religious Divisions

After Ferdinand I's death in 1564, the Habsburg lands were divided among his sons. The main Austrian territories went to **Maximilian II**, who also became Holy Roman Emperor. Maximilian II was somewhat more open to Protestant ideas than his father, though he remained a Catholic officially.

- **Religious Leanings**: Maximilian II was rumored to hold private sympathy for Lutheranism. He relaxed some persecutions, allowing Protestant nobles and towns a bit more freedom to worship. This policy of relative moderation prevented immediate revolts but also frustrated Catholic hardliners.
- **Ottoman Threat Continues**: The Ottoman Empire under Sultan Selim II still posed a risk, although major campaigns slowed after a series of costly wars. Austria had to maintain frontier defenses, particularly in Royal Hungary.

- **Intellectual Climate**: Vienna continued to attract scholars, including moderate reformers. The University of Vienna had professors sympathetic to Protestant theology, although official policy remained Catholic.

Maximilian II's reign demonstrated the difficulty of ruling a religiously divided land while facing external threats. His balancing act kept Austria from the kind of prolonged religious warfare seen in parts of Germany, but it was clear that tensions could erupt if the monarchy shifted too strongly toward either side.

8.10 Rudolf II

Maximilian II's son, **Rudolf II** (r. 1576–1612), brought a different style to the Habsburg court. Educated in Spain, Rudolf was a devout Catholic yet held a fascination for astrology, alchemy, and the arts. Though he spent much of his reign in Prague, he remained ruler of Austria and Emperor of the Holy Roman Empire.

1. **Artistic and Scientific Patronage**
   Rudolf's court in Prague became a renowned center for artists and intellectuals. Figures like astronomers Tycho Brahe and Johannes Kepler found patronage under Rudolf's sponsorship. This cultural flowering touched Vienna as well, though Rudolf preferred Prague as his main residence.
2. **Religious Conflicts Deepen**
   While Rudolf was personally devout, many of the Estates in Lower and Upper Austria, as well as in Bohemia, pressed for greater religious freedoms. Rudolf oscillated between concessions—such as the Letter of Majesty in Bohemia, granting some religious rights—and attempts at re-Catholicization.
3. **Internal Habsburg Friction**
   Rudolf's eccentricities and perceived inaction on pressing matters, like the Ottoman frontier, angered his more pragmatic relatives. His brother Matthias eventually challenged Rudolf's authority, leading to a family power struggle.

Although Rudolf's reign saw cultural brilliance, the religious polarization in the Habsburg lands continued to grow. Protestant nobles, especially in Austria and Bohemia, were ready to defend their rights by force if necessary, while the monarchy's Catholic faction planned to roll back Protestant gains when they had sufficient power to do so.

8.11 Matthias and Ferdinand II

Matthias took over much of the government from Rudolf II by 1608, eventually becoming Holy Roman Emperor in 1612. He tried to maintain control by making compromises with Protestant Estates, especially in Bohemia and Austria. However, his successor, **Ferdinand II** (crowned King of Bohemia in 1617 and Emperor in 1619), had a strong commitment to the Counter-Reformation.

- **Strict Catholic Policies**: Ferdinand II believed in forcibly returning Protestant lands to the Catholic Church. This approach alarmed Protestant nobles who felt betrayed after decades of relative tolerance.
- **The Defenestration of Prague (1618)**: In Bohemia, tensions exploded when Protestant nobles threw the emperor's representatives out of a window in Prague Castle, igniting the **Thirty Years' War** (1618–1648). Although the war is beyond the immediate scope of this chapter's timeframe, it is important to note that these events grew out of the conflicts brewing in Austria and neighboring regions during the early modern period.

For Austria, Ferdinand II's reign signaled the monarchy's final rejection of religious pluralism. The country would soon become a stronghold of Catholicism, with the monarchy using all means—legal, financial, and military—to suppress Protestant opposition.

8.12 Society and Daily Life in Turbulent Times

Amid these religious and political upheavals, ordinary Austrians carried on with their lives:

1. **Urban Guilds and Crafts**: Guilds remained the backbone of artisanal production in towns. Some guild members embraced Protestant teachings, forming clandestine groups to study the Bible.
2. **Peasant Conditions**: Rural peasants still owed dues to landlords, whether Catholic or Protestant. Some lords who converted to Protestantism treated their peasants with varying degrees of tolerance, while Catholic lords sometimes forced their tenants to attend Catholic Mass.
3. **Witch Hunts**: Like in many parts of Europe, fears of witchcraft occasionally surfaced. Trials occurred sporadically, with both religious and social tensions fueling accusations.

4. **Festivals and Customs**: Despite conflicts, festivals like **Fasching** (Carnival) continued, offering a break from daily hardships. Religious feasts—Catholic or Protestant gatherings—remained central to communal identity.

While Austrian towns benefited from trade and cultural exchange, the countryside often faced local power struggles, especially when lords of different faiths competed for loyalty or imposed strict rules on worship.

8.13 The Legacy of the Early Modern Period in Austria

By the early 17th century, Austria had undergone significant transformation:

- **Habsburg Ascendancy**: Austria lay firmly under Habsburg control, tied to a vast network of dynastic possessions. Although the monarchy faced internal divisions, the idea of a strong, centralized Habsburg realm had taken hold.
- **Religious Division**: Protestant communities existed in many areas, though Catholic rulers tried to suppress them. This religious rift would profoundly shape the political and cultural landscape, erupting into full-blown conflict during the Thirty Years' War.
- **Ottoman Standstill**: The Ottoman Empire remained a major threat, but Austria had proven it could defend Vienna with sufficient resources and strategic alliances. Sporadic truce agreements and shifting front lines in Hungary kept the conflict simmering.
- **Cultural and Intellectual Growth**: The University of Vienna and various monastic schools produced scholars influenced by Renaissance humanism and Counter-Reformation ideals. Artistic patronage, especially under rulers like Maximilian I and Rudolf II, introduced a blend of late Gothic, Renaissance, and early Baroque styles in architecture, painting, and music.

This period set the stage for Austria's future developments: it would become a leading Catholic power in Central Europe, deeply involved in continental conflicts over religion and territory. The seeds of the modern Austrian state—central administration, a professionalized military, and court culture—were planted in these early modern decades.

CHAPTER 9: THE OTTOMAN WARS AND TERRITORIAL ADJUSTMENTS

9.1 Introduction

By the early to mid-17th century, the Austrian Habsburgs had solidified their hold on the Austrian hereditary lands but still faced major challenges both internally and externally. Internally, the aftermath of the Reformation continued to fuel tension between Catholic rulers and Protestant Estates. Externally, the biggest threat came from the **Ottoman Empire**, whose ambitions in Central Europe had already been demonstrated by the siege of Vienna in 1529. Conflicts continued in phases, sometimes called the "Long Turkish War" or subsequent wars that persisted well into the late 17th century.

In this chapter, we will trace how Austria, under Habsburg leadership, dealt with repeated Ottoman aggression, culminating in the **siege of Vienna in 1683**, and how success in these wars allowed Austria to expand its territories significantly—especially in Hungary, Transylvania, and other lands previously under Ottoman control. These victories reshaped Austria's power and status in Europe. We will also look at the broader social and economic consequences of these military struggles, highlighting the ways in which they prepared the stage for the Baroque cultural wave and the transformation of the Austrian state.

9.2 The Long Turkish War

Before the famous siege of 1683, Austria (and the Holy Roman Empire more widely) was already engaged in a series of conflicts known collectively as the **Long Turkish War** (1593–1606). This period overlapped with a time of religious strife in the empire, including the early phases of the Thirty Years' War (1618–1648), which would soon devastate much of Germany. Austria, stuck between internal concerns about Protestant-Catholic hostility and the external Ottoman threat, had to manage resources and alliances carefully.

9.2.1 Causes and Early Campaigns

A mix of factors fueled the Long Turkish War:

- **Ottoman Pressure in Hungary**: The Ottomans controlled much of central Hungary since the Battle of Mohács (1526) and continued to press into border territories. While Royal Hungary recognized Habsburg rule, Ottoman frontier raids persisted, straining the local population.
- **Habsburg Defense**: Austria's strategic priority was to maintain a defensive line along the border regions of Royal Hungary, fortifying towns and castles.
- **Christian Alliances**: The Papacy and other European powers occasionally rallied behind the Habsburgs, providing subsidies or troops to fend off the "Turkish menace." Yet religious divisions within the empire often limited the kind of united front that might have prevented these protracted wars.

Major battles saw both sides gain and lose ground. The Austrians sometimes captured Ottoman forts, only to be pushed back in subsequent campaigns. The war inflicted severe damage on Hungarian and Croatian lands, turning many areas into devastated border zones.

9.2.2 The Peace of Zsitvatorok (1606)

After 13 years of fighting, both the Ottomans and the Habsburgs were exhausted and economically strained. The **Peace of Zsitvatorok** (1606) effectively ended the Long Turkish War, though it did not resolve all territorial issues. It did, however, yield some important outcomes:

1. **Recognition of Habsburg Status**: The Sultan recognized the Habsburg emperor as a legitimate counterpart (although the Ottomans typically avoided using the exact title "Emperor" for European rulers). This diplomatic milestone, while subtle, helped elevate the Habsburgs' prestige.
2. **Temporary Halt in Major Hostilities**: The peace stabilized the border for a while, allowing local communities in Hungary, Croatia, and Austria to begin rebuilding.
3. **Financial Relief**: Both sides reduced immediate expenditures on war, though they remained wary of each other's ambitions.

Despite this treaty, minor skirmishes and raids continued. The uneasy peace would last only a few decades before a new wave of conflict erupted, culminating in the Great Turkish War of the late 17th century.

9.3 The Thirty Years' War and Austria's Predicaments

Though focused primarily on the Ottoman conflicts in this chapter, it is impossible to ignore the **Thirty Years' War (1618–1648)** raging across much of the Holy Roman Empire. Austria, as the seat of Habsburg power, was at the heart of this Catholic-Protestant struggle. The emperor—initially Ferdinand II—tried to maintain Catholic hegemony in the empire, clashing with Protestant princes and their foreign allies (Sweden, France, and others).

1. **Internal Pressures**: Many Austrian nobles had Lutheran sympathies or had converted outright. Ferdinand II's push for Counter-Reformation measures triggered resistance. However, fear of the Ottomans often forced the Estates to supply money and troops to the Habsburg cause in exchange for certain concessions.
2. **Military Focus**: While large parts of the empire were devastated by Swedish, French, and other armies, Austria itself was less directly impacted by the worst ravages of the war. Yet maintaining armies on multiple fronts—against Protestant German states, rebellious Bohemians, and potential Ottoman incursions—proved financially crippling.
3. **Outcome for Austria**: The Peace of Westphalia (1648) ended the Thirty Years' War. Austria emerged more centralized in some respects (in Bohemia, for instance, the Habsburgs tightened their grip), but heavily indebted and militarily strained.

With the empire's religious balance more or less settled—Protestant states recognized in the north, Catholic states like Austria and Bavaria prevailing in the south—the Habsburg monarchy could reorient its energies toward the continuing Ottoman threat on its southeastern frontier.

9.4 Renewed Conflict with the Ottomans

9.4.1 Shifting Alliances and European Diplomacy

By the mid-17th century, the Ottoman Empire faced internal reforms and power struggles, but it remained a formidable force in Southeastern Europe. In Central Europe, the Habsburgs recalibrated their foreign policy, seeking alliances with:

- **Poland-Lithuania**: A significant Christian power to the northeast of the Ottomans.
- **Various German Princes**: Even though some were Protestant, mutual fear of Ottoman expansion could override religious animosities.
- **Venice and Other Italian States**: Venice, long in conflict with the Ottomans over Mediterranean trade routes, had an interest in keeping the Ottoman army busy on land rather than focusing on naval ventures in the Aegean or Adriatic.

Despite these diplomatic maneuvers, the Ottoman Empire found opportunities to press deeper into Hungarian lands once it regained stability under strong sultans like Mehmed IV (r. 1648–1687). This led to a series of campaigns culminating in a direct threat to the Austrian heartland again.

9.4.2 The Decisive 1663–1664 Campaigns

One of the more notable preludes to the Great Turkish War was the conflict of 1663–1664. The Ottomans advanced through Hungary, capturing fortresses and threatening regions close to Austria. Habsburg forces, under the command of generals like Raimondo Montecuccoli, managed to halt the advance at the **Battle of Saint Gotthard** (1664). A hastily arranged peace (the Peace of Vasvár) angered many in Austria, as it granted the Ottomans modest territorial gains and was seen as too lenient. However, Emperor Leopold I (r. 1658–1705) believed the empire was not yet ready for a prolonged war, especially given lingering financial burdens from the Thirty Years' War.

This uneasy truce set the stage for a much larger confrontation when the Ottomans renewed their offensive in the early 1680s, encouraged by internal strife among the Hungarian nobility and new opportunities to press advantage against the Habsburgs.

9.5 The Siege of Vienna

The year **1683** remains one of the most pivotal in Austrian and European history, marking the **second Ottoman Siege of Vienna**. This event, more than any other, galvanized Christian states to form a unified resistance and ultimately reversed the tide of Ottoman expansion in Central Europe.

9.5.1 Ottoman Advance Under Kara Mustafa

Grand Vizier Kara Mustafa led a massive Ottoman army—estimates range from 90,000 to 150,000 troops—into Hungary, swiftly overpowering local fortresses and allies. Encouraged by Hungarian rebels who opposed Habsburg rule, Kara Mustafa aimed to seize Vienna, the symbolic and strategic seat of the Habsburg monarchy. If Vienna fell, Ottoman influence could spread deeper into Central Europe, potentially threatening the German states and beyond.

By July 1683, Ottoman forces reached the outskirts of Vienna. The city's defenses, improved since the 1529 siege, still faced formidable odds. Governor Count Ernst Rüdiger von Starhemberg led roughly 15,000 defenders—including local militia, Imperial troops, and volunteers—against the besiegers. Intense artillery bombardment and tunneling operations placed the city on the brink of collapse by early September.

9.5.2 Relief Forces: Jan Sobieski and the Holy League

What saved Vienna was the **relief army** assembled under the Polish King **John (Jan) III Sobieski**, in alliance with Emperor Leopold I and various German princes. Sobieski's cavalry—the famed "Winged Hussars"—and Imperial contingents converged on the Kahlenberg heights north of Vienna on September 12, 1683. In a swift and decisive battle, the Ottoman lines were broken. Kara Mustafa's army retreated in disarray, leaving behind tents, artillery, and provisions. Vienna was spared.

The victory was celebrated as a monumental event in the Christian world. It signaled that the Ottoman Empire, though still powerful, could be defeated when European states united. For Austria, the relief of Vienna cemented the Habsburgs' position as defenders of Christendom and reshaped the power dynamics in Southeastern Europe.

9.6 The Great Turkish War and Beyond

The relief of Vienna did not end hostilities. Instead, it launched the **Great Turkish War** (1683–1699), also known as the War of the Holy League. Austria, Poland-Lithuania, Venice, and later Russia formed a united front against the Ottomans. Over the next 16 years, the Habsburg military, led by generals such as Charles of Lorraine and Prince Eugene of Savoy, made significant gains in Hungary and the Balkans.

9.6.1 Prince Eugene of Savoy's Role

Prince Eugene of Savoy, a French-born nobleman who entered Habsburg service, quickly became one of the most talented military commanders of his age. He contributed significantly to Habsburg victories:

- **Battle of Mohács (1687)**: A second Mohács (not to be confused with the 1526 battle) ended in a major Ottoman defeat, pushing Ottoman forces further south.
- **Campaigns in Serbia and Bosnia**: Austrian armies occupied Belgrade at times, though some territories changed hands multiple times during the war.

These successes boosted the morale of Imperial forces and established Prince Eugene's reputation as a brilliant strategist, a figure who would remain crucial in subsequent conflicts.

9.6.2 The Treaty of Karlowitz (1699)

The **Treaty of Karlowitz** (1699) ended the Great Turkish War. It was a diplomatic triumph for Austria and its allies, resulting in major territorial concessions by the Ottoman Empire:

1. **Hungary and Transylvania**: Large parts of Hungary, including the entire region of Royal Hungary plus the central territories that had been under Ottoman control, were ceded to the Habsburgs. Transylvania, historically a semi-independent principality under Ottoman suzerainty, also acknowledged Habsburg rule.
2. **Croatia and Slavonia**: These regions, heavily devastated, also fell under Habsburg administration.
3. **Venetian Gains**: Venice received territory in Dalmatia and the Peloponnese, further shrinking Ottoman holdings in Europe.

For Austria, the Treaty of Karlowitz transformed the monarchy into a multi-ethnic empire stretching from the Alps to the Carpathians and the Balkans. This expansion laid the basis for what would become the "Austrian Empire" in the centuries ahead, though it also introduced new administrative challenges as the Habsburgs now ruled over numerous ethnic groups—Magyars, Slavs, Romanians, and others—each with distinct traditions and local elites demanding privileges.

9.7 Social and Economic Impact of the Ottoman Wars

9.7.1 The Frontier Societies

For decades, the southeastern borderlands of the Habsburg monarchy functioned as frontier regions shaped by perpetual conflict. Fortified towns, such as Győr and Pressburg (Bratislava), and a network of smaller fortresses served as defensive outposts. Rural communities faced repeated destruction; peasants sometimes fled into more secure Austrian territories, leaving farmland abandoned. Over time, these same frontiers developed a martial culture where local populations, including Croats, Serbs, and others, served in "Grenzer" units (border troops) with unique privileges.

9.7.2 Economic Burden and Reconstruction

Prolonged warfare demanded massive financial resources. The monarchy collected extraordinary taxes from both Estates and commoners. Debts soared, and currency debasement occasionally shook economic stability. However, the end of major Ottoman threats allowed Habsburg rulers to focus on reconstruction:

- **Repopulating Hungary**: The monarchy encouraged settlers—Germans, Slovaks, Serbs, Romanians, and others—to move into devastated areas. Grants of land and tax exemptions lured many to rebuild farmland.
- **Agricultural Revival**: With relative peace after 1699, grain production expanded, turning parts of Hungary into the "breadbasket" of the monarchy.
- **Urban Growth**: Towns on the Danube and along major trade routes revived. Vienna, already a significant city, grew further as it absorbed administrative responsibilities for these new territories.

9.7.3 Shifts in Feudal Relations

In newly acquired regions like Hungary, local nobles negotiated to preserve traditional rights, including the privileges of the Magyar aristocracy. While the monarchy aimed to streamline governance—reflecting more absolutist tendencies in Western Austria—Hungary remained a separate kingdom within the Habsburg domain, retaining its own diet (parliament) and laws. This compromise foreshadowed future tensions between central imperial authority and local autonomy, an issue that would recur repeatedly in Austrian history.

9.8 Religious Dimensions

9.8.1 The Catholic Church and Eastern Provinces

As Habsburg power extended into areas previously under Ottoman rule, the Catholic hierarchy saw opportunities to re-establish or expand dioceses. Missionary orders, especially Jesuits, Franciscans, and Capuchins, founded schools, built churches, and launched campaigns to convert Orthodox Christians, Muslims (in areas with leftover Ottoman populations), and any lingering Protestants. This re-Catholicization drive encountered varied responses:

- **Orthodox Communities**: Many Orthodox Serbs and Romanians had fled Ottoman territory, settling in Habsburg lands. They received certain religious freedoms if they served in the military or contributed taxes. Complete assimilation was never fully achieved, but Catholic authorities tried to forge unions (e.g., the Greek Catholic Churches).
- **Protestant Resurgence Stifled**: In Austrian "core" provinces, the monarchy remained vigilant against Protestant gatherings, but some Hungarian and Transylvanian nobles insisted on toleration for their Reformed or Lutheran faith. A delicate balance arose, shaped by local bargains and the monarchy's need for loyalty in newly integrated lands.

9.8.2 Jesuit Education and Cultural Influence

Throughout the 17th century, Jesuit colleges multiplied. In newly reclaimed Hungarian towns, these institutions combined religious indoctrination with advanced curricula in rhetoric, philosophy, and sciences. This contributed to a more uniform Catholic elite across the monarchy. The clergy played a growing role in administration, promoting the Baroque style in architecture and liturgy, further cementing the Catholic identity of the expanding Habsburg realm.

9.9 Vienna as a Political and Cultural Hub

With the Ottoman threat rolled back, **Vienna** solidified its status as a major European capital:

1. **Imperial Residence**: Since Emperor Leopold I and his successors governed an enlarged monarchy, the Hofburg in Vienna became the seat of an increasingly centralized administration, at least for the German-speaking provinces.

2. **Defense to Ornament**: The city's fortifications, which had saved it during the siege, were modernized or, over the next century, partially replaced by grand boulevards. Palaces and churches sprang up in the Baroque style, funded by both noble families and the imperial court.
3. **Population Growth**: Refugees from war-ravaged areas and migrants seeking opportunities in administration, crafts, or trade swelled the city's population. Suburbs grew beyond the old city walls, setting the stage for even more dramatic urban expansions in the 18th century.

Vienna's transformation symbolized Austria's shift from a frontier fortress to the core of a confidently expanding empire. The upcoming Baroque era would see the city flourish in music, architecture, and courtly spectacle, reflecting the monarchy's newfound security and ambitions.

9.10 The Role of Key Habsburg Rulers

The late 17th century saw a series of Habsburg emperors who guided Austria through the wars with the Ottomans and subsequent consolidation:

- **Ferdinand III (r. 1637–1657)**: Oversaw Austria's conclusion of the Thirty Years' War. Stabilized internal affairs enough to keep focus on the Ottoman border.
- **Leopold I (r. 1658–1705)**: Central figure during the siege of Vienna in 1683 and the Great Turkish War. A staunch supporter of the Counter-Reformation, he also became a major patron of Baroque culture.
- **Joseph I (r. 1705–1711)** and **Charles VI (r. 1711–1740)**: Continued to defend and administer the newly acquired lands. Charles VI, in particular, attempted to solidify a legal basis for Habsburg succession through the **Pragmatic Sanction (1713)**—a topic we will examine in later chapters.

These rulers faced constant financial strains and local rebellions. Yet their overall success in containing the Ottomans and managing a complex empire paved the way for the monumental cultural era to come.

9.11 Shifting Balance of Power in Europe

With the Treaty of Karlowitz and subsequent treaties like Passarowitz (1718), Austria emerged as a leading Central European power. The empire's frontiers pushed deeper into Southeastern Europe, and the Ottoman retreat created a new balance of power:

- **France vs. Habsburgs**: On the western front, France under Louis XIV and Louis XV became the main rival to Austrian influence. The Spanish Succession War (1701–1714) demonstrated the broad competition between Bourbon and Habsburg claims in Europe.
- **Rise of Russia**: In the east, Russia under Peter the Great began to challenge the Ottomans in the Black Sea region. This opened possibilities for the Habsburgs to coordinate with Russia against the Ottomans, but also introduced a new power dynamic that Austria would need to navigate in the 18th century.
- **Internal Consolidation**: With reduced Ottoman pressure, the monarchy could concentrate on building an administrative state, fostering trade, and harnessing the resources of Hungary and other acquisitions.

These changes set the stage for Austria's involvement in major 18th-century conflicts, like the War of Austrian Succession, but they also enabled a period of relative peace in which arts, music, and architecture could flourish—the hallmark of the Baroque era.

9.12 Everyday Life in the Late 17th Century

While statecraft and warfare shaped the grand narrative, everyday life for most Austrians evolved in the aftermath of repeated conflicts:

1. **Agricultural Patterns**: As farmland in Hungary reopened, peasants there found new opportunities, but also faced feudal obligations to local nobles. In Lower Austria, stable conditions led to improved yields and surpluses for trade, particularly in grain.
2. **Urban Guilds and Crafts**: Towns like Vienna, Graz, and Pressburg saw an expansion of guild-regulated crafts—smithing, weaving, tailoring—providing goods for both the local populace and the military.

3. **Trade Routes**: The Danube became a crucial artery connecting Austrian lands to the Black Sea region. With Ottoman control receding, merchants explored markets once cut off by conflict, facilitating the spread of goods like spices, coffee, and textiles.
4. **Cultural Blending**: Regions reclaimed from Ottoman rule contained diverse populations—Magyars, Slavs, Germans, Romanians, Serbs, and others. Daily interactions in border areas led to a blend of traditions. For instance, coffee, introduced to Vienna by Ottoman traders and soldiers, soon became a local obsession, sparking the famous coffeehouse culture.

9.13 Austria's Military Evolution

The repeated wars with the Ottomans necessitated a more professional and permanent military structure. Key developments included:

- **Standing Army**: Austria moved away from relying solely on feudal levies. Habsburg rulers established a core standing army with standardized training and equipment.
- **Fortification Systems**: Frontier fortresses in Hungary were modernized with bastions and star forts, reflecting the latest military engineering from Italy and the Low Countries.
- **Officer Corps**: Noble families increasingly sent sons into military service as officers, tying their status to loyalty to the Habsburg crown. Prince Eugene of Savoy exemplified the era's new breed of career commanders who combined battlefield prowess with strategic planning.

This modernized army stood in contrast to the earlier ad hoc forces that struggled during the Long Turkish War. By the early 18th century, the Habsburg Monarchy boasted one of the more formidable militaries in Europe, setting the foundation for further expansions of influence.

9.14 Integration of New Territories

9.14.1 Hungary's Position in the Monarchy

Perhaps the most significant outcome of the wars was Hungary's integration. While Hungarian nobles accepted Habsburg sovereignty—often ratified in coronations in

Pressburg or later in Pozsony—they insisted on preserving the Kingdom of Hungary's constitutional traditions. This arrangement became a model of a "composite monarchy," where different regions within the empire retained distinct legal frameworks.

- **Diet of Hungary**: Met periodically, resisting attempts at full centralization.
- **Religious Tensions**: Many Hungarian nobles adhered to Protestant faiths, fueling friction with the Catholic monarchy's re-Catholicization efforts.
- **Economic Development**: By harnessing Hungary's agricultural wealth, the Habsburg state grew stronger. But resentment lingered over heavy taxes and mandatory military service.

9.14.2 Transylvania and Border Regions

Transylvania, long a principality under Ottoman suzerainty, became a Habsburg domain with a measure of autonomy. Its prince and Estates negotiated to keep some local privileges, especially concerning the rights of Romanian Orthodox, Hungarian Reformed, and Saxon Lutheran communities. The monarchy hoped to pacify the region by honoring these arrangements, though Catholic influence steadily grew.

Border regions in Croatia and the Military Frontier (Vojna Krajina) also took shape as heavily militarized zones, populated by communities that served as border guards (Grenzer). In exchange for defending the frontier, these communities received certain exemptions from feudal dues, forging a unique frontier culture.

9.15 Shaping a Multi-Ethnic Empire

By 1700, Austria had transformed into a multi-ethnic mosaic under Habsburg rule. This posed administrative and cultural challenges:

- **Languages**: German was the language of court and administration in the core provinces, but Latin, Hungarian, Croatian, Romanian, Slovak, and other languages prevailed locally.
- **Noble Cooperation**: The Habsburgs relied on local aristocracies (Magyar magnates, Transylvanian princes, Croatian bans) to govern effectively. A delicate balance of power, patronage, and negotiation kept these elites loyal.

- **Religious Pluralism** (to a limited extent): While the monarchy aimed for Catholic uniformity, certain regions retained recognized Protestant or Orthodox communities. The monarchy's approach varied from outright suppression (in core Austrian lands) to grudging tolerance (in Hungary and Transylvania) where local elites were too powerful to ignore.

Thus, the wars with the Ottomans not only shifted borders but also forged the complex social and political structure that would characterize the Habsburg realms for centuries. Austria, no longer just a "German" duchy, now straddled East and West in a real sense.

CHAPTER 10: THE BAROQUE ERA AND THE RISE OF IMPERIAL CULTURE

10.1 Introduction

Having fended off the Ottoman threat and expanded into vast new territories by the end of the 17th century, the Habsburg Monarchy in Austria entered a period of relative stability and prosperity. This environment allowed for the flourishing of **Baroque culture**, characterized by grandeur, dramatic artistry, and a close connection to Catholic spirituality. The imperial court in Vienna, alongside aristocratic patrons, funneled resources into architecture, music, painting, and literature. Lavish church buildings, palaces, and musical compositions became defining features of Austrian society, reflecting both the triumph of the Counter-Reformation and the monarchy's ambition to project power.

In this chapter, we will explore how the Baroque movement took hold in Austria, shaping public spaces, religious life, and courtly expression. We will also see how the Habsburgs used cultural patronage to unify their diverse empire, forging a shared identity that transcended regional differences. This Baroque splendor was not merely decorative: it served as a political tool that reinforced loyalty to the Catholic Church and to the House of Habsburg.

10.2 The Context of the Baroque in Austria

10.2.1 European Baroque Influences

The Baroque style in art and architecture developed in Italy during the late 16th century, partly as a product of the Counter-Reformation. It then spread across Catholic Europe. In the German-speaking lands, and especially in Austria, it arrived in full force during the reign of Emperor Leopold I (r. 1658–1705) and continued under his successors. Key elements included:

- **Ornamentation and Drama**: Baroque designs favored sweeping curves, elaborate decorations, and dynamic forms that aimed to evoke awe and emotion.
- **Religious Fervor**: Many Baroque churches used architecture and interior design—frescoes, gilded altars, sculptures—to draw worshippers into a mystical experience of faith, aligning well with the Catholic Church's emphasis on majesty and devotion.
- **Courtly Splendor**: Secular architecture, such as imperial palaces and aristocratic residences, displayed a grandeur that symbolized the owner's status and authority.

Austria, freshly triumphant against the Ottomans, embraced the Baroque style as a means to celebrate Catholic victory and highlight imperial authority. The monarchy's success in Southeastern Europe provided the wealth needed to fund ambitious building projects and artistic commissions.

10.2.2 The Habsburgs' Catholic Identity

Since the Reformation, the Habsburgs had championed the Counter-Reformation, seeing themselves as the "sword of Catholicism." Baroque art and architecture perfectly expressed the movement's ideals: splendor, emotional depth, and a strong narrative content that could stir devotion. This synergy between monarchy and Church found expression not just in grand cathedrals but also in rural parish churches, monasteries, and pilgrimage sites across the Austrian lands.

10.3 Architecture

10.3.1 Baroque Churches

In post-1683 Austria, many older Gothic churches were remodeled or expanded in the Baroque style. New churches were erected in regions integrated after the Ottoman Wars, reinforcing Catholic presence and celebrating Habsburg rule. Common features included:

1. **Dramatic Facades**: Curved pediments, statues of saints, and ornamental columns greeted the faithful.
2. **Illusionistic Frescoes**: Ceilings often depicted biblical scenes or the triumph of the Church, painted to give an impression of opening up to heaven.

3. **Use of Light**: Large windows and carefully placed domes flooded interiors with light, enhancing the emotional experience of worship.

Monastic orders, especially the Benedictines, Cistercians, and Jesuits, were major patrons. Famous examples range from Melk Abbey, perched above the Danube with its striking façade and richly decorated interior, to the pilgrimage church at Mariazell, which underwent Baroque remodeling during this era.

10.3.2 Palaces and Residences

Austria's aristocracy and the imperial family vied to display their wealth and prestige by constructing or renovating palaces in Vienna and the countryside. Notable among these projects was the **Hofburg** in Vienna, which evolved from a medieval fortress into a sprawling complex with Baroque wings and courtyards. Equally significant:

- **Schönbrunn Palace**: Initially a hunting lodge, it was rebuilt under Emperor Leopold I and later expanded under Maria Theresa (in a period slightly beyond the scope of this chapter, but the origins lay firmly in the Baroque age). Schönbrunn's design and lavish gardens were meant to rival other European monarchs' residences, such as Versailles in France.
- **Belvedere Palace**: Commissioned by Prince Eugene of Savoy, who used his military fortunes to create a grand summer residence. The lower and upper Belvedere structures, set amid formal gardens, exemplify high Baroque design and remain among Vienna's architectural gems.

These palaces served multiple functions: residences for the court or nobility, stages for grand receptions, and visual statements of power that greeted foreign diplomats. Baroque theatrics extended to the design of staircases, ceremonial halls, and gardens, each intended to evoke wonder and admiration.

10.4 Music and Performance at the Imperial Court

10.4.1 Court Composers and Chapel Masters

Music held a prominent place in Baroque Austria. The imperial court in Vienna maintained a chapel (Hofkapelle) and an orchestra of professional musicians. Emperors like Leopold I were themselves musically inclined, occasionally composing or performing. Composers from Italy, Bavaria, and other parts of the empire converged in Vienna:

- **Johann Heinrich Schmelzer**: An Austrian violinist and composer who served at the Habsburg court, contributing instrumental works that shaped the Baroque violin tradition.
- **Antonio Bertali** and **Marc-Antoine Charpentier** (the latter more closely associated with France, but his style influenced composers who visited or studied in Vienna).
- **Later Figures**: Although slightly beyond the strict chronological focus of this chapter, the tradition paved the way for composers like Johann Joseph Fux, who would become a leading figure in Austrian sacred music and counterpoint teaching.

Operas and oratorios, often in Italian or Latin, were performed at the court as well. Elaborate stage machinery, costumes, and set designs demonstrated the monarchy's commitment to spectacle and cultural sophistication. Music was not just entertainment; it reinforced the ruler's prestige and divine right to govern.

10.4.2 Public Festivities and Church Music

Public celebrations—such as the emperor's name day, major weddings, or religious festivals—featured processions, open-air concerts, and fireworks. Liturgical music in churches mirrored this grandeur, with choirs, orchestras, and organs combining for a richly layered sound. The Jesuits, in particular, used theatrical productions and polyphonic music to attract congregations and deepen religious sentiment.

Vienna's musical life gradually extended beyond the palace gates. Wealthy burghers and guilds organized civic festivities, hiring court musicians or commissioning works for special occasions. Thus, a vibrant urban musical culture took root alongside the courtly sphere.

10.5 Painting, Sculpture, and Decorative Arts

10.5.1 Celebrating the Habsburg Dynasty

Artists across Austria painted portraits of Habsburg rulers, saints, and allegorical scenes depicting victories over the Ottomans. Court painters received commissions to immortalize the monarchy's achievements in epic cycles:

- **Ceiling Frescoes**: Palaces and churches alike displayed monumental frescoes glorifying the imperial house. Angels might hold the Habsburg coat of arms, and allegorical figures would present the monarchy as chosen by God to defend Christianity.

- **Portraiture**: Emperors and archdukes were depicted in armor or regalia, emphasizing martial prowess or divine sanction. Women of the court were shown in sumptuous gowns, reflecting both status and the era's ideal of elegance.

10.5.2 Prominent Artists and Patronage

While some leading Baroque artists like Caravaggio or Bernini remained in Italy, Austria cultivated its own talents and attracted foreign masters. Italian architects and fresco painters traveled north to work on large-scale commissions. Central figures included:

- **Martino Altomonte**: Born in Naples but active in Vienna and the Austrian lands, painting historical scenes and altarpieces that combined Italianate drama with local themes.
- **Paul Troger**: A Tyrolean painter who created grandiose frescoes and altarpieces in monasteries across Austria, known for bright color palettes and expressive faces.
- **Georg Raphael Donner**: A sculptor whose works bridged Baroque and early Rococo styles, celebrated for statues that adorned palaces and fountains.

Such artists operated within a well-organized system of patronage. Nobles, bishops, and the imperial court competed to commission the most impressive works, ensuring that Baroque aesthetics permeated both secular and religious buildings.

10.6 The Catholic Church and Baroque Spirituality

10.6.1 The Role of Monasteries

Monastic orders—Benedictines, Cistercians, Augustinians, Capuchins, and Jesuits—played a crucial part in spreading Baroque culture. Their monasteries served as both spiritual centers and cultural hubs:

1. **Architectural Masterpieces**: Abbeys like Melk, Göttweig, and Kremsmünster underwent extensive Baroque remodeling. Their libraries, refectories, and churches showcased frescoes and stucco decorations that illustrated biblical scenes, Church history, and moral lessons.

2. **Learning and Scholarship**: Monastic schools taught not only theology but also the arts. Skilled craftsmen, including woodcarvers and metalworkers, were often trained by or employed in monasteries. Music was cultivated for liturgical purposes, with choirs and orchestras enriching worship.
3. **Pilgrimages and Festivals**: Pilgrimage churches, adorned with miraculous images, thrived in Baroque Austria. Local populations flocked to such sites on feast days, greeted by processions, music, and dramatic sermons. The entire spectacle reinforced communal identities centered on Catholic devotion.

10.6.2 Popular Devotions

Beyond grand architecture, Baroque Catholicism fueled grassroots devotions:

- **Marian Cult**: Veneration of the Virgin Mary soared, with processions, rosary confraternities, and new shrines dedicated to her. Images of the Madonna became focal points in both city churches and rural chapels.
- **Saints and Relics**: The Church showcased relics in elaborate reliquaries, often crowned with precious metals and ornamentation. Feast days of local saints spurred town-wide festivities.
- **Theatrical Preaching**: Preachers, notably Jesuits, employed dramatic gestures, rhetorical devices, and stage-like pulpits to captivate congregations, turning sermons into quasi-performances that stirred strong emotional responses.

All these elements worked in tandem to present a cohesive vision of Catholic faith where art, music, ritual, and monarchy supported one another.

10.7 Court Life and Social Hierarchies

10.7.1 Etiquette and Ceremonial Protocols

With the triumph of the monarchy came an intensified focus on **court ceremony**. Protocols regulated every aspect of imperial audiences, banquets, and daily life in the Hofburg:

- **Rank and Precedence**: Nobles were ranked carefully according to lineage, offices held, and proximity to the imperial family.

- **Sumptuary Laws**: Some forms of dress were restricted to certain ranks, ensuring that one's status was immediately visible.
- **Elaborate Rituals**: From the emperor's morning lever (rising ceremony) to the distribution of official titles, every event followed a script designed to reinforce the mystique of Habsburg sovereignty.

These practices not only impressed foreign ambassadors but also disciplined the nobility, reminding them that their privileges stemmed from the emperor's favor. Baroque etiquette thus served as a political instrument, knitting the aristocracy into a hierarchy with the monarch at its apex.

10.7.2 The Aristocracy and Patron-Client Relations

Austrian nobles, whether they held ancestral titles or were newly elevated for military or administrative service, participated eagerly in Baroque cultural life. To maintain favor, they sponsored operas, built sumptuous town palaces, and hosted lavish balls. This competition for display also nurtured patron-client relationships: lesser nobles or talented artists relied on powerful aristocrats for protection and advancement, while the aristocrats gained prestige through their retinues and sponsored talents.

In the countryside, castles and manor houses reflected scaled-down versions of Baroque opulence—perhaps a Baroque chapel, a grand salon, or formal gardens. The aristocratic lifestyle, though not as ostentatious as in Vienna, mirrored courtly values and rituals.

10.8 Economic Foundations of the Baroque Splendor

10.8.1 Agricultural Wealth

A significant portion of the resources fuelling Baroque construction and patronage came from agriculture, especially in newly acquired territories such as Hungary, where fertile plains produced surplus grains. Nobles shipped grain along the Danube, sold it domestically or to neighboring regions, and reinvested profits in building projects. The monarchy also taxed rural production to fund its military and cultural endeavors.

10.8.2 Mercantile Enterprises

While Austria was not a major maritime trading power like the Dutch Republic or England, it participated in continental trade networks. Merchants in Vienna, Linz, and Trieste (the latter under Habsburg rule in the 18th century) imported luxury goods—textiles, spices, fine furniture—that fed aristocratic tastes. Even small merchants benefited from the capital's demand for ornate furnishings, clothing, and decorative arts.

10.8.3 The Role of Guilds and Skilled Artisans

Skilled artisans in guilds thrived on commissions for church altars, palace interiors, and musical instrument production. Woodcarvers, goldsmiths, stonemasons, tapestry weavers, and organ builders found steady work. This in turn stimulated apprenticeship systems, passing down specialized crafts from generation to generation, ensuring a high standard of quality.

10.9 Intellectual Currents

Baroque Austria was not solely about visual and musical grandeur. Intellectual life also evolved:

1. **Catholic Universities**: The University of Vienna remained a stronghold of Catholic doctrine, with Jesuits heavily involved in teaching theology and philosophy. Scholastic debates continued, but humanist influences and new scientific ideas slowly filtered in from abroad.
2. **Scientific Societies**: Although overshadowed by the monarchy's religious priorities, small circles of scholars studied astronomy, mathematics, and natural science. Some aristocrats sponsored private observatories or "cabinets of curiosities," collecting minerals, exotic animals, and scientific instruments.
3. **Early Enlightenment**: By the early 18th century, seeds of Enlightenment thought appeared. Travelling intellectuals brought new methods of inquiry, though the monarchy and the Church kept tight control over censorship. A tension emerged between the desire for knowledge and the fear that unbridled inquiry might challenge established doctrines.

10.10 Cultural Integration Across the Empire

As the Habsburg domain spanned multiple regions—German Austria, Bohemia, Moravia, Silesia, Hungary, Croatia, Transylvania—Baroque culture became a vehicle for forging unity:

- **Architectural Consistency**: Each region's capital witnessed Baroque building projects, partially funded by local Estates or the monarchy, creating a shared aesthetic that linked Prague, Pressburg, Budapest (Buda), and Graz to Vienna.
- **Administrative Outreach**: Officials traveling from the imperial capital carried courtly manners and tastes, encouraging local elites to adopt Vienna's fashions and ceremonials.
- **Ecclesiastical Networks**: The archbishoprics and bishoprics under Habsburg influence promoted Baroque religious art, ensuring a relatively uniform style and liturgical practice across Catholic enclaves.
- **Festivals Celebrating Imperial Victories**: Anniversaries of the 1683 siege relief or other key battles were observed in multiple cities, with fireworks, processions, and Masses highlighting the monarchy's protective role.

This cultural integration did not eradicate local identities, but it did create an overarching sense of belonging to a grand Catholic empire that projected unity and power through its Baroque aesthetic.

10.11 Notable Figures of the Austrian Baroque

- **Ferdinand II and Leopold I**: Emperors who strongly endorsed the Counter-Reformation and oversaw major expansions in architecture and music.
- **Prince Eugene of Savoy**: While best known as a military commander, he was also a noted patron of the arts. His Belvedere Palace exemplifies the synergy of martial success and cultural ambition.
- **Johann Bernhard Fischer von Erlach (1656–1723)**: Perhaps the most influential Baroque architect in Austria, responsible for designing parts of the Hofburg, the Karlskirche in Vienna, and other monumental buildings.
- **Lukas von Hildebrandt (1668–1745)**: Another leading architect who worked on the Belvedere and many aristocratic palaces, employing a lighter, more ornamental take on the Baroque style that anticipated the Rococo.

- **Johann Joseph Fux (1660–1741)**: A composer and music theorist known for his influential treatise *Gradus ad Parnassum*, which guided generations of European composers in counterpoint.

Together, these and other figures transformed Austria into a powerhouse of Baroque expression, setting standards that would influence future generations of artists and architects.

10.12 Critiques and Challenges

Not everyone adored the lavish expenditures or the heightened emotional tenor of Baroque art. Certain critics—often members of more austere religious orders or those carrying proto-Enlightenment ideas—argued that:

1. **Excessive Ornamental Spending**: The monarchy and high nobility poured money into monumental buildings while peasants still lived in poverty, fueling occasional resentment.
2. **Heavy-Handed Religious Zeal**: Protestant minorities or secular thinkers found the swirling angels and golden altars overwhelming, questioning whether such display overshadowed genuine faith.
3. **Absolutist Overtones**: The pomp of the court sometimes signified an all-powerful ruler, raising concerns about personal freedoms and the autonomy of local Estates. Over time, these critiques would feed into Enlightenment-era calls for reform.

Nonetheless, these challenges did little to halt the Baroque wave, which remained dominant in Austrian high culture through the first half of the 18th century.

10.13 The Transition Toward the 18th Century

By the early 1700s, the Baroque style in Austria reached its zenith. Emperor **Charles VI (r. 1711–1740)** continued patronizing grand projects. His **Pragmatic Sanction (1713)**, which ensured that his daughter Maria Theresa could inherit the Habsburg lands, set the stage for the next era. Under Maria Theresa, many reforms would occur—economic, administrative, and educational—but the Baroque cultural legacy remained palpable in the architecture, music, and social norms of mid-18th-century Austria.

Meanwhile, external challenges persisted:

- **French Rivalry**: Wars of Spanish and later Polish Succession tested Austrian resources.
- **Ottoman Tensions**: Although the Ottomans had retreated, conflicts intermittently flared until treaties like Passarowitz (1718) and Belgrade (1739) fixed boundaries for a time.
- **Rising Prussia**: A new German rival in the north emerged under the Hohenzollerns, eventually clashing with Austria over influence in the empire.

Yet for ordinary Austrians, the early 18th century was a time when stable frontiers and the brilliance of Baroque achievements at court gave an impression of magnificence and divine favor.

10.14 Everyday Life in the Baroque Era

Amid the splendor, daily life for most people in the Habsburg realms involved:

1. **Agrarian Cycles**: Peasants toiled under feudal obligations, but some found improved conditions through expanded markets for surplus grain.
2. **Guild and Craft Routines**: In towns, guilds regulated apprenticeship, ensuring a continuous supply of artisans to meet the high demand for Baroque finery.
3. **Public Festivals**: Church calendars punctuated the year with feasts that combined religious worship and communal celebration. Magnificent processions in city streets exemplified Baroque theatricality reaching beyond the aristocracy.
4. **Social Mobility Limits**: While a few talented individuals rose through church or court patronage, most lived within the constraints of their birth status. The hierarchy was rigid, though occasional expansions of bureaucracy or the army offered some upward paths for the educated or militarily skilled.

The Baroque environment shaped tastes in clothing (voluminous fabrics, bright colors, elaborate wigs), fueled a desire for public spectacle, and reinforced the strong links between religion and everyday life.

CHAPTER 11: THE AGE OF MARIA THERESA AND ENLIGHTENMENT REFORMS

11.1 Introduction

When **Charles VI** died in 1740, his only surviving child was a daughter: **Maria Theresa**. To secure her succession, Charles VI had proclaimed the **Pragmatic Sanction (1713)**, requiring Europe's powers—and the local Estates—to accept that a female could inherit the Habsburg lands if there were no male heirs. Despite these preparations, the monarchy found itself in a precarious position upon Charles VI's death. Various powers questioned the legality of a female ruler, while Austria's finances and army were weaker than they appeared.

Maria Theresa would reign from 1740 to 1780, becoming one of the most significant figures in Austrian history. She faced immediate wars that threatened to dismember her lands, but she also enacted wide-ranging reforms that modernized the state. Her reign is associated with the early spread of **Enlightenment ideas**—yet she remained a devout Catholic who resisted certain liberal philosophies. This chapter explores the War of the Austrian Succession, her attempts to strengthen central authority, the cultural and social transformations under her rule, and the gradual emergence of Enlightenment reforms.

11.2 Prelude: The Pragmatic Sanction and Its Challenges

11.2.1 Charles VI's Efforts

Charles VI spent much of his reign persuading foreign courts and local Estates to recognize the **Pragmatic Sanction**. Through diplomatic efforts, marriages, and sometimes bribes or territorial concessions, he secured (at least on paper) an agreement that the Habsburg lands must remain indivisible. In theory, this meant if Charles died without a son, his eldest daughter could inherit them all, ensuring the monarchy's unity.

However, Charles VI's policies left Austria in a difficult position:

1. **Financial Strain**: The monarchy was heavily indebted due to constant military expenditures and lavish court expenses.
2. **Army's Condition**: Although reforms had begun, the Austrian army was smaller and less modern than that of emerging powers like Prussia.
3. **Diplomatic Vulnerability**: Some European states signed the Pragmatic Sanction only to keep Austria friendly or to gain short-term concessions. They did not necessarily intend to uphold the agreement once Charles VI died.

11.2.2 The European Powers Eye an Opportunity

When Charles VI died in October 1740, many rulers saw a chance to challenge Austria's hold over valuable regions. Prussia, Bavaria, France, Spain, and Saxony all had varying motives to test the new ruler, Maria Theresa. Some claimed distant rights to parts of the Habsburg inheritance (like the Duchy of Milan, the Austrian Netherlands, or Bohemia); others aimed to limit Habsburg power.

Maria Theresa, just 23 years old, inherited a complex realm that spanned Austria, Bohemia, Hungary, parts of Italy, and the Austrian Netherlands. She also married **Francis Stephen of Lorraine**, who became Grand Duke of Tuscany. But in 1740, few believed that a young woman could maintain the monarchy's integrity against seasoned male monarchs determined to seize territory.

11.3 The War of the Austrian Succession (1740–1748)

11.3.1 Prussia's Seizure of Silesia

The first and most shocking blow came from **Frederick II of Prussia** (later known as Frederick the Great). In December 1740, he invaded **Silesia**, a prosperous Habsburg province in the northeast. Frederick justified his move with old claims, but the real reason was Silesia's economic and strategic value. Austria's unprepared army could not stop the Prussians.

Maria Theresa refused to cede Silesia, thus beginning the broader **War of the Austrian Succession**. Prussia's success encouraged other states—Bavaria, France, and Spain—to join in the struggle, hoping to pick off portions of Habsburg territory. This multifront conflict engulfed much of Europe, drawing in Britain and the Dutch Republic on Austria's side, as they opposed French expansion.

11.3.2 Early Struggles and Maria Theresa's Appeal to Hungary

Faced with invasion from multiple directions, Maria Theresa took bold steps:

1. **Hungarian Support**: She traveled to the Hungarian Diet in Pressburg (today's Bratislava), appealing to the Magyar nobility's tradition of loyalty. Holding her infant son Joseph, she pleaded for help to defend the monarchy. According to reports, the Hungarian nobles pledged their "lives and blood" for their queen. This rallying cry helped raise troops and funds.
2. **British and Dutch Aid**: Britain, worried about French dominance on the Continent, supported Austria financially and sent troops. The Dutch also participated, fearing a French push into the Low Countries.

Despite some early defeats, Maria Theresa's determination and these new alliances prevented a total collapse. Austria managed to hold Bohemia against Bavarian and French forces, though at great cost.

11.3.3 Diplomatic Balances

The War of the Austrian Succession became a complex web of alliances. Key developments included:

- **Allied vs. French Blocs**: Austria, Britain, the Dutch Republic, and Hanover (in personal union with Britain) faced France, Prussia, Bavaria, and Spain.
- **Battles from Bohemia to Belgium**: Major engagements raged in Bohemia (Prague threatened), in the Austrian Netherlands (modern Belgium), and along the Rhine. Naval warfare between Britain and France spilled over into colonial theaters.
- **Maria Theresa's Tenacity**: Although lacking direct military experience, she was a capable organizer. She replaced incompetent generals, improved supply systems, and negotiated with aristocrats to secure loyalty. Over time, the Austrian forces became more disciplined, though Prussia retained the advantage in training and leadership under Frederick II.

11.3.4 The Treaty of Aix-la-Chapelle (1748)

By 1748, all sides were weary, and the war had reached a stalemate. The **Treaty of Aix-la-Chapelle** ended the conflict:

1. **Silesia's Loss**: Austria had to accept the permanent loss of most of Silesia to Prussia. This was a significant economic blow and a major humiliation for Maria Theresa.
2. **Recognition of Maria Theresa's Rule**: Her status as the legitimate ruler of the Habsburg lands was reaffirmed. No partition of the monarchy occurred, thus preserving its essential unity.
3. **Restoration of Occupied Territories**: Some conquests on both sides were returned to their original owners under the principle of "status quo ante bellum."

Although Maria Theresa emerged from the war with her monarchy largely intact, she never forgave the loss of Silesia. The outcome set the stage for an intense rivalry between Austria and Prussia, which would shape German and European politics for generations. Nonetheless, the war also showcased Maria Theresa's leadership capacity and secured a degree of internal unity.

11.4 Internal Reforms After the War

11.4.1 Centralization and Administrative Overhaul

Maria Theresa realized that the monarchy's chaotic administration had almost led to its downfall. She and her advisors, like **Friedrich Wilhelm von Haugwitz** and **Count Kaunitz**, introduced reforms designed to strengthen central authority:

1. **Unified Chancellery**: Instead of each province (Austria, Bohemia, Hungary) running entirely separate administrations, she pushed for more coordination from Vienna. While Hungary resisted complete integration, the Austrian and Bohemian chancelleries merged, streamlining decision-making.
2. **Taxation**: She negotiated "perpetual" or longer-term tax agreements with Estates, reducing the need to beg each province's diet for yearly funds. She also tried to standardize tax collection, reducing tax evasion by noble estates.
3. **Professional Bureaucracy**: Maria Theresa hired well-educated civil servants, many from middle-class backgrounds rather than solely from the nobility. Salary-based officials were more loyal and consistent, establishing a stronger state apparatus.

These measures aimed to create a more modern, capable government. Nonetheless, local aristocrats, especially in Hungary, guarded their privileges. The crown had to compromise to maintain their support, guaranteeing that the monarchy remained a "composite state" with various legal traditions intact.

11.4.2 Military Reforms

Having faced Prussia's superior army, Maria Theresa prioritized building a more effective force:

- **Conscription Systems**: The monarchy introduced modest forms of conscription or quotas in certain provinces, though aristocrats managed to exempt many peasants from service.
- **Officer Training**: New military academies were founded, and stricter discipline was enforced. She also encouraged a merit-based promotion system, though noble birth remained important.
- **Supply and Armaments**: She invested in better arsenals, uniforms, and training exercises, trying to catch up to Prussia's well-drilled infantry. Over time, the quality of Austrian artillery improved significantly, which would prove essential in future wars.

These reforms did not transform Austria's army overnight, but they laid the groundwork for stronger performance in the next major conflict—one Maria Theresa was already planning: a chance to retake Silesia from Prussia.

11.5 Diplomatic Revolution and the Seven Years' War

11.5.1 Count Kaunitz's Grand Strategy

Maria Theresa's chief minister, **Wenzel Anton von Kaunitz**, recognized that Austria needed a new diplomatic configuration to challenge Prussia effectively. Traditionally, Austria had allied with Britain against France. But Britain's main concern was colonial rivalry with France, not regaining Silesia for Austria. Kaunitz proposed an **about-face**:

- **Ally with France**: Despite centuries of Habsburg-Bourbon enmity, he believed a Franco-Austrian alliance could isolate Prussia.
- **Secure Russian Support**: He also worked to bring Russia into the coalition, further encircling Frederick II of Prussia.

This approach, which became known as the **Diplomatic Revolution of 1756**, flipped the old alliances: Britain joined forces with Prussia, while Austria, France, and Russia aligned together.

11.5.2 Outbreak of the Seven Years' War

In 1756, Frederick II, suspecting encirclement, launched a preemptive strike against Saxony, igniting the **Seven Years' War**. The conflict played out on multiple continents—Europe, North America (the "French and Indian War"), India, and elsewhere—but the central European theater pitted Prussia against the Austro-French-Russian coalition.

Key aspects in central Europe:

1. **Initial Prussian Success**: Frederick's military genius, combined with Britain's financial support, allowed Prussia to hold off numerically superior enemies.
2. **Austrian Struggles and Gains**: Although Austria won some victories (e.g., at the Battle of Kolin, 1757), they could not decisively break Prussia's resistance.
3. **Russia's Shifting Involvement**: Russian armies invaded East Prussia, threatening Berlin at times, but Russia's Empress Elizabeth died in 1762. Her successor, Peter III, admired Frederick II and withdrew from the war, gutting the anti-Prussian coalition.

11.5.3 Treaty of Hubertusburg (1763)

By 1763, both sides were drained. The **Treaty of Hubertusburg** ended the war in central Europe, returning everything largely to the status quo. Maria Theresa once again failed to recover Silesia. Prussia solidified its status as a great power, while Austria's monarchy learned how difficult it was to conquer Frederick's well-led forces.

Nevertheless, Austria's performance was more respectable than in the War of the Austrian Succession, thanks to improved organization and the Franco-Austrian alliance. The monarchy retained its core territories, and Maria Theresa emerged with a stable realm, albeit still overshadowed by the humiliating permanent loss of Silesia.

11.6 Social and Economic Reforms Under Maria Theresa

11.6.1 Serfdom and Peasant Relief

Maria Theresa, motivated by both moral and practical concerns, introduced measures to protect peasants from the harshest abuses of serfdom. She believed that overexploited peasants would not produce enough revenue for the state, nor supply enough healthy recruits for the army. Her reforms included:

- **Robot Patents**: These decrees regulated the amount of unpaid labor (robot) peasants owed to their lords. Though not abolishing serfdom, they placed some limits on forced labor.
- **Land Registers**: Attempts were made to document landholdings and prevent nobles from arbitrarily increasing dues.
- **Partial Freedoms**: In the Bohemian and Austrian lands, peasants gained a bit more freedom to move or to marry without the lord's absolute veto.

These policies varied by region, as Hungary and other provinces retained strong noble privileges. Still, they represented a step towards more centralized oversight and an early expression of Enlightenment-influenced paternalism, in which the monarch saw herself as responsible for the common welfare.

11.6.2 Education and Bureaucratic Expansion

Maria Theresa and her advisors also saw education as key to forming a loyal, productive society:

1. **School Reforms**: They promoted primary education for children, especially in core Austrian and Bohemian regions. Though the system was rudimentary, parish schools or state-sponsored institutions taught basic literacy and religious instruction.
2. **Joseph von Sonnenfels**: A leading public intellectual who advocated administrative improvements and the moral betterment of society through state intervention. His writings influenced policies that aimed to reduce corruption in officialdom.
3. **Growth of Government Departments**: The monarchy required more skilled clerks, accountants, and legal experts. Bureaucratic offices in Vienna grew, employing educated individuals from the middle class who formed a new administrative elite.

At the same time, the monarchy censored books deemed dangerous to the faith or to the state's authority. Maria Theresa believed in controlling the flow of radical Enlightenment ideas while embracing moderate reforms that strengthened her rule.

11.6.3 Economic Stimulation

Maria Theresa encouraged domestic production and trade:

- **Manufacturing Initiatives**: She granted privileges to local textile, glass, and iron industries. Austrian and Bohemian factories produced uniforms, cannons, and everyday goods, reducing reliance on imports.
- **Internal Customs Barriers**: Some barriers among the Habsburg lands were lowered to create a larger domestic market. This was an early step toward a more unified economic space, though local traditions still slowed full integration.
- **Mercantilist Tendencies**: Like most 18th-century rulers, she favored mercantilism—protecting local industries with tariffs and supporting them with subsidies. This approach improved self-sufficiency but sometimes clashed with Hungary's preference for agricultural exports.

These measures, along with the partial relief of peasants, gradually strengthened the monarchy's tax base and resource pool, fueling further reforms and military readiness.

11.7 Religious Policies

11.7.1 Maria Theresa's Catholic Convictions

Maria Theresa remained a devout Catholic, suspicious of extreme Enlightenment skepticism. She supported the Church's moral authority and believed that a united Catholic faith bolstered the monarchy's stability. However, her faith did not stop her from curbing some church privileges where they interfered with state goals:

- **Bishops and Monasteries**: She subjected many church institutions to state oversight. Monasteries had to keep clear financial records, and the crown regulated new foundations.

- **Censorship**: Books that challenged Catholic doctrine or threatened the monarchy's image were heavily censored. Some Enlightenment works, especially those from France, were banned unless carefully vetted.
- **Toleration?**: Maria Theresa was not inclined toward religious tolerance. Protestants in Austria faced ongoing restrictions. Jews were subject to special taxes and residency limitations, though she did not expel them entirely as some earlier Habsburgs had done.

In short, her approach to religion can be termed a "conservative Enlightenment": modernizing the administrative aspects of the Church but not embracing the broader Enlightenment call for religious pluralism.

11.7.2 Jesuits and Educational Impact

The Jesuits had long played a leading role in Austrian education and the Counter-Reformation. Maria Theresa initially supported them wholeheartedly, but the **Suppression of the Jesuits** by Pope Clement XIV in 1773 (influenced by various European powers suspicious of Jesuit political influence) forced the monarchy to reorganize some educational institutions. She replaced Jesuit-led schools with state-controlled structures, ensuring that the monarchy, not the Church alone, guided curriculum and doctrine. This transition, though done carefully, reflected a broader shift in power from ecclesiastical authorities to the centralized state.

11.8 Court Life and Cultural Flourishing

11.8.1 From Baroque to Rococo and Early Classical Styles

The court of Maria Theresa, building upon the Baroque traditions established in the previous century, gradually incorporated **Rococo** elements—more playful, light, and ornate. Palaces like **Schönbrunn** in Vienna were renovated, showcasing:

1. **Intricate Interiors**: Curved lines, pastel color schemes, gilded decorations, and delicate motifs.
2. **Expanding Gardens**: The famous gardens at Schönbrunn, complete with the Gloriette pavilion, symbolized regal taste and an embrace of "enlightened" nature shaping.
3. **Musical Innovations**: Viennese culture increasingly turned toward forms that would later be known as **Classical**. Composers like Christoph Willibald Gluck reformed opera, while Joseph Haydn gained fame at the Hungarian Esterházy court (closely tied to Vienna).

11.8.2 Court Etiquette and Family

Maria Theresa's court remained elaborate but was also influenced by her personal emphasis on family virtue. She bore 16 children, many of whom she married off to various European dynasties to secure alliances—most famously, **Marie Antoinette**, who wed the future Louis XVI of France. Court ceremony continued to feature strict protocols, but Maria Theresa was known to be more modest in some respects than her predecessors, discouraging overt extravagance and maintaining certain moral standards.

11.8.3 Patronage of the Arts

Maria Theresa and Francis Stephen funded portraitists, sculptors, and architects to decorate imperial residences. While the Empress enjoyed music and drama, she was also conscious of budget constraints, trying to avoid the lavish spending that had plagued earlier reigns. Still, the royal family's presence at opera performances, balls, and receptions kept artistic life in Vienna vibrant. These cultural forms would flourish further under her successors, as Vienna evolved into a center of the Classical music tradition.

11.9 Foreign Policy Beyond Prussia

11.9.1 Ongoing Rivalry with Prussia

Even after the Seven Years' War, Maria Theresa kept a wary eye on Frederick II. Periodic tensions flared over smaller German states. She also recognized that direct confrontation with Prussia was too costly, so she switched to a defensive posture, investing in alliances (with Saxony, Bavaria, or minor principalities) to contain Prussia's influence.

11.9.2 Expansion in Southeastern Europe

Austria participated in further wars against the Ottoman Empire during Maria Theresa's reign, albeit on a smaller scale than earlier. Gains were modest: some fortresses in the Balkans or adjustments of border lines. Nonetheless, these expansions consolidated Habsburg control in parts of Croatia and strengthened the Military Frontier.

Maria Theresa also had to deal with **Russian expansion** and the **Partitions of Poland** (1772, 1793, 1795). In the first partition (1772), Austria took **Galicia**, a Polish region. Though Maria Theresa reportedly felt uneasy about dismantling Poland, she agreed to secure Austria's strategic interests. This acquisition, while beneficial economically (Galicia had salt mines and agricultural lands), added yet another distinct ethnic and cultural group to the monarchy's population.

11.10 The Later Years and the Co-Regency with Joseph II

By the 1760s and 1770s, Maria Theresa's health began to decline, and she gradually involved her son **Joseph II** in governance. In 1765, after Francis Stephen died, Joseph II was elected Holy Roman Emperor while Maria Theresa retained control over the Habsburg lands. The two exercised a "co-regency," though Maria Theresa held the decisive voice. Their relationship was sometimes tense, as Joseph leaned toward more radical Enlightenment reforms, while Maria Theresa stayed more conservative.

11.10.1 Further Reforms in Taxation and Administration

In the final phase of her reign, Maria Theresa continued to refine the bureaucracy:

- **State Councils**: She established specialized councils for war, finance, and justice, staffed by professionals.
- **Provincial Integration**: Though not eliminating local diets, she tried to place more power in the hands of royal commissioners (Gubernien) who reported directly to Vienna.
- **Legal Codification**: Efforts were made to standardize criminal codes and judicial procedures, culminating in more rational, uniform laws—though many exceptions remained.

Joseph II supported these changes but pushed for faster, more radical action, particularly regarding the Church.

11.10.2 Economic and Social Climate in the 1770s

Austria's population steadily grew, aided by agricultural improvements and relative peace after the Seven Years' War. Some regions saw the beginnings of proto-industrial activity, especially in textiles or ironworks. Urban centers like Vienna, Prague, and Pressburg were buzzing with new ideas—German translations of Enlightenment works circulated discreetly, stirring discussions among the educated.

Yet the monarchy remained cautious about freedom of expression. Maria Theresa believed in guiding reforms from above, not unleashing revolutionary impulses. She compromised with the aristocracy to ensure political stability. This stable environment paved the way for Joseph II to attempt a much broader reform agenda once he assumed sole power.

11.11 Impact and Legacy of Maria Theresa

Maria Theresa passed away in 1780. Her four decades on the throne shaped Austria in profound ways:

1. **Preservation of the Habsburg Monarchy**: Despite two major wars with Prussia, she held the empire together, refusing to let opportunistic rivals carve it up.
2. **Modernizing the State**: Her administrative, military, and economic reforms laid the groundwork for a more centralized, coherent government. Future rulers, especially Joseph II, would build on these foundations.
3. **Cultural Vitality**: The monarchy's cultural scene thrived, moving from Baroque to Rococo, setting the stage for the Classical era in music. Courtly life balanced piety with spectacle.
4. **Mixed Approach to Enlightenment**: Maria Theresa selectively embraced Enlightenment-inspired efficiency and paternalistic social improvements while rejecting religious tolerance and broader liberal freedoms.

Her reign ended the old notion of a static, feudal monarchy. She launched Austria on a path toward a more "enlightened absolutism," though she never fully relinquished traditional Catholic and aristocratic values. The next chapter will examine how her son, **Joseph II**, took this project further, attempting sweeping changes that tested the very limits of imperial authority and triggered significant social reactions.

CHAPTER 12: JOSEPH II AND THE QUEST FOR MODERNIZATION

12.1 Introduction

When **Maria Theresa** died in 1780, her son **Joseph II** became the sole ruler of the Habsburg Monarchy. He had already served as Emperor and co-regent but now possessed full authority. Joseph II (r. 1780–1790) is remembered as the epitome of an **"enlightened absolutist"**—a monarch who embraced Enlightenment ideals of reason, progress, and rational administration, yet held firm to the principle of centralized monarchical power.

His ten-year reign was marked by a whirlwind of ambitious reforms touching every aspect of society: religion, administration, legal systems, agriculture, and more. Yet, Joseph II's rapid pace and lack of compromise often provoked opposition, leading to a mixed legacy of achievements and failures. This chapter explores his major reform programs, the resistance he faced from nobles and even commoners, and how his policies reflected Enlightenment thought. We also look at the broader European context, as the French Revolution broke out near the end of his reign, foreshadowing dramatic changes in the continent's political landscape.

12.2 Joseph II's Personality and Outlook

12.2.1 Enlightenment Influences

Joseph II was deeply influenced by **Voltaire**, **Montesquieu**, and other Enlightenment thinkers. While his mother, Maria Theresa, had been selective and cautious about these ideas, Joseph was far more open to them:

1. **Reason and Utility**: He believed that policies should be guided by rational principles and aimed at the "greatest good for the greatest number."
2. **State above Privilege**: Joseph disliked feudal privileges that hindered a more efficient state, seeing them as irrational relics of the past.

3. **Centralized Control**: He shared his mother's desire for a strong monarchy but went further in trying to impose uniform laws and institutions across his diverse empire.

12.2.2 Personal Qualities

Joseph II was diligent and energetic, often working long hours on state business. He traveled incognito to observe local conditions, speaking directly with peasants or city dwellers. However, he could be impatient and stubborn. Critics noted he rarely consulted those actually affected by his decrees, and he struggled with the delicate art of political compromise. His sense of urgency, while admirable, generated friction as he tried to overhaul centuries of custom in just a few years.

12.3 Religious Reforms: Toleration and the Church

12.3.1 Edict of Toleration (1781–1782)

One of Joseph II's boldest moves was his **Edict of Toleration**, granting non-Catholics—Lutherans, Calvinists, and Orthodox Christians—greater freedom of worship. They could establish their own schools, own property, and practice professions without the severe limitations imposed earlier. In 1782, he extended limited toleration to Jews, easing residency restrictions and taxes aimed at them.

These decrees reflected Joseph's belief that religious uniformity was not necessary for a loyal, productive society. He saw religious persecution as wasteful, harmful to economic growth, and contrary to Enlightenment principles of individual conscience. Nonetheless, full equality did not exist. Catholics retained a privileged status, and many local officials resisted implementing the reforms in practice.

12.3.2 Church Under State Control

Going beyond toleration, Joseph II pursued a policy sometimes called **"Josephinism,"** which sought to subordinate the Catholic Church to the state:

1. **Monastic Suppressions**: He closed hundreds of monasteries that he deemed unproductive—those not involved in education, healthcare, or parish work. The proceeds from their assets were funneled into a "Religious Fund" to pay for parish priests and social needs.

2. **Regulation of Worship**: Joseph mandated shorter, more simplified church services, reduced feast days, and limited pilgrimages. He believed elaborate devotions wasted time and clashed with rational efficiency.
3. **State-Run Seminaries**: He created new seminaries under government oversight to ensure clergy were educated in line with state interests rather than strict ecclesiastical tradition.

These policies provoked an outcry from many clergy and devout Catholics who saw Joseph's intrusions as a direct assault on the Church's autonomy. Even Pope Pius VI visited Vienna in 1782, hoping to moderate Joseph's actions, but the emperor remained firm. Tension grew between Catholic conservatives and the imperial government.

12.4 Administrative Centralization

12.4.1 Uniform Governance Across the Empire

Joseph II believed that his mother's cautious approach to integrating the monarchy's regions had not gone far enough. He aimed for uniformity:

- **New Districts**: He redrew provincial boundaries into "circles" governed by appointed officials reporting to Vienna. Traditional diets (like the Hungarian Diet) found their powers reduced, sparking opposition.
- **German as Administrative Language**: Joseph insisted on using German in official business throughout the empire, including in Hungary, Bohemia, and Galicia. He argued that a single language would streamline administration. But non-German elites, especially Hungarian magnates, saw this as an attack on their identity.

12.4.2 Bureaucracy and Meritocracy

Building on Maria Theresa's reforms, Joseph expanded the civil service:

1. **Promotion by Merit**: He tried to ensure that capable individuals rose in the ranks, regardless of noble birth. This created some opportunities for educated commoners.
2. **Financial Efficiency**: Joseph introduced new tax structures that aimed to include nobility's lands under consistent rules, reducing feudal exemptions.

3. **Census and Cadaster**: He commissioned population counts and land surveys (cadaster) to rationalize tax collection. However, local nobles often resisted, fearing higher burdens if their land was fully registered.

Overnight changes to centuries-old privileges alienated many powerful interest groups. While Joseph saw his approach as modern and equitable, Hungarian and Bohemian aristocrats saw it as an assault on their historic liberties.

12.5 Legal and Social Policies

12.5.1 Abolition of Serfdom (1781 in Bohemia; 1785 in Galicia, etc.)

One of Joseph II's most significant acts was to curtail or abolish serfdom in various parts of the monarchy:

- **Emancipation Edicts**: He declared that peasants should be free to marry, move, and choose occupations without their lord's permission. They were also permitted to own property.
- **Retained Obligations**: While ending the personal bondage aspect of serfdom, Joseph did not entirely remove feudal dues. Peasants still owed rents or labor services, but these were more regulated and supposedly fairer.

These moves pleased many peasants, at least in theory, but enraged landowning nobles who relied on cheap labor. Implementation varied widely by region, and many local officials dragged their feet. In Hungary, Joseph delayed fully implementing the reforms until 1785, prompting further controversy.

12.5.2 Criminal Law and Judicial Modernization

Joseph II pursued a more rational legal system:

- **Torture Abolished**: He formally prohibited the use of torture as a means of investigation or punishment, aligning with Enlightenment ideals of humane justice.
- **Death Penalty Limited**: Joseph was influenced by thinkers like Cesare Beccaria, who argued against capital punishment. The emperor restricted its use, though he did not ban it outright.

- **Unified Codes**: He aimed for a single set of legal codes across the monarchy, diminishing regional legal variations. This again met resistance from local elites who were used to their own laws.

These changes improved legal fairness in some areas. They also spurred an expansion of the legal profession and the centralized court system, furthering the monarchy's control over local jurisdictions.

12.6 Economic and Educational Reforms

12.6.1 Commercial Freedoms and Guild Reforms

Joseph wanted a more dynamic economy:

- **Guild Restrictions Eased**: He reduced the power of guilds, believing they stifled competition and innovation. People could practice trades with fewer guild regulations, encouraging entrepreneurship.
- **Internal Tariffs**: Following mercantilist logic, Joseph still used protective measures for certain industries, but he tried to eliminate some internal barriers between Habsburg provinces to create a larger single market.

12.6.2 Agricultural Improvements

Continuing and deepening Maria Theresa's approach, Joseph promoted better farming methods, drainage of wetlands, and crop diversification. Some model farms were established with government backing. The partial liberation of peasants was intended to encourage them to work more efficiently, though many peasants lacked capital or knowledge to significantly expand production.

12.6.3 Education and Enlightenment Ideals

Joseph advanced a universal schooling policy:

- **Primary Schools**: Building upon Maria Theresa's basic system, he sought to make elementary education accessible to boys and girls. The curriculum often combined basic literacy, arithmetic, and Catholic moral teaching, though with less emphasis on Church dogma than before.
- **State Universities**: He reorganized universities to reduce church influence, introducing secular subjects like science, law, medicine, and political economy. This produced a new generation of professionals who could staff the bureaucracy or the expanding army's officer corps.

Nevertheless, the scope of these changes outpaced the monarchy's capacity to implement them evenly. Rural areas often lacked enough teachers or resources, and local elites—secular or clerical—resisted outside interference.

12.7 Reactions and Resistance

12.7.1 Aristocratic Opposition

Nobles in Hungary, Bohemia, and other provinces fiercely resented Joseph's centralization, language policy, and the weakening of feudal privileges. The Hungarian Diet refused to recognize many of his decrees. In retaliation, Joseph ruled Hungary by decree, refusing to be crowned with the Holy Crown of St. Stephen so that he might bypass certain constitutional restraints. This heavy-handed approach only deepened noble anger.

12.7.2 Clerical Discontent

Joseph's closure of monasteries and regulation of church activities alienated many bishops and parish priests. They complained to Rome and to sympathetic Catholic monarchs. While Joseph insisted the changes were "useful" for the people and the state, traditionalist clergy believed he was undermining Christian piety and ignoring local devotions. The "Josephinist" liturgical reforms—like banning certain processions—provoked resentment among common folk who valued these longstanding traditions.

12.7.3 Peasant Unrest and Implementation Gaps

Though some peasants welcomed the end of serfdom, confusion over new responsibilities led to local conflicts. In some areas, peasants misunderstood reforms as the complete abolition of feudal dues, clashing with nobles who insisted that rent and labor obligations remained. Joseph's administration struggled to communicate the nuances of the new edicts effectively. Where local officials resisted, the reforms remained on paper only, breeding frustration among peasants who had hoped for genuine freedom.

12.8 Foreign Policy During Joseph II's Reign

12.8.1 Alliance with Russia and Conflicts with the Ottomans

Like his mother, Joseph looked to expand Habsburg influence in Southeastern Europe. He formed an alliance with **Catherine the Great** of Russia, planning to partition Ottoman territories. In 1787, Austria and Russia went to war against the Ottoman Empire:

- **Mixed Results**: Joseph's armies had some successes but also suffered setbacks, partly due to poor coordination and local disease outbreaks.
- **Costly Strain**: Maintaining large forces in the Balkans drained the treasury, and discontent at home rose. Meanwhile, Prussia watched for an opportunity to undermine Austria again.

12.8.2 Attempted Annexations and Diplomatic Maneuvers

Joseph also eyed Bavaria, hoping for a "swap" that would give Austria contiguous German lands in exchange for some eastern territories. This plan—known as the **Bavarian Exchange**—met resistance from the Bavarian elector and from Prussia, which insisted on preserving the balance of power in the Holy Roman Empire. Joseph's overreach thus came to nothing, harming his reputation as a skilled diplomat.

12.9 The Shadow of the French Revolution

In 1789, as Joseph's reforms already faced intense opposition, the **French Revolution** began. Although early revolutionaries cited Enlightenment ideals that Joseph himself admired, the radical turn in France—dethroning a king and challenging aristocratic privilege—frightened European monarchs. Joseph's own health declined, and he worried about revolutionary contagion spreading to his provinces, particularly given the widespread dissatisfaction with his policies.

Though the French Revolution would not directly consume Austria until after Joseph's death, it symbolized how Enlightenment ideas could lead to upheaval rather than top-down reforms. Joseph found himself in the paradoxical position of championing rational, centralized changes while also having to suppress demands for more radical or democratic transformations.

12.10 The Final Year and Joseph's Death

Overwhelmed by war expenses, administrative turmoil, and resistance on every side, Joseph II began to repeal some of his decrees in 1790, seeking to prevent the monarchy from fracturing. He restored certain Hungarian privileges and moderated religious reforms. Ill with tuberculosis, he died in February 1790 at the age of 48.

In a final, somewhat tragic note, Joseph reportedly asked that his epitaph read: "Here lies Joseph II, who failed in all he undertook." This self-criticism reflected the disappointment of seeing many reforms undone or watered down. Yet, his legacy is more complex than failure:

1. **Laying the Foundation for Modernization**: Even undone decrees left lasting impressions. Many officials trained under Joseph's system continued to push for rational governance.
2. **Stimulating Debate**: Joseph's boldness forced aristocrats, clerics, and commoners to confront new ideas of state, society, and individual rights.
3. **Prototype of Enlightened Absolutism**: His reign exemplified the best and worst of trying to impose top-down Enlightenment: visionary reforms met by practical constraints and cultural resistance.

12.11 Evaluating Joseph II's Impact

12.11.1 Lasting Reforms

Some of Joseph's initiatives endured in modified forms:

- **Toleration**: Even if partially rolled back, Joseph's Toleration Edict paved the way for future religious freedoms.
- **Peasant Rights**: Full serfdom would be gradually dismantled. His laws at least made it impossible to return to older forms of bondage.
- **Centralized Administration**: Austria remained more centralized than it had been before 1740. Joseph's concept of a unified, modern bureaucracy influenced successors like Leopold II and Francis II (later Emperor Francis I of Austria).

12.11.2 Seeds of Future Tension

Joseph's confrontation with Hungarian, Bohemian, and Austrian nobles foreshadowed ongoing struggles between central rulers and local elites. National sentiments stirred by his attempt to impose German language policies also reappeared in the 19th century, fueling the rise of ethnic nationalism.

Moreover, by interfering so heavily in the Church, Joseph triggered a debate about the boundary between ecclesiastical authority and state power. Later 19th-century controversies—like those over state education or civil marriage—would echo these tensions.

12.12 Aftermath

Joseph II's brother, **Leopold II** (r. 1790–1792), succeeded him. Leopold quickly tried to calm the unrest by restoring some local rights and reversing certain controversial decrees. He also ended the Ottoman war. His short reign stabilized the monarchy internally. Leopold upheld some of Joseph's progressive ideas but proceeded more carefully.

When Leopold II died in 1792, his son **Francis II** (later Emperor Francis I of Austria) confronted the challenge of the French Revolutionary Wars, which soon embroiled Austria in continuous conflict. Thus, Joseph's dream of a peaceful, enlightened monarchy was overshadowed by decades of warfare and conservative backlash. Over time, many would look back on Joseph's reign with nostalgia for progressive possibilities that Europe's turmoil had cut short.

12.13 Cultural Developments Under Joseph II

Despite the political turbulence, cultural life in Vienna and other Austrian cities thrived:

- **Music**: The era saw the height of **Haydn**'s career and the early maturity of **Wolfgang Amadeus Mozart**, both associated with the Viennese Classical style that shaped Western music. Joseph II personally attended some performances, famously quipping about Mozart's "too many notes" in *The Abduction from the Seraglio*, though he appreciated the composer's talent.

135

- **Theater and Opera Reform**: Joseph believed in making opera more accessible and moral. He commissioned **German-language operas**, hoping to move away from exclusively Italian works. The result was a flowering of Singspiel (a form of German light opera), culminating in Mozart's *Die Zauberflöte* near the end of the century.
- **Artists and Intellectuals**: Viennese salons grew as centers of discussion among nobles, bourgeois intellectuals, and visiting scholars. Though censorship remained in place, some works of the French Enlightenment circulated discreetly, influencing a new generation of writers.

Thus, Joseph's quest for modernization ran parallel with an extraordinary blossoming of Austrian cultural achievements, bridging Baroque traditions and the dawn of a more rational, classicist aesthetic.

CHAPTER 13: THE NAPOLEONIC ERA AND THE RESHAPING OF EUROPE

13.1 Introduction

By the final decade of the 18th century, Austria stood at a crossroads. The energetic but controversial reign of **Joseph II (1780–1790)** had stirred hopes of modernization while provoking resistance among nobles, clergy, and other interest groups. In the broader European context, the **French Revolution (1789–1799)** erupted, ultimately transforming France into a formidable republic and then an empire under **Napoleon Bonaparte**. For the Austrian Habsburg Monarchy—a leading Catholic power long invested in preserving the old order—French revolutionary zeal posed not just a diplomatic challenge, but an existential threat.

Over the next two decades, Austria would fight multiple coalitions against revolutionary and Napoleonic France. The wars tested the monarchy's political will, financial capacity, and military structure. These upheavals contributed to the dissolution of the Holy Roman Empire in 1806 and the redefinition of Austria under a new imperial title. They also catalyzed internal reforms, as Austrian leaders realized they had to strengthen and modernize the state to survive. By 1815, after the fall of Napoleon, Austria helped orchestrate the **Congress of Vienna**, reshaping Europe's borders and diplomatic systems for decades to come.

This chapter examines Austria's role during the **Napoleonic Wars**, describing how repeated conflict both weakened and, paradoxically, revitalized the monarchy. We will see the monarchy's military struggles, key treaties with Napoleon, the complex alliances that arose, and the final push that saw Austria join in the defeat of the French Empire.

13.2 Austria on the Eve of Revolutionary Turmoil

Before France's dramatic changes, Austria had already experienced transitions under Joseph II, followed by a brief, more cautious reign of **Leopold II (1790–1792)**.

Then, **Francis II** (later Emperor Francis I of Austria) ascended the throne in 1792. Francis II was no ardent reformer like Joseph II; he preferred stability and tradition, especially in the face of growing radical currents emanating from France.

1. **Societal Pulse**: The monarchy's nobility had regained some of its old privileges, pushing back against Joseph's centralization. At the same time, some intellectuals within Austria felt drawn to Enlightenment ideals, sympathetic to aspects of the French revolutionary message. The government, however, clamped down on political dissent.
2. **Military Condition**: Austria's military reforms were incomplete. Although Joseph II had tried to modernize the army, the officer corps remained dominated by noble families, and logistical systems were still outdated. Many Austrian generals were cautious or conservative tacticians, occasionally outpaced by the more dynamic approaches that would soon emerge in revolutionary France.
3. **Economic Constraints**: War debts from earlier conflicts, including the War of the Austrian Succession and the Seven Years' War, persisted. The monarchy's finances were fragile, complicating any large-scale military mobilization.

Thus, when revolutionary France began challenging monarchies across Europe, Austria was both a prime target and somewhat ill-prepared for the ideological and military shock to come.

13.3 Early Conflicts with Revolutionary France

13.3.1 The First Coalition

Fearing that the French Revolution would spread subversive ideas throughout Europe, Austria joined **Prussia** and other states in the **First Coalition (1792–1797)** against the young French Republic. Initially, the coalition forces expected a quick victory over what they saw as a chaotic, inexperienced French army. However, revolutionary fervor spurred mass conscription in France (the **levée en masse**), generating large, motivated armies.

- **Campaigns of 1792–1794**: Austrian forces fought in the Austrian Netherlands (modern Belgium), along the Rhine, and in northern Italy. Early successes gave way to setbacks once the French restructured their army and adopted more flexible tactics.

- **Political Tensions**: Prussia pursued separate interests in Poland, weakening the coalition's focus. Austria, for its part, was drawn into internal issues, including concerns about Hungarian loyalty and finances.
- **Emergence of New Generals**: Though many Austrian commanders stuck to traditional methods, some younger officers started paying attention to French innovations in divisional structures and mobility. This slow internal shift foreshadowed eventual Austrian military reforms.

Ultimately, France pushed coalition forces back. By 1795–1796, French armies pressed into the Rhineland and Northern Italy, scoring major breakthroughs. The Austrian Netherlands fell, and the monarchy lost important revenues from that prosperous region.

13.3.2 Bonaparte in Italy

A young French general named **Napoleon Bonaparte** rose to prominence by leading a bold campaign in **Northern Italy** (1796–1797). Facing Austrian and Piedmontese troops, Napoleon's forces repeatedly defeated them, culminating in Austrian retreats. The once-strong Habsburg foothold in Lombardy collapsed.

In 1797, **Austria** signed the **Treaty of Campo Formio** with France, ceding the **Austrian Netherlands** and recognizing French client republics in Northern Italy. In exchange, Austria acquired most of the **Republic of Venice**, dividing Venetian territories with France. This arrangement reorganized parts of the Italian peninsula but at the expense of Austrian prestige: the monarchy ceded swaths of territory to an aggressive new republic that was only a few years old.

Campo Formio also hinted at Napoleon's cunning: despite being a general in the French Republic, he negotiated personally with Austrian diplomats, revealing his individual power. The stage was set for further confrontation.

13.4 The Second Coalition and Renewed Warfare

13.4.1 Austrian Hopes for Revenge

Austria reeled from its losses and sought another chance to regain territory. Together with **Britain**, **Russia**, and other powers, it formed the **Second Coalition (1798–1802)** to challenge French expansion. Francis II and his advisors believed that a multi-pronged assault might overturn France's hold on Italy, Switzerland, and the Rhineland.

- **Early Victories**: Coalition forces initially recaptured parts of Northern Italy. Russian General **Aleksandr Suvorov** achieved stunning successes, pushing the French out of Lombardy. Austria briefly felt vindicated.
- **Setbacks**: Frictions arose between Austrian and Russian command. The coalition soon faltered after disagreements on strategy. Russia pulled out, disillusioned by Austria's moves in the region. The French rallied under capable generals like **Jean Moreau** and **André Masséna**, reversing coalition gains.

13.4.2 Napoleon's Coup and the Peace of Lunéville

Back in France, Napoleon seized power via the **Coup of 18 Brumaire (1799)**, installing himself as **First Consul** and effectively ending the revolutionary government. This transition gave France more stable leadership with a sharp focus on military victory. In 1800, Napoleon led a surprise crossing of the Alps, defeating Austrian forces at **Marengo**. Another French army under Moreau bested the Austrians at **Hohenlinden**.

Exhausted and isolated after Russia's withdrawal, Austria sued for peace. The **Treaty of Lunéville (1801)** confirmed French gains: Austria again lost territory in Italy and along the Rhine. The monarchy faced another blow to prestige, as well as large indemnities.

13.5 Interlude and the Formation of the Third Coalition

13.5.1 Austrian Reforms Under Archduke Charles

Repeated defeats convinced some Austrian leaders that comprehensive military reform was overdue. One influential figure was **Archduke Charles**, Emperor Francis II's brother, who had shown glimpses of skilled leadership. He advocated changes in:

1. **Army Organization**: Promoting flexible corps structures, improved artillery, and better cavalry coordination.
2. **Officer Training**: He established the **Theresian Military Academy** to produce well-rounded officers, hoping to embed modern tactics.
3. **Conscription**: Austria experimented with a landwehr (militia) concept, though it was never as far-reaching as the French levée en masse.

These reforms proceeded slowly, hampered by conservative attitudes, financial strains, and political caution. Yet they did yield incremental improvements, ensuring that Austria would not be as unprepared in the next war.

13.5.2 Diplomatic Maneuvers and Napoleon's Empire

In 1802, Britain and France signed the **Peace of Amiens**, briefly halting war. But tensions persisted. Napoleon consolidated power, proclaiming himself **Emperor of the French** in 1804. By crowning himself in Notre-Dame Cathedral, he sent a clear message that the era of republican France was over; an imperial France had emerged.

Alarmed by Napoleon's growing influence—especially after he reorganized German states in the **Confederation of the Rhine**—Austria and Britain drew closer. Russia joined them, forming a new **Third Coalition** in 1805 to contain Napoleon. Francis II, who feared France's meddling in Germany and Italy, prepared for yet another showdown.

13.6 Creation of the Austrian Empire

Fearing that Napoleon might claim the legacy of the Holy Roman Empire for himself, **Francis II** took a decisive step in 1804: he proclaimed himself **Francis I, Emperor of Austria** (Kaiser von Österreich). This move preemptively secured a separate imperial title for the Habsburg family, distinct from Francis's existing title as Holy Roman Emperor.

1. **Motives**: Francis recognized that if Napoleon sought to dismantle or supplant the Holy Roman Empire, the Habsburg monarchy needed a new identity to preserve its rank among Europe's great powers.
2. **International Recognition**: Most European courts recognized Francis's new title, though it underscored that the Holy Roman Empire's days were likely numbered, given Napoleon's manipulation of German states.

Thus, from 1804 onward, Austria was formally styled as an empire, with Francis as its emperor. This nomenclature encompassed all the Habsburg territories—Austria proper, Bohemia, Hungary, and various other lands—under a single imperial designation, even while the Holy Roman Empire continued in name.

13.7 The War of the Third Coalition

13.7.1 Ulm and Austerlitz

As the Third Coalition mobilized, Napoleon struck swiftly against Austrian forces in Bavaria. In a masterful campaign, the **French army** encircled an Austrian contingent at **Ulm**, compelling its surrender in October 1805. This victory opened the path to Vienna, which Napoleon's troops entered in November without a major fight.

However, the culminating clash occurred at **Austerlitz** (December 2, 1805), also known as the **Battle of the Three Emperors**: Napoleon (France) vs. Francis II (Austria) and Tsar Alexander I (Russia). The French won a decisive victory. Austerlitz destroyed the coalition's immediate hopes, exposing Austrian weaknesses yet again and severely undermining Francis II's standing.

13.7.2 Treaty of Pressburg

Forced to negotiate, Austria signed the **Treaty of Pressburg** (December 1805). The monarchy surrendered control of territories in **Tyrol** and **Vorarlberg** to Bavaria (Napoleon's ally) and gave up Venice, Istria, and Dalmatia to the **Kingdom of Italy**, a Napoleonic creation. Austria also paid a large indemnity. The humiliation of Pressburg left the monarchy smaller and fractured.

In short, the War of the Third Coalition ended with a catastrophic defeat for Austria. Napoleon's dominance on the continent seemed near total. Many in Vienna's court wondered if the Habsburg monarchy could survive more wars or whether it might end up partitioned like Poland had been.

13.8 The Dissolution of the Holy Roman Empire

One of the profound consequences of the Austerlitz triumph was the **dissolution of the Holy Roman Empire** in 1806. Napoleon organized numerous German states into the **Confederation of the Rhine**, effectively removing them from the empire's authority. Facing this reality, **Francis II** abdicated his Holy Roman imperial crown, bringing the first German Reich—already anachronistic—formally to an end after nearly a thousand years of existence.

1. **Symbolic Shift**: The demise of the Holy Roman Empire severed centuries-old feudal bonds and reconfigured central Europe into a simpler mosaic of Napoleonic client states and a few independent powers (Prussia, Austria).
2. **Rise of the Austrian Empire**: While this event was traumatic in some respects, Austria's new imperial title (adopted in 1804) gave the Habsburg monarchy a fresh identity. It could now stand as a fully sovereign empire without the cumbersome medieval structures that Napoleon so easily manipulated.

Though the Holy Roman Empire was defunct, Austria's struggle to survive was far from over. The monarchy remained overshadowed by Napoleon's power, and further confrontations loomed.

13.9 The War of the Fourth Coalition and Austria's Wait

Although **Prussia** entered the fray against Napoleon in 1806, Austria initially stayed on the sidelines. Exhausted and financially strained, Francis and his ministers recognized they had neither the resources nor the public appetite for immediate war. Napoleon swiftly defeated Prussia at **Jena–Auerstedt (1806)** and confronted the Russians again, concluding with the **Treaties of Tilsit (1807)**.

During this interval, Austria tried to rebuild:

1. **Military Reorganization**: Under Archduke Charles, the general staff refined training, introduced new regulations, and improved the landwehr concept. Morale needed bolstering after Austerlitz.
2. **Diplomatic Observations**: Austria watched how Napoleon ruled conquered areas, from the Netherlands to Poland, searching for vulnerabilities. Some Austrian policymakers realized that Napoleon's hold depended on continuous victories and tribute from client states.
3. **Economic Hardships**: The monarchy struggled with rampant inflation and war debts. Francis II's government resorted to devaluing currency, deepening social discontent.

By 1809, events emboldened Austria to try once more to challenge Napoleon.

13.10 The War of the Fifth Coalition

13.10.1 The Austrian Offensive

Despite still recovering from prior defeats, Austria believed it had to act before Napoleon consolidated further. Encouraged by Britain (which hoped to weaken Napoleon's Continental dominance), Austria declared war in April 1809. Archduke Charles led the Austrian army into Bavaria, hoping for a quick strike.

Initially, Austrian forces made some progress, but Napoleon, returning from campaigns in Spain, quickly reorganized his **Grande Armée**. He launched a series of counterattacks, culminating in battles around **Eckmühl** and **Regensburg**. Pushed back, the Austrians retreated toward the Danube.

13.10.2 Aspern-Essling and Wagram

Near Vienna, however, came a glimmer of hope for Austria:

- **Battle of Aspern-Essling (May 1809)**: Archduke Charles forced Napoleon's army, attempting to cross the Danube, into a precarious position. In a two-day struggle, the Austrians inflicted considerable losses on the French. While not a total victory, it was the first time a Napoleonic army had been significantly checked in a major set-piece battle, boosting Austrian morale.
- **Battle of Wagram (July 1809)**: The success at Aspern-Essling proved short-lived. Napoleon regrouped, brought reinforcements, and faced Charles again at Wagram. After a ferocious engagement, Austrian lines broke. The monarchy sued for peace yet again, undone by the superior numbers, artillery, and tactics of the French.

13.10.3 Treaty of Schönbrunn

The subsequent **Treaty of Schönbrunn (October 1809)** exacted another heavy price: Austria lost Salzburg and parts of Carinthia and Carniola, along with territory along the Adriatic coast (creating the **Illyrian Provinces** under French control). A humiliating clause also required Francis II to marry his daughter, **Archduchess Marie Louise**, to Napoleon, forging a dynastic link that Napoleon believed would legitimize his empire.

At this juncture, Austria appeared near ruin. Yet the monarchy persisted, partially because Napoleon's ambitions were overextended. Ironically, the alliance cemented by this forced marriage would play a role in future shifts of loyalty once Napoleon's fortunes changed.

13.11 Austria Between 1809 and 1812

13.11.1 Internal Reassessment

After yet another defeat, Francis II and his ministers recognized the urgent need for deeper reforms. A new wave of administrators, some influenced by Enlightenment thought, advocated modern governance:

1. **Economic and Fiscal Adjustments**: Austria introduced new taxes, tried to standardize tariffs, and sought foreign loans to stabilize finances. Wartime devastation in regions like Lower Austria and Tyrol demanded reconstruction efforts.
2. **Societal Morale**: War fatigue was high. Peasants and townsfolk suffered from conscription, property seizures, and inflation. Yet many still harbored resentment toward France, fueling a nascent sense of German/Austrian patriotism that reformers tapped into.
3. **Army Modernization**: Archduke Charles's influence remained strong, but friction with conservative courtiers slowed drastic changes. Still, Austrian artillery improved, the landwehr system expanded, and new training doctrines spread across regiments.

13.11.2 The Marriage Alliance with Napoleon

Napoleon's marriage to Marie Louise in 1810 briefly made Austria a reluctant ally of France. This bond theoretically obliged Austria to contribute forces for French campaigns, such as the war in Spain and preparations for conflict with Russia. However, Francis II and his ministers quietly braced for a future opportunity to break free from Napoleon's dominance.

Meanwhile, the French emperor, busy with the Iberian Peninsula War, the Continental Blockade against Britain, and designs on Russia, grew overconfident. Austria bided its time, wary of direct confrontation but willing to exploit any French missteps.

13.12 The Russian Campaign and Austria's Cautious Participation

13.12.1 Austria's Role in the Invasion

In 1812, Napoleon embarked on his grand invasion of Russia, aiming to force Tsar Alexander I to comply with the Continental System against Britain. By treaty, Austria was compelled to provide an auxiliary corps under **Prince Karl Schwarzenberg**, though Francis II insisted on limiting Austria's involvement.

- **Minimal Engagement**: Schwarzenberg's corps, numbering around 30,000 men, operated on the southern flank, engaging mostly in minor actions. Francis II's strategy was to appear loyal to Napoleon while preserving his forces.
- **Napoleon's Catastrophe**: The campaign turned disastrous for the French. The Grande Armée marched to Moscow but found it burned and untenable. Forced to retreat amid harsh winter conditions, Napoleon lost the bulk of his army.

13.12.2 Shifting Alliances

As the French retreated from Russia, Austrian leaders recognized the moment to act. Their carefully preserved troops remained relatively intact. Diplomatic backchannels opened with the Russian court and with Prussia—long resentful of French domination. Even Britain, which had financed coalitions before, was eager to see Austria rejoin the anti-French cause.

Yet Francis II still hesitated. If Napoleon recovered, a premature Austrian break could again invite invasion. The monarchy thus sought to mediate at first, offering proposals for peace that might curtail Napoleon's ambitions without requiring a total break. But the dynamic moved swiftly toward outright war as the allied momentum grew irresistible.

13.13 The War of the Sixth Coalition

13.13.1 Austria's Return to the Anti-French Fold

By mid-1813, with Prussia and Russia already in open conflict against Napoleon, Austria entered negotiations with the allies. **Foreign Minister Klemens von**

Metternich became a central figure, orchestrating a diplomatic approach that gave Napoleon a chance to accept reduced borders. When Napoleon refused, Metternich aligned Austria fully with the coalition.

- **Austrian Mobilization**: A revitalized Austrian army, under capable generals like Schwarzenberg, marched alongside Russian and Prussian columns. The monarchy's improved artillery and better morale made a difference.
- **Key Battles**: Napoleon won early encounters such as **Dresden**, but his forces were outnumbered and outmaneuvered. By October 1813, the **Battle of Leipzig** (also known as the **Battle of Nations**) sealed Napoleon's fate in central Europe. Allied armies forced the French to withdraw west of the Rhine.

13.13.2 Invasion of France and Napoleon's Abdication

Allied forces, including Austrian contingents, advanced into France during early 1814. Despite stiff resistance, the allies captured Paris in March. Napoleon abdicated in April, going into exile on Elba. The victorious powers began outlining a new European order to prevent the resurgence of French hegemony.

For Austria, this outcome was a triumph. The monarchy regained lost territories, reestablished an influential role in Germany and Italy, and saw the end of Napoleon's challenge. However, the cost in lives, resources, and social disruption was immense. The monarchy needed a stable peace to rebuild.

13.14 The Hundred Days and Final Defeat of Napoleon

Napoleon's escape from Elba in March 1815 briefly reignited war. Austria again joined the coalition, though Prussia and Britain took the lead at Waterloo (June 1815). With Napoleon's final defeat, he was exiled to Saint Helena. The Napoleonic Wars were definitively over.

Austria now had a seat at the negotiating table for a grand reorganization of Europe. The monarchy aimed to ensure no single power would dominate the Continent again and that revolutionary ideologies would be contained. These priorities shaped the subsequent **Congress of Vienna**, which Metternich largely directed.

13.15 The Congress of Vienna

Though begun before Waterloo, the **Congress of Vienna** concluded after Napoleon's final defeat. For months, diplomats from across Europe negotiated territories, spheres of influence, and alliances. Metternich served as a principal architect, determined to:

1. **Restore Balance of Power**: So no single state (like France under Napoleon) could assert hegemony again.
2. **Legitimize Dynasties**: The Bourbon monarchy was restored in France. Other old royal families returned to their thrones if possible.
3. **Prevent Revolutionary Upheaval**: The monarchy and other conservative powers agreed to suppress liberal nationalist movements.

Key outcomes regarding Austria included:

- **Territorial Recoveries**: Austria regained Lombardy and Venetia in northern Italy, plus Tirol and Salzburg. These acquisitions reinforced Austrian influence south of the Alps.
- **German Confederation**: The Holy Roman Empire was not revived. Instead, a loose German Confederation formed, with Austria presiding but not dictating.
- **Legitimacy of the Austrian Empire**: The final treaties acknowledged Francis as Emperor of Austria, solidifying the monarchy's new identity.

By 1815, Austria emerged not as the old feudal monarchy but a somewhat modernized empire. Despite heavy costs, it regained status as a major European power. The policies hammered out in Vienna would guide continental diplomacy for decades, inaugurating the so-called **Concert of Europe** and ushering in the next period of Austrian history, often associated with **Prince Metternich's** conservative order.

13.16 Consequences for Austrian Society and Governance

The Napoleonic Wars had profound implications for Austria's internal structure:

- **Military Lessons**: Repeated defeats triggered partial modernization of the army, including better training and use of corps-level operations. By the final campaigns, Austria's forces matched up more effectively with French armies.
- **Proto-National Sentiments**: Although the monarchy was officially multinational, elements of German cultural patriotism emerged among Austrian officers and middle classes, fueled by hostility to French occupation. Similar sentiments grew in Hungarian and other ethnic groups, though these often clashed with Habsburg centralism.
- **Economic Strains**: War debts soared, inflation and forced loans burdened peasants and urban dwellers alike, setting the stage for socio-political tensions in the years to come. Reconstruction demanded strong state intervention and further administrative adaptation.

Nevertheless, Austria's survival and eventual success in the coalition that overthrew Napoleon validated the monarchy's enduring place in Europe. Under Francis II (Francis I of Austria), the monarchy concluded this tumultuous era with renewed diplomatic clout but also an entrenched suspicion of liberal or nationalist movements—suspicions that would shape the postwar order.

CHAPTER 14: THE METTERNICH SYSTEM AND THE AUSTRIAN EMPIRE

14.1 Introduction

With the defeat of Napoleon and the resolutions of the **Congress of Vienna (1814–1815)**, Austria regained its standing as a great power in Europe. The monarchy's foreign minister (and later state chancellor), **Prince Klemens von Metternich**, emerged as the principal architect of the post-Napoleonic order. Under Metternich's guidance, Austria strove to maintain a conservative equilibrium designed to thwart revolutionary ideologies and preserve the authority of Europe's monarchies.

During the period often called the "**Metternich System**" or the "**Concert of Europe**," Austria championed a policy of collective security among European powers, mutual intervention against revolutions, and rigorous censorship at home. While this system did bring relative peace in the decades following the Napoleonic Wars, it also stifled political reform, breeding discontent among liberals and nationalists.

In this chapter, we explore how Metternich's diplomacy shaped the Austrian Empire's role in Europe, focusing on international congresses, internal repression of dissent, and the monarchy's cautious balancing act among its diverse territories. We also trace the social and economic trends of early 19th-century Austria—trends that fueled eventual unrest despite the superficial calm, culminating in the revolutions of 1848 (which, while beyond our final stopping point, form the logical outcome of these tensions).

14.2 Metternich's Rise and Principles

14.2.1 Metternich Before 1815

Born into a Rhenish noble family, **Klemens Wenzel Lothar von Metternich** quickly climbed diplomatic ranks. He represented Austria at key negotiations, including the

Treaty of Lunéville (1801) and in Paris (1806). His successes and close association with Emperor Francis II (Francis I of Austria) earned him the post of **Foreign Minister** in 1809. After the War of the Sixth Coalition, Metternich orchestrated the Congress of Vienna, showcasing both diplomatic skill and a vision for Europe's conservative restoration.

By 1821, Metternich was appointed **State Chancellor**, wielding tremendous influence over Austria's foreign and domestic policies until his downfall in 1848. His worldview:

- **Anti-Revolutionary**: He believed French revolutionary ideals threatened European civilization and monarchy.
- **Balance of Power**: He wanted no single state—neither France nor Russia—to dominate.
- **Conservative Morality**: Metternich upheld a paternalistic monarchy, with strong ties to the Catholic Church, as a bulwark against societal upheaval.

14.2.2 The Metternich System at Home

Internally, Metternich strove to curb liberal and nationalist ideas. He saw any relaxation of press laws or expansion of civil rights as a slippery slope toward rebellion. Thus, he promoted **censorship**, **police surveillance**, and a network of informants to root out suspected revolutionaries. These policies would define Austrian politics in the first half of the 19th century and also help shape the German Confederation's approach to dissent.

14.3 The Congress System and the Concert of Europe

14.3.1 A Framework for Peace

The **Congress of Vienna** had established new frontiers and validated dynastic legitimacy in places like France, Spain, and German principalities. To preserve this settlement, Metternich championed periodic meetings—**Congresses**—where major powers could coordinate responses to crises. This arrangement became known as the **Concert of Europe**.

1. **Key Members**: Austria, Russia, Prussia, Britain, and, later, restored Bourbon France.
2. **Collective Security**: The powers agreed to intervene if revolutions threatened monarchical rule.

In practice, each power had its own interests. Britain favored maritime and trading freedoms, Russia eyed expansion or influence in the Balkans, and Prussia sought leadership in German affairs. Metternich's skill lay in balancing these rivalries to maintain Austrian preeminence in Central Europe.

14.3.2 The Congresses of Aachen, Troppau, Laibach, and Verona

Several congresses in the years after 1815 tested the system:

- **Aachen (1818)**: France was readmitted into the Concert after paying reparations. Metternich welcomed France as a conservative partner against radicalism.
- **Troppau (1820) and Laibach (1821)**: These meetings addressed revolutionary unrest in Naples and Piedmont. Austria, with Metternich's encouragement, intervened militarily to restore the status quo. The principle that the great powers could invade a state to quell revolutions emerged, known as the **Troppau Protocol**.
- **Verona (1822)**: Focused on Spain and Greek independence movements. Metternich opposed recognizing Greek insurgents against the Ottoman Empire, seeing any national uprising as a dangerous precedent. Meanwhile, France intervened in Spain to prop up the Bourbon monarchy.

These congresses underscored the tension: while the powers cooperated to suppress liberal movements, they also pursued individual agendas. Over time, Britain grew uneasy with frequent interventions, preferring a more liberal stance that let constitutional reforms proceed if local rulers agreed.

14.4 The German Confederation and Austria's Dominance

14.4.1 Creation of the German Confederation

After dissolving the Holy Roman Empire in 1806, German states needed a new framework. The **German Confederation (Deutscher Bund)** formed in 1815 under the presidency of Austria. It was a loose association of 39 states, including Prussia, Bavaria, Saxony, and Hanover. The federal assembly (Bundestag) met in Frankfurt, with Austrian diplomats chairing sessions.

1. **Goals**: Maintain independence of member states, preserve monarchical authority, and coordinate defense.

2. **Weaknesses**: Lacking an executive or real central power, the confederation relied on consensus. This suited Austria's interest in preventing a powerful, unified Germany under another state's leadership (especially Prussia).

14.4.2 The Carlsbad Decrees (1819)

Rising nationalist and liberal sentiments in the German states alarmed Metternich. After a student activist assassinated a conservative writer (August von Kotzebue) in 1819, Metternich seized the opportunity to push through the **Carlsbad Decrees**:

- **Press Censorship**: Newspapers, pamphlets, and books faced stringent controls.
- **University Supervision**: Professors suspected of liberal or national ideas were dismissed, and student societies (Burschenschaften) were outlawed.
- **Federal Commission**: A body oversaw the suppression of subversive activities within the Confederation.

These decrees symbolized Metternich's determination to stifle any threat to the old order, reinforcing Austria's leadership in conservative repression across the German lands. Yet, in the long run, they built resentment among educated middle classes, sowing seeds for future revolutionary waves.

14.5 Austria's Internal Structure under Metternich

14.5.1 Emperor Francis I's Role

Though Metternich often took center stage in foreign policy, Emperor Francis I (the former Francis II, Holy Roman Emperor) retained ultimate authority. He shared Metternich's distrust of liberalism. Throughout the 1820s and 1830s, Francis supported strict policing, secret censorship offices, and minimal constitutional concessions in the monarchy's diverse provinces.

1. **Centralized Administration**: The monarchy further centralized under Francis, with bureaucrats loyal to the imperial court. Hungary, Bohemia, Lombardy-Venetia, and other crown lands had local diets but limited real power.
2. **Noble Influence**: Aristocrats held top civil and military posts. Although Joseph II's attempts to erode feudal privileges had been partially reversed,

the monarchy still needed noble cooperation to collect taxes and govern effectively.

3. **Fiscal Pressures**: War debts and reconstruction after Napoleonic devastation remained issues. The monarchy introduced some protective tariffs to foster domestic industry, particularly in Bohemia's textile and iron sectors.

This stable but repressive system functioned relatively well as long as major external conflicts did not arise and the population remained too scattered in grievances to mount organized resistance.

14.5.2 Policing and Surveillance

Metternich's approach to internal security included:

- **State Police**: Agents monitored coffeehouses, universities, theaters, and Masonic lodges. Reports on suspicious discussions circulated among ministers.
- **Censorship**: Foreign books, especially from France or Britain, were reviewed. Writings with liberal, democratic, or nationalistic content were confiscated or heavily redacted.
- **Clergy Involvement**: Some Catholic clerics cooperated with the state in identifying "dangerous" ideologies. However, the monarchy also wanted to keep church influence in check, recalling the conflicts under Joseph II.

These methods fostered a climate of caution. Critics of the regime either self-censored or met in secret. Intellectual life did not vanish—literary salons and romantic cultural movements thrived in certain circles—but overt political dissent was stifled.

14.6 Social and Economic Trends After 1815

14.6.1 Population Growth and Rural Changes

The early 19th century saw a steady population rise across the Habsburg lands. This put pressure on agricultural resources. In many rural areas, peasants still lived under vestiges of feudal obligations, although the monarchy had placed some limits on forced labor. Some peasants migrated to emerging industrial centers for work:

- **Bohemia**: Notable for early industrial development, particularly in textile mills and ironworks around regions like Pilsen and the Erzgebirge.
- **Lower Austria**: Saw a gradual rise in mechanized production.
- **Hungary**: Large estates continued focusing on grain exports. Local aristocrats blocked extensive reforms that would free peasants or modernize agriculture on a large scale.

Though wealth slowly increased, inequality remained entrenched. The monarchy's paternalist approach provided minimal social services, leaving many peasants vulnerable to poor harvests or fluctuations in grain prices.

14.6.2 Proto-Industrialization

In city suburbs and small towns, domestic workshops spread, producing textiles, glass, and consumer goods. Some wealthy families (like the Rothschilds, who gained influence in Austrian finance) invested in nascent factories or railroads. Infrastructure improvements were modest but notable:

1. **Road Building**: The monarchy extended roads connecting Vienna to major provincial centers.
2. **Early Railways**: The first horse-drawn railway in Austria appeared in the 1820s (the Linz–Budweis line), followed by steam-powered lines in the 1830s.
3. **Danube Navigation**: Steamboats started plying the Danube, boosting trade flows from Hungary to Vienna.

Urban living conditions slowly changed as the population grew, leading to overcrowding in some districts. While not yet an "industrial revolution" on the British scale, these developments created a new social stratum of factory workers and entrepreneurial bourgeoisie, some of whom held liberal political aspirations.

14.7 Cracks in the Metternich System

14.7.1 Greek War of Independence (1821–1830)

The Greek rebellion against the Ottoman Empire tested Metternich's anti-revolution stance. While many Europeans sympathized with Greek Christians, Metternich worried that supporting a national revolt would legitimize similar uprisings. Austria officially maintained neutrality, though Russia and others eventually intervened on behalf of Greece. The success of the Greek cause indicated that nationalist sentiments could triumph, undermining the universal principle of monarchical legitimacy that Metternich championed.

14.7.2 Belgian Revolt (1830)

When the Belgians rose against Dutch rule, forming an independent Belgium in 1830, Metternich again faced the challenge of a nationalist movement. The powers eventually recognized Belgian independence as part of a compromise. For Austria, it confirmed that the Concert of Europe had limits: not all revolutionary or nationalist pressures could be suppressed by force if the great powers disagreed.

14.7.3 Revolutions in France (1830) and Elsewhere

The **July Revolution** in France (1830) ousted the Bourbon king Charles X, replacing him with the more liberal **Louis-Philippe**. Metternich recognized Louis-Philippe's regime to maintain stability but lamented the blow to the principle of hereditary legitimacy. Meanwhile, Poland briefly rebelled against Russia, though that uprising was crushed. Each wave of disturbances reinforced Austrian conservatives' fear that such movements might spread into Habsburg territories.

14.8 Nationalist and Liberal Currents in the Monarchy

While the Metternich System strove to stifle dissent, ideas of **national identity** grew among various ethnic groups in the empire:

1. **German Liberals**: Middle-class professionals and intellectuals in Vienna or Prague read about constitutionalism and yearned for representative assemblies. They also championed German cultural unity, though they still accepted Habsburg leadership in the German Confederation.
2. **Hungarian National Awakening**: Influential figures like **Count István Széchenyi** and later **Lajos Kossuth** pressed for Hungarian autonomy, language rights, and economic modernization. Though cautious at first, Hungarian reformers increasingly resented Austrian centralism.
3. **Czechs, Slovaks, and Other Groups**: In Bohemia, the Czech language revival gained momentum. Cultural societies promoted literature and history in the local language, hinting at political demands for more autonomy.

While these movements generally avoided open confrontation, the monarchy's unyielding censorship only pushed activism underground, fostering frustration. By the 1840s, calls for constitutional reforms grew louder across Europe, amplified by a new generation of educated youth.

14.9 The Later Reign of Francis I and the Accession of Ferdinand I

14.9.1 Francis I's Conservative Consolidation

Emperor Francis I died in 1835. His final years were spent reinforcing Metternich's system, tightening police measures, and blocking any constitutional developments. He left behind a monarchy outwardly stable but rife with tensions. Industrialization advanced slowly, the treasury remained precarious, and popular discontent simmered under heavy censorship.

14.9.2 Ferdinand I (1835–1848)

Francis's son, **Ferdinand I**, succeeded him. Physically and mentally fragile, Ferdinand delegated much governance to a "State Conference" dominated by Metternich, Archduke Ludwig, and other conservative dignitaries. Under this arrangement, Metternich's influence peaked, but so did the monarchy's rigidity:

1. **Little Reform**: The government introduced mild improvements to administration and infrastructure but refused major political changes.
2. **Mounting Pressures**: Revolutions elsewhere in Europe stirred demands for a constitution, freedom of the press, and broader civil liberties. The monarchy's refusal to adapt made an eventual confrontation more likely.

14.10 Cultural and Intellectual Life Under Censorship

14.10.1 The Biedermeier Era

Despite constraints, Austria saw a **Biedermeier** cultural phase (1815–1848), emphasizing domesticity, family, and a romanticized simplicity in art, music, and literature. Middle-class salons thrived on intimate gatherings where safe, apolitical topics like landscape painting, sentimental poetry, or dance music (e.g., the waltz) flourished. Composers like **Franz Schubert** created works beloved in private circles, though Schubert's circle sometimes clashed with censors over liberal associations.

Johann Strauss I popularized dance music, providing lighthearted entertainment that matched the monarchy's preference for avoiding political subjects. Meanwhile, in architecture, a subdued neoclassicism or romantic style replaced flamboyant Baroque, reflecting a calmer, inward focus after decades of war.

14.10.2 Scientific and Intellectual Developments

While radical political treatises were banned, scientific and technical fields enjoyed relative freedom:

- **Medicine**: Vienna's medical school gained renown, pioneering research in pathology and surgery.
- **Mathematics and Natural Sciences**: A small but growing community of scholars studied astronomy, geology, and botany, often with the monarchy's quiet support, as these areas posed no ideological threat.
- **Economic Thought**: Some officials studied Adam Smith's liberal economic theories. However, implementing free trade conflicted with the monarchy's mercantilist instincts and the protection of certain noble interests.

In the underground realm, liberal pamphlets circulated discreetly, fueling discontent among educated city dwellers who craved more personal and political freedoms.

14.11 Metternich's Foreign Affairs After 1830

14.11.1 Balancing Act with Russia and France

Metternich found himself in delicate equilibrium:

1. **Russia**: Under Tsar Nicholas I, Russia aligned with Austria in suppressing revolutions (the Holy Alliance). Yet differences over Balkan influence emerged. Metternich tried to keep Russia engaged in the Concert while preventing unilateral Russian expansion into the Ottoman sphere.

2. **France**: The July Monarchy under Louis-Philippe was more liberal, but also not entirely revolutionary. Metternich maintained wary relations, ensuring that France would not reignite a major European conflict.
3. **Britain**: Took a more hands-off approach, focusing on colonial expansion. Metternich relied on Britain to moderate Russian ambitions.

This diplomacy managed to avert large-scale European wars, but local uprisings (e.g., in Italy, Poland, or the German states) tested the system. Austria intervened in Italy several times to quell risings in places like Modena or the Papal States, reinforcing its image as the policeman of the peninsula.

14.12 Toward an Inevitable Crisis?

14.12.1 Socio-Economic Pressures

By the 1840s, poor harvests, rising food prices, and early industrial unrest combined to strain Metternich's system. Rural misery mixed with urban unemployment. Intellectuals demanded an end to feudal remnants, the establishment of constitutional government, and the freedom to publish political thoughts.

In **Hungary**, the reform faction led by **Lajos Kossuth** pressed for Hungarian autonomy, a national assembly with legislative power, and the replacement of Latin with Hungarian as the official language. Austrians in Vienna, particularly university students and middle-class professionals, debated constitutional monarchies in private gatherings. As the monarchy refused to concede, frustration grew.

14.12.2 The Reform Debates

Some moderate officials around Archduke Franz Karl and his son, the future Emperor Franz Joseph, suggested partial liberalization to stave off a major crisis—such as adopting a consultative assembly or relaxing press laws. But Metternich opposed these moves, convinced that any concession would ignite unstoppable demands.

By early 1848, the monarchy's intransigence collided with a Europe-wide revolutionary wave. France overthrew Louis-Philippe, establishing the Second Republic. This shock reverberated across Germany and Italy. Austrian society stood on the brink of upheaval, though few realized just how swiftly events would unfold.

14.13 Legacy of the Metternich System

14.13.1 Achievements

- **Continental Stability**: For roughly three decades after 1815, Europe avoided major continent-wide wars. Metternich's congress diplomacy succeeded in containing conflicts, especially in Germany and Italy.
- **Diplomatic Prestige**: Austria regained leadership in central European affairs. Foreign courts looked to Vienna as the pivot of conservative governance.
- **Internal Consolidation**: The monarchy expanded administrative structures, developed a better-trained bureaucracy, and revived economically from Napoleonic devastation—though gradually and unevenly.

14.13.2 Shortcomings

- **Repression and Intellectual Stagnation**: Censorship hindered political debate and creative expression, sowing resentment. Some of Austria's brightest minds emigrated or self-censored.
- **Neglect of Democratic Aspirations**: Metternich's refusal to grant even mild constitutional reforms ensured that once revolution erupted, it would be radical.
- **Emerging Nationalism**: Diverse ethnic groups under Habsburg rule increasingly sought cultural and political recognition. By stifling these demands, the monarchy invited future turmoil.

14.14 The End of an Era: 1848 in Sight

When revolution broke out in Paris (February 1848), it triggered protests in the German states and the Habsburg Empire itself. By March, Vienna was in an uproar, with students and workers demanding a constitution. The monarchy, paralyzed by internal divisions, failed to contain the protests. Metternich, the symbol of repression, was forced to resign and flee the city on March 13, 1848.

Though the revolutions of 1848 go beyond our concluding historical scope, they mark the downfall of the system Metternich had so painstakingly upheld. In that sense, the events of 1848 stand as a direct result of the tensions accumulated during his era: the monarchy's unwillingness to accommodate moderate reform eventually catalyzed a far larger crisis.

CHAPTER 15: THE REVOLUTIONS OF 1848 AND THEIR AFTERMATH

15.1 Introduction

By the early 1840s, the Austrian Empire—under the conservative system championed by Prince Klemens von Metternich—appeared stable on the surface. Censorship and police surveillance kept overt dissidence in check, while the monarchy avoided major wars abroad through careful diplomacy. Beneath this calm, however, socioeconomic and ideological tensions steadily mounted. Economic hardships such as poor harvests and rising food prices, the frustrations of a growing middle class shut out of political power, and the burgeoning sense of cultural-linguistic awareness among various ethnic groups all converged.

In 1848, these pressures exploded into a series of upheavals that rocked Europe. Starting with the February Revolution in France, revolt spread swiftly across the German states, Italy, and the Habsburg lands themselves. Within weeks, the old order that Metternich had labored to preserve teetered on the brink of collapse. Riots in Vienna forced Metternich to flee, peasant and liberal demands shook the monarchy to its core, and national movements flared up in Hungary, Bohemia, and beyond.

This chapter explores the dramatic course of the **Revolutions of 1848** in the Austrian Empire, detailing how they began, how various factions pressed for reform, and how the monarchy responded with a mix of concessions and military force. We will also examine the revolution's aftermath: the empire's attempts to return to absolutism under Emperor Franz Joseph, the short-lived constitutions, and the "neoabsolutist" era that followed. These events would transform Austrian politics, society, and the relationship between Vienna and the empire's diverse nationalities, setting the stage for the eventual Austro-Hungarian Compromise of 1867.

15.2 The Preludes to 1848

15.2.1 Economic Discontent

The 1840s brought a series of poor grain harvests across Europe, including in the Austrian crown lands. Rising bread prices, unemployment, and widespread misery fueled anger at noble landowners and an indifferent bureaucracy:

1. **Rural Hardships**: Many peasants still owed feudal dues—labor services or rent—while facing mounting debts. In some regions, conditions approached crisis levels, with peasant families pushed off land or forced into wage labor under harsh terms.
2. **Urban Pressures**: Vienna, Prague, and other cities had small but growing industrial sectors, employing weavers, spinners, and ironworkers. These workers experienced low wages and job insecurity. Artisans, once protected by guilds, found themselves unable to compete with proto-industrial factories. Economic anxieties fed into broader political discontent.

15.2.2 Growing Middle-Class and Student Liberalism

A new educated middle class—lawyers, civil servants, professors, and merchants—emerged in Austrian cities, influenced by the spread of German liberal thought and occasional foreign publications that slipped past censorship. These liberals demanded:

- **Constitutional Governance**: They yearned for a representative assembly to limit imperial arbitrariness and shape legislation.
- **Civil Rights**: Freedoms of the press, speech, and association, all severely curbed under Metternich's watch.
- **Economic Modernization**: The middle class wanted fewer internal trade barriers and more rational legal structures to encourage commerce and entrepreneurship.

University students, especially in Vienna, rallied around these ideas, organizing underground reading clubs to debate liberal and nationalist concepts. The monarchy's clampdown on such discussions only heightened their allure.

15.2.3 National Movements within the Empire

Another powerful current was nationalism among the empire's non-German populations:

- **Hungary**: Politicians like István Széchenyi and Lajos Kossuth advocated the use of Hungarian (Magyar) in administration, greater legislative authority for the Hungarian Diet, and an end to feudal privileges.
- **Czechs in Bohemia**: Intellectuals championed the revival of the Czech language and culture, seeing themselves as distinct from the German-speaking ruling circles.
- **Italians in Lombardy-Venetia**: Some looked to the rising "Italian national awakening," resentful of Austrian rule from Milan to Venice.
- **Other Slavic Groups**: Slovaks, Slovenes, Croats, and others also began articulating cultural-linguistic identities, though not all advanced overt political demands in 1848.

While these national movements did not always share a unified agenda—indeed, they often clashed with each other's territorial aspirations—they unanimously resented the empire's centralized and German-dominated bureaucracy. The year 1848 would provide them a moment to push for autonomy or independence.

15.3 The Outbreak

15.3.1 French Uprising as Catalyst

In February 1848, protestors in Paris toppled King Louis-Philippe, establishing the French Second Republic. News of this event galvanized liberals and radicals across Europe, proving that a monarchy could be overturned within days. Austrian censors tried to suppress the information, but rumors spread quickly, reaching universities, coffeehouses, and aristocratic salons.

15.3.2 First German States to Revolt

Following France, the southern German states—Baden, Württemberg, and Bavaria—saw demonstrations demanding constitutions and unity for Germany. Alarmed by these developments near its western frontier, Austria prepared to tighten security. However, the monarchy itself was not immune: on March 13, protests erupted in Vienna, taking authorities by surprise and triggering the revolution in the empire's capital.

15.4 The March Revolution in Vienna

15.4.1 Street Protests and Student Demonstrations

On March 13, large crowds of students, artisans, and some middle-class citizens gathered in Vienna's center, chanting for "Freedom!" and "Constitution!" Initially peaceful, the demonstrations escalated when security forces attempted to disperse them. Barricades went up in some streets, and rumors spread that the imperial court might call in the army to crush the movement. Tension soared.

Students from the University of Vienna formed a central force, demanding freedom of the press, an end to censors, and a representative assembly. The court was stunned by the scale of unrest.

15.4.2 Metternich Resigns and Flees

As violence mounted, Emperor Ferdinand I and his advisors recognized that sacrificing Metternich might placate the protesters. On March 13, the once all-powerful statesman resigned. By night, he fled the city disguised, eventually seeking exile in England. To many revolutionaries, Metternich's fall symbolized the end of an era of police-state conservatism.

The monarchy hoped that dismissing Metternich would calm the crowds. However, the revolution's demands went far beyond removing one man; they called for structural reforms. With Metternich gone, cracks in the old system were laid bare.

15.5 Concessions and Chaos

15.5.1 The "March Laws" and the Constitution Plan

Ferdinand I issued a series of hurried decrees:

1. **Abolition of Censorship**: Temporary freedom of the press was proclaimed to ease tensions. Periodicals mushroomed overnight, fueling further debate.
2. **Promise of a Constitution**: The imperial court announced it would draft a constitution that guaranteed a parliament and some civil liberties. A hastily prepared "Pillersdorf Constitution" emerged in April, attempting to create a bicameral legislature and preserve monarchical authority.

3. **Student Guards**: Students organized a National Guard (Akademische Legion) to keep order, ironically giving them arms and official standing. This measure ironically empowered radical voices who now felt legitimate in policing the capital.

These moves aimed to buy time and fragment the revolutionaries. But they were insufficient for many liberals, who saw them as half measures. Meanwhile, peasants clamored for the complete end of feudal dues, and other regions demanded more autonomy.

15.5.2 Rural Revolts and Serfdom Abolition

Peasant uprisings erupted in Lower Austria, Bohemia, Galicia, and elsewhere. They attacked manor houses, refusing to perform feudal labor. Terrified aristocrats pressed the emperor to quell these disorders, yet also realized partial concessions were inevitable. In April 1848, the government decreed the abolition of remaining feudal obligations, seeking to undercut rural support for the revolution.

Although peasants welcomed the move, confusion persisted over compensation for landowners. Some peasants discovered they were free but still owed redemption payments. This compromise ended the most severe aspects of serfdom, though disputes over property rights continued for years.

15.6 National Movements

15.6.1 Hungary's March Demands

In the Kingdom of Hungary, a separate revolution unfolded. On March 15, inspired by Vienna's example, Hungarian reformers led by Lajos Kossuth forced the Habsburg-appointed Palatine to accept a list of 12 demands, including:

- **A Responsible Hungarian Ministry**: Executive power in Hungarian hands rather than Viennese absolutism.
- **Freedom of the Press**: End of censorship.
- **National Guard Formation**: Hungarian militia.
- **Full Abolition of Feudal Privileges**.
- **Union with Transylvania**: Unifying territories with a Hungarian majority.

Ferdinand I conceded many points, appointing a Hungarian cabinet under Count Lajos Batthyány. This effectively made Hungary a semi-autonomous realm. But friction loomed: minority groups within the Hungarian Kingdom (Croats, Romanians, Slovaks) had their own aspirations, leading to complex tensions. Vienna's acceptance was also reluctant—only granted due to the empire's crisis and a desire to avoid another front of conflict.

15.6.2 Czech Aspirations in Bohemia

In Bohemia, Czech intellectuals demanded equality of the Czech language, an end to German administrative dominance, and a form of autonomy within the empire. A Pan-Slav Congress convened in Prague in June 1848, inviting Slavic leaders from across the monarchy to discuss common goals. However, the monarchy cracked down when radical voices in Prague's streets clashed with local authorities. Troops under General Windisch-Grätz bombarded parts of the city, dispersing the Pan-Slav Congress.

These events underscored how ethnic and national goals could conflict with each other and with the monarchy. While Hungarian liberals wanted independence from Vienna, Czech liberals feared Hungarian dominance in their territories. Meanwhile, the monarchy maneuvered to exploit these divisions to its advantage.

15.7 The Frankfurt Parliament and German Unity Debates

15.7.1 The German National Assembly

Elsewhere in the German Confederation, revolutionaries convened a National Assembly in Frankfurt in May 1848, aiming to draft a constitution for a united Germany. Representatives included liberals from Austrian and Prussian territories. Some Austrian German liberals hoped that the monarchy's German-speaking provinces might join a new, liberal Germany. But this posed a dilemma: could Austria, with its vast non-German lands, fully integrate into a "Greater Germany"?

Two main visions emerged:

1. **"Grossdeutsch"** (Greater German) solution: Include all German-speaking parts of the Austrian Empire, thus uniting them with Germany. This would have made Austria central but entangled the new Germany with millions of non-German subjects.

2. **"Kleindeutsch"** (Lesser German) solution: Exclude Austria, forming a smaller Germany led by Prussia. This avoided mixing in Austria's non-German lands.

The question plagued the Frankfurt Parliament, which hesitated to impose a solution that risked conflict with the Habsburg monarchy or Prussia.

15.7.2 Austrian Position on Frankfurt

Initially, Austrian liberals at Frankfurt supported a "Grossdeutsch" plan, hoping to transform the monarchy into a constitutional empire aligned with German unity. However, the monarchy's official stance was cautious: Vienna signaled it would not break up the empire or cede non-German crown lands to remain in the German union. As months passed, the monarchy regained confidence and distanced itself from the Frankfurt Assembly's radical or liberal agenda.

Eventually, the Frankfurt Parliament's efforts faltered. Prussia refused the parliamentary-offered crown for Germany, and Austria resumed a more conservative line, rejecting the subordination of the empire to any all-German body. By mid-1849, the Frankfurt experiment collapsed without unifying Germany.

15.8 The Radical Turn and Military Responses

15.8.1 Vienna Uprising, October 1848

Throughout the summer of 1848, the imperial government made some reforms but was uneasy about the continuing radical climate. When Emperor Ferdinand I replaced liberal ministers with more conservative ones, unrest flared anew. In October, the monarchy ordered troops from Vienna to help suppress the Hungarian revolutionaries. Viennese radicals, outraged, rose up again, hoping to prevent the departure of these soldiers.

The confrontation escalated, and after days of street fighting, imperial troops under General Windisch-Grätz besieged Vienna. By October's end, the city was bombarded into submission. This brutal retaking signaled the monarchy's shift to open counterrevolution. Many revolutionaries were arrested, some executed, and the city was placed under martial law.

15.8.2 Abdication of Ferdinand I and Rise of Franz Joseph

In December 1848, as the monarchy struggled to reassert control, Emperor Ferdinand I abdicated in favor of his 18-year-old nephew, **Franz Joseph**. Ferdinand, mentally and physically frail, was deemed unable to navigate the crisis. The new emperor, guided by reactionary advisors, moved to restore authoritarian rule, though he initially kept the veneer of constitutional promises.

Franz Joseph's accession marked a critical turning point. Young and resolute, he would rule until 1916, shaping the empire's fate through the latter 19th century.

15.9 The Hungarian War for Independence

15.9.1 From Autonomy to Break with the Habsburgs

Hungary had won significant autonomy in March–April 1848. However, conflicts with Vienna deepened as Hungarian radicals insisted on controlling the kingdom's finances and army. Non-Magyar minorities—especially Croats led by Ban Jelačić—revolted against Hungarian authority, receiving tacit support from Vienna.

When the monarchy, under Franz Joseph, rescinded the "March Laws," Hungarians saw this as a betrayal. In April 1849, the Hungarian Diet proclaimed independence from the Habsburgs, naming Lajos Kossuth as Governor-President. This bold step alarmed Vienna, which then launched a full-scale military campaign to crush the Hungarian revolution.

15.9.2 Austrian and Russian Intervention

Faced with a determined Hungarian army, Franz Joseph sought help from Tsar Nicholas I of Russia. In mid-1849, a massive Russian force invaded Hungary from the northeast, coordinating with Austrian troops. Though Hungarian fighters achieved some victories, they were eventually overwhelmed by the two great imperial armies converging on them. By August 1849, Hungarian forces surrendered at Világos, effectively ending their war of independence.

In the aftermath, the monarchy imposed harsh reprisals: leading Hungarian generals were executed or imprisoned, and civil liberties across the kingdom were curtailed. This brutal crackdown—epitomized by the executions at Arad—left deep scars on Hungarian society.

15.10 Bohemia, Italy, and Other Fronts

With Vienna subdued and Hungary on the path to defeat, the monarchy also dealt with lingering unrest in Bohemia and Italy:

1. **Bohemia**: Having suppressed the June 1848 uprising in Prague, the monarchy maintained tight control. Czech political societies were dissolved or forced underground.
2. **Italian Lands (Lombardy-Venetia)**: Encouraged by the Kingdom of Sardinia-Piedmont and local patriots, Milan and Venice rose against Austrian rule in early 1848. Field Marshal Radetzky, an experienced Austrian commander, withdrew temporarily but later regrouped and decisively defeated the Piedmontese at battles like Custoza (July 1848) and Novara (March 1849). Venice held out under siege until August 1849. Austrian authority was thus restored, albeit at great cost, inflaming Italian nationalism.

By late 1849, the monarchy had managed to crush revolutions across its domains through force of arms, aided by foreign intervention (Russia in Hungary) and internal divisions among revolutionaries.

15.11 Outcomes of 1848

15.11.1 The Imposed Constitution of March 1849

To salvage the promise of reform while preserving absolute power, Franz Joseph issued the so-called **March Constitution** of 1849. Drafted by conservative ministers, it centralized the empire, reaffirmed the emperor's strong prerogatives, and left only a narrow legislative role for a Reichsrat (Imperial Council). Implementation was delayed, and it was suspended later in 1851, reinforcing a fully neoabsolutist regime.

15.11.2 Return to Absolutism: The Bach System

Alexander Bach, the new interior minister, oversaw this "neoabsolutist" regime:

- **Police State Methods**: Press restrictions tightened, and the monarchy continued to watch over universities, clubs, and social gatherings.

- **Centralization**: Hungary lost its special status, forcibly integrated under direct rule from Vienna. The German language dominated administration across the empire, fueling discontent among various nationalities.
- **Legal and Economic Reforms**: Interestingly, the monarchy used authoritarian powers to push modernizing changes, such as standardizing the legal code, promoting building of railways, and fostering commerce. This top-down modernization aimed to bolster state power and revenue.

Despite these achievements, the monarchy's heavy-handed approach reignited national tensions, especially in Hungary, where resentment smoldered. The empire remained perched on a precarious balance of forced loyalty.

15.12 Why the Revolutions Failed and Their Lasting Impact

Although the monarchy overcame the revolutionary movements by 1849, the aftermath cannot be seen purely as a conservative victory. Several factors explain both the revolutions' failure and their partial successes:

1. **Lack of Unity**: Liberals, radicals, and nationalists often pursued conflicting goals. For example, Hungarian independence clashed with the autonomy desires of Croats and Romanians. Viennese liberals disagreed with working-class radicals over social demands.
2. **Monarchy's Military Strength**: The empire's standing army, combined with Russian intervention in Hungary, outmatched the uncoordinated revolutionary forces.
3. **Partial Reforms**: Feudal obligations were largely abolished. Even with a reactionary turn, the monarchy did not restore serfdom. Middle-class liberals gained some recognition of commerce and property rights.
4. **Emergence of National Consciousness**: Despite defeat, the events of 1848 sowed deeper seeds of nationalism and liberal constitutionalism. Over the next decades, these ideas would resurface, compelling further reforms.

Thus, the revolutions forcibly ended Metternich's old system but replaced it with a new era of centralized, militarized rule under Franz Joseph, ironically labeled "neoabsolutist." A final resolution to demands for constitutional governance and ethnic autonomy would wait until the later 1850s and 1860s.

15.13 The Neoabsolutist Period

15.13.1 Austria's Tight Grip

During the 1850s, the Habsburg state exercised unprecedented control over its domains:

- **Civil Bureaucracy**: District commissioners replaced local autonomy. In Hungary, especially, Austrian officials oversaw administration, ignoring previous legal traditions.
- **Catholic Church**: The concordat of 1855 reinforced the Church's influence in education and moral regulation, though the monarchy never relinquished final authority.
- **Economic Development**: Railway construction accelerated, linking Vienna to Prague, Budapest, and Trieste. A stable currency replaced war-ravaged finances, aided by alliances with major banking families.

15.13.2 Cracks Appear: Foreign Policy Setbacks

Despite internal control, the monarchy faced new foreign challenges:

1. **Crimean War (1853–1856)**: Austria remained neutral but alienated Russia by occupying the Danubian Principalities, previously under Russian influence. As a result, the old Holy Alliance with Russia frayed.
2. **Italian Ambitions**: Piedmont-Sardinia, allied with France under Napoleon III, prepared to challenge Austrian rule in Lombardy-Venetia. This looming conflict threatened Austria's prestige and highlighted the empire's vulnerabilities.

By the late 1850s, Emperor Franz Joseph recognized that harsh centralism was unsustainable, especially with foreign foes looming. A new approach to governance would soon follow.

CHAPTER 16: AUSTRIA-HUNGARY AND THE DUAL MONARCHY

16.1 Introduction

The decade after crushing the 1848 revolutions saw Austria's leadership cling to centralized, absolutist methods under Emperor Franz Joseph. But as the 1850s advanced, internal strains and foreign policy setbacks piled up, forcing the monarchy to reconsider its approach. In the early 1860s, new constitutional experiments emerged, seeking to balance demands for representation with continued imperial authority.

A pivotal turning point came in the 1860s, when Austria's power in Germany declined after a swift war with Prussia, culminating in the **Battle of Königgrätz (1866)**. Confronted with the collapse of its influence in German affairs and intensifying Hungarian demands for autonomy, the monarchy negotiated the **Ausgleich (Compromise) of 1867**, transforming itself into the **Dual Monarchy of Austria-Hungary**. Under this arrangement, Austria and Hungary each gained distinct political structures and substantial independence in internal matters, while sharing a common monarch and joint ministries for war, foreign affairs, and finance.

This chapter traces the evolution of Austrian governance from the twilight of neoabsolutism to the formation of Austria-Hungary in 1867, examining how war with Sardinia-Piedmont, conflict with Prussia, and persistent Hungarian pressures shaped the empire's reorganization. We will also explore the new constitutional framework, the complexities of dual governance, and the varied experiences of other nationalities within this restructured monarchy. While the Dual Monarchy resolved some immediate crises, it also left important questions of ethnic representation unanswered, setting the stage for future tensions in the late 19th and early 20th centuries.

16.2 From Neoabsolutism to Constitutional Experiments

16.2.1 The Demise of Neoabsolutism

After 1849, Austria's neoabsolutist system under Franz Joseph concentrated power in Vienna, relying on a large bureaucracy and the army to suppress dissent. However, multiple factors eroded this setup by the late 1850s:

1. **Growing Public Discontent**: Middle-class liberals, especially in the empire's German-speaking provinces, chafed under restrictions on press and assembly. Meanwhile, Hungarian resentment lingered, and other ethnic groups also wanted reforms.
2. **Financial Strains**: Military expenditures and grand building projects weighed on the treasury. While the monarchy modernized roads and railways, the cost was high, and economic growth could not keep pace.
3. **Deteriorating Foreign Ties**: Austria's neutrality during the Crimean War alienated Russia, and unresolved tensions in Lombardy-Venetia made another conflict in Italy likely.

In 1859, the monarchy faced a humiliating defeat in the **Second Italian War of Independence** against Sardinia-Piedmont, allied with France under Napoleon III. The battles of **Magenta** and **Solferino** led to Austria losing Lombardy (including Milan), revealing the fragility of neoabsolutism when confronted by external challenges.

16.2.2 Initial Constitutional Reforms (the October Diploma and February Patent)

Sobering foreign losses pushed Emperor Franz Joseph to seek domestic legitimacy. Advisors argued that reintroducing some form of parliament might rally elites to the throne.

- **October Diploma (1860)**: This decree proposed a federal structure, granting provincial diets more power, especially in Hungary. However, Hungarian leaders deemed it insufficient, wanting full restoration of 1848 principles. Many German-speaking liberals disliked the plan's strong nod to federalism.
- **February Patent (1861)**: Attempted a more centralized approach, creating a bicameral Reichsrat (Imperial Council) in Vienna. Provincial diets would elect representatives, but ultimate authority remained with the emperor. Hungary boycotted this arrangement, refusing to send delegates to what they saw as an illegal assembly.

These half-hearted reforms satisfied few. Hungarians demanded autonomy; Austrian Germans demanded real parliamentary power. Tensions simmered, with the monarchy still relying on bureaucratic rule and limiting press freedoms.

16.3 Foreign Crises and the Road to 1866

16.3.1 The German Question and Rivalry with Prussia

After 1848, Austria remained the nominal leader of the German Confederation, yet Prussia's rising economic strength (through the Zollverein customs union) and military modernization threatened Austrian supremacy. Both states vied for influence among the smaller German principalities.

Key flashpoints:

- **Schleswig-Holstein Dispute**: Both Austria and Prussia intervened against Denmark in 1864 to protect the German-speaking duchies of Schleswig and Holstein. Initially victorious, Austria and Prussia then quarreled over how to administer the conquered lands.
- **Diplomatic Maneuvers**: Austria sought allies in southern Germany; Prussia courted Italy, promising Venice if Italy would attack Austria. Emperor Franz Joseph faced the possibility of a two-front war.

By early 1866, the friction over Schleswig-Holstein and German leadership had become untenable. Prussia, under King Wilhelm I and Prime Minister Otto von Bismarck, prepared for open confrontation. Austria recognized the peril but refused to cede leadership of the Confederation.

16.3.2 War with Italy: Loss of Venice

Simultaneously, Italy yearned to complete its unification by seizing Venetia, still under Austrian control. If war broke out in Germany, Italy would exploit the chance to open a southern front. Austria's situation thus mirrored 1859: fighting on two fronts with uncertain allies. The monarchy hoped for French neutrality or support, but Napoleon III demanded concessions in return—Vienna remained wary of such deals.

16.4 The Austro-Prussian War

16.4.1 Outbreak of Hostilities

In June 1866, after diplomatic efforts collapsed, Prussia declared war on Austria. Most smaller German states sided with Austria, though some (like Hanover and Saxony) were swiftly overrun by the highly efficient Prussian army. Meanwhile, Italy declared war to gain Venetia.

Austrian forces marched north under General Ludwig Benedek, an officer with experience in Italy but less familiarity with the northern terrain. Morale was mixed; Austria's army was large but organizationally behind the Prussian model, which boasted breech-loading needle guns and modern mobilization.

16.4.2 The Decisive Battle of Königgrätz (Sadowa)

On July 3, 1866, Austrian and Prussian armies clashed near Königgrätz (Sadowa) in Bohemia. Despite initial Austrian positions on higher ground, the superior Prussian strategy and firepower tipped the scales. Heavy rains hampered Austrian artillery, and confusion plagued their command structure. By late afternoon, the Austrian lines collapsed.

Königgrätz was a decisive defeat, shattering Austria's German leadership. Benedek's forces retreated in disarray, leaving the monarchy vulnerable to a Prussian advance toward Vienna. Italy also scored some victories in the south, though Austrian forces held off major Italian incursions at sea (notably at Lissa). Faced with looming disaster, Emperor Franz Joseph sought an armistice.

16.4.3 Treaty of Prague and Consequences

In August 1866, the **Peace of Prague** ended the Austro-Prussian War:

- **Dissolution of the German Confederation**: Prussia replaced it with the North German Confederation under its dominance, excluding Austria.
- **Loss of Venetia**: Austria ceded Venetia to Napoleon III, who then transferred it to Italy, fulfilling Italy's unification dream in the north.
- **Reduced Influence**: Austria was formally barred from German affairs, marking a historic shift in Central Europe's power balance.

Though the treaty was comparatively lenient—Bismarck did not want to destroy Austria, preferring it as a future ally—Vienna emerged humiliated and reeling from the cost of war. It was clear that a fundamental reorientation was needed, especially regarding Hungary, whose cooperation was crucial for internal stability.

16.5 The Ausgleich (Compromise) of 1867

16.5.1 Pressures for Reform in Hungary

Hungary's refusal to accept the post-1849 settlement persisted, with many leaders in exile or passive resistance at home. Hungarian nobility demanded the 1848 "March Laws" be recognized and the monarchy scale back centralized control. After 1866's defeat, the empire faced a dire financial and military situation, so Franz Joseph recognized he could not hold Hungary by force.

Key Hungarian figures—Count Gyula Andrássy, Ferenc Deák, and others—were willing to negotiate if the monarchy restored a constitution and recognized Hungary's special status. Deák's moderate platform advocated for a dual arrangement: full internal autonomy for Hungary, joint oversight of foreign affairs, defense, and finances with the Austrian half.

16.5.2 Negotiations and Terms

Talks in early 1867 yielded the **Ausgleich (Compromise)**:

1. **Dual Monarchy**: Austria and Hungary became two distinct states, each with its own parliament and government. They shared the same monarch, now titled Emperor of Austria and King of Hungary, crowned separately in each realm.
2. **Joint Ministries**: Three critical areas—foreign affairs, military, and part of the finance ministry—remained common. A joint delegations system from both parliaments oversaw these matters.
3. **Economic Union**: A customs union linked the two halves for 10-year periods, renewable by agreement. This fostered integrated markets.
4. **Language and Administration**: German dominated in the Austrian half, Hungarian in the Hungarian half. Each recognized the other's language within its domain.

This settlement restored Hungary's constitution and recognized many 1848 reforms, minus some radical elements like total independence. For Austria, the Ausgleich ended years of confrontation in Hungary, enabling it to focus on rebuilding after the defeat of 1866. Emperor Franz Joseph was crowned King of Hungary in June 1867, symbolically sealing the compromise.

16.6 Structure and Functioning of the Dual Monarchy

16.6.1 The Austrian Half (Cisleithania)

The monarchy's western and northern provinces— including Lower and Upper Austria, Bohemia, Moravia, Silesia, Salzburg, Tyrol, Carinthia, Carniola, Trieste, and some Polish-speaking territories like Galicia—formed the Austrian half, often called **Cisleithania** (lands on the "this" side of the River Leitha, from the Viennese perspective).

- **Austrian Parliament (Reichsrat)**: Composed of two chambers, though initially dominated by German-speaking elites. Over time, other national groups—Czechs, Poles—entered if they chose to participate.
- **Constitution of 1867**: Guaranteed civil rights, the rule of law, and limited parliamentary representation. However, the emperor retained significant powers, including control over the army and foreign policy (shared with the Hungarian partner).
- **Ethnic Tensions**: Czechs in Bohemia demanded equal standing for the Czech language in schools and administration. Poles in Galicia also sought autonomy. The monarchy tried to handle these demands through incremental concessions or occasional compromise.

16.6.2 The Hungarian Half (Transleithania)

On the eastern side—**Transleithania**—the Kingdom of Hungary ruled over present-day Hungary, Transylvania, Croatia-Slavonia, and parts of what is now Serbia. The Hungarian parliament in Pest gained broad legislative authority, though the monarchy oversaw the army's top command and foreign policy in conjunction with Austrian representatives:

- **Dominance of the Magyar Elite**: Hungarian aristocrats and a burgeoning Magyar middle class controlled politics, pushing Magyarization on minority nationalities (Slovaks, Romanians, Croats, Serbs).
- **Croatian Autonomy**: A separate compromise (the Nagodba of 1868) granted Croatia limited self-government, but it remained within the Kingdom of Hungary. Tensions persisted over linguistic and administrative questions.

- **Economic Development**: The Hungarian half promoted agriculture, rail expansion, and some industry, spurred by the joint customs union. A wave of modernization soon improved Budapest's infrastructure, making it a rival to Vienna.

16.6.3 The Shared Ministries

Both halves financed and directed common military, foreign affairs, and partial financial policy. The system required each parliament to send delegates to a joint committee, which managed the budget for the army, diplomatic corps, and debt. This arrangement demanded continuous negotiation, often leading to political struggles each time the 10-year economic union needed renewal.

While the Dual Monarchy stabilized relations between Vienna and Budapest, it left unresolved the aspirations of many other nationalities—Slavs, Romanians, Italians—who found themselves overshadowed by German or Magyar elites.

16.7 Emperor Franz Joseph's Role

Having ruled since 1848, Franz Joseph became the central figure of the Dual Monarchy. His personal authority and sense of dynastic duty contributed to the system's longevity:

1. **Balancing Act**: He presided as Emperor in Austria and King in Hungary, traveling frequently between Vienna and Budapest. His presence lent legitimacy to both parliaments.
2. **Conservative Outlook**: While the 1867 compromise was pragmatic, Franz Joseph remained a conservative. He tolerated constitutional forms but retained a strong monarchy.
3. **Symbol of Unity**: For many citizens, the emperor embodied continuity and tradition, a unifying figure above partisan politics. Still, critics noted that real reforms often lagged behind social and economic changes.

16.8 Consequences of the 1867 Settlement

16.8.1 Renewed Stability

The Ausgleich ended the immediate Hungarian threat of secession, ensuring internal peace. The monarchy could refocus on foreign policy and economic modernization without fear of another Hungarian war:

- **Industrial Growth**: Both halves pursued rapid industrialization, especially from the 1870s onward, building railways and factories. A stable political framework encouraged foreign investment.
- **Diplomatic Maneuvering**: Freed from German entanglements, Austria-Hungary eventually formed new alliances in the 1870s and 1880s. The monarchy remained a major player in Balkan affairs, particularly contending with Russian influence over Slavic peoples.

16.8.2 Dissatisfaction Among Other Nationalities

While Austria recognized Hungary as a co-equal partner, other ethnic groups felt marginalized:

- **Czechs**: They demanded a similar "trialist" compromise, making Bohemia the third pole of the monarchy. These pleas were largely ignored. Sporadic efforts for a "Bohemian Compromise" foundered on Hungarian and German opposition.
- **South Slavs (Croats, Serbs, Slovenes)**: Subordinate to Budapest or Vienna, they resented forced assimilation. Over time, such discontent would fuel movements for broader autonomy or a separate South Slav unity.
- **Poles in Galicia**: Gained limited autonomy in local administration, but poverty and socio-political tensions persisted. Some Polish conservatives allied with Vienna in exchange for privileges.

Thus, the Dual Monarchy recognized only one major nationality conflict—Hungary—while ignoring others. This partial solution sowed seeds for future crises, as the monarchy tried to manage an array of national demands without a consistent framework.

16.9 The Constitutional Dynamics in Cisleithania

After 1867, the Austrian half established a parliamentary life known as the **Reichsrat**:

1. **Limited Suffrage**: Initially, voting rights were restricted by property qualifications, giving the German-speaking bourgeoisie disproportionate influence.

2. **Rise of Political Clubs**: Liberals formed the majority in the early years (the "German Liberal" era), pushing economic modernization and civic freedoms, but also blocking Czech language equality or broader minority rights.
3. **Conflict over Federalism**: Czechs demanded that Bohemia be recognized similarly to Hungary, but the Austrian Germans resisted ceding power. Periodically, the Czechs boycotted the Reichsrat, leading to "empty seats" controversies.

Over time, moderate conservative and Catholic parties also grew in strength, further complicating the Reichsrat's politics. The monarchy's prime ministers alternated between seeking German liberal support and more conservative alliances, as Emperor Franz Joseph strove to maintain his role above partisan divisions.

16.10 Hungarian Politics After the Ausgleich

16.10.1 The Hungarian Constitutional System

In the Hungarian half, a new constitution reaffirmed the dominance of the Magyar elite:

- **Parliament (Országgyűlés)**: Bicameral, with an upper house (House of Magnates) including aristocrats and high clergy, and a lower house (House of Representatives).
- **Restricted Franchise**: Voting rights favored landowners and the educated. Rural masses and non-Magyar groups had minimal representation.
- **Cultural "Magyarization"**: The government promoted Hungarian as the official language in administration, courts, and education, often at the expense of local languages like Croatian, Slovak, or Romanian.

While moderate liberals and aristocrats governed under a consensus that upheld the monarchy's foreign policy partnership, radical nationalists occasionally pressed for further independence, though they typically found little traction among the elite.

16.10.2 Growth and Tensions

Hungary experienced economic growth—grain exports, rail expansion, and Budapest's transformation into a major urban center. Yet large peasant populations outside the Hungarian core felt excluded from the political process. Slavic and Romanian communities resented forced assimilation. Periodic local disturbances or cultural boycotts emerged, though these did not threaten the monarchy's stability in the near term.

16.11 Austria-Hungary's Place in Europe After 1867

16.11.1 Shift Away from Germany

With Prussia dominating the new North German Confederation, and later the German Empire (1871), Austria-Hungary turned more attention to the Balkans and Southeastern Europe. The monarchy considered itself the heir to centuries of Habsburg influence in the region, even as neighboring powers—particularly Russia—also vied for ascendancy.

16.11.2 The Balkan Interests and Conflicts

Austria-Hungary's strategic focus on the Balkans led to future clashes with expansionist Russian policy. Many South Slavs under Ottoman or Austro-Hungarian rule looked to Pan-Slavic ideals. Tension escalated after the 1870s, culminating in crises that are beyond our current scope. Yet the seeds of conflict were present: Austria-Hungary believed controlling or influencing the Balkans was vital to empire security and trade, while local nationalist movements demanded autonomy or union with related Slavic states.

16.11.3 Economic Cooperation and Internal Development

Despite looming challenges, the Dual Monarchy enjoyed a period of relative stability in the late 19th century. The customs union between Austria and Hungary fostered economic synergy. Rail networks expanded further, industry developed in both halves, and cities modernized. Cultural life blossomed in Vienna, Budapest, Prague, and elsewhere. The monarchy seemed to have found an equilibrium, albeit precarious, among its many nationalities.

16.12 Internal Debates on National Autonomy and Federalization

16.12.1 Bohemia's Unresolved Status

Czech leaders in Bohemia consistently argued for a third crown or a "Bohemian Compromise" akin to Hungary's arrangement. Some Austrian politicians toyed with the idea of "trialism," creating a triune monarchy. But Hungarian politicians vehemently opposed any revision that might dilute the dual structure. Emperor Franz Joseph, wary of alienating Hungary or fueling demands from other groups, never conceded a fundamental reorganization along these lines.

16.12.2 Southern Slavs and Romanians

Croats achieved partial autonomy under the 1868 Nagodba within Hungary, but Serbian and Slovenian populations felt overshadowed. Romanian communities in Transylvania also yearned for cultural rights, facing Magyar assimilation policies. Tensions simmered, with local elites appealing either to Vienna or to other external powers for support.

Over time, the monarchy's refusal to systematically address these grievances would accumulate, leaving potential for future unrest. For the moment, the monarchy's focus on external alliances and moderate domestic reforms staved off major crises.

16.13 Cultural Flourishing in the Dual Monarchy

Despite political complications, the final decades of the 19th century saw major cultural and intellectual achievements:

1. **Vienna's Golden Age**: A hub of music, science, and arts. Composers like Johann Strauss II advanced the Viennese waltz tradition, while the city's café culture nurtured diverse literary talents.
2. **Budapest's Transformation**: Unified from separate towns (Buda, Pest, Óbuda) in 1873, the capital rapidly modernized, constructing grand boulevards, public buildings, and universities.
3. **National Revivals**: Czechs, Poles, and Southern Slavs built theaters, schools, and learned societies to promote their languages and cultural traditions, leading to a renaissance in literature and scholarship that shaped future nationalist movements.

This dual monarchy environment produced dynamic cross-cultural exchanges, even while fuelling political friction. Cities boomed, attracting migrants from rural areas, forging new social classes and forging an urban intelligentsia that often embraced liberal or socialist ideas.

16.14 The Legacy of the Ausgleich

16.14.1 Strengths

- **Stabilizing Factor**: By acknowledging Hungarian autonomy, the monarchy avoided another insurrection on the scale of 1848. This co-opted Hungarian elites into the imperial system.
- **Institutional Flexibility**: The dual arrangement allowed each half to pursue internal reforms tailored to its preferences while remaining united for foreign policy and defense.
- **Economic Growth**: A larger internal market encouraged industrialization. Austria's advanced manufacturing complemented Hungary's agricultural base, fostering interdependence.

16.14.2 Weaknesses and Unresolved Questions

- **Exclusion of Other Nationalities**: The monarchy effectively recognized only German Austrians and Magyar Hungarians as "constitutive" peoples. Others lacked comparable political mechanisms, breeding dissatisfaction.
- **Complex Joint Governance**: Continuous negotiation was required to maintain the customs union and shared ministries. Occasional deadlocks or crises arose whenever renewal terms were disputed.
- **Potential for National Conflict**: The monarchy's reliance on two dominant groups aggravated minority resentments, sowing seeds for later instability.

In sum, the Ausgleich provided a crucial respite from internal revolt and external defeat, yet it laid out a structure that demanded perpetual compromises. The monarchy succeeded in the short to medium term, but deeper tensions lingered beneath the surface.

CHAPTER 17: THE LATE 19TH CENTURY AND GROWTH OF NATIONAL TENSIONS

17.1 Introduction

With the **Ausgleich of 1867**, Austria-Hungary stabilized itself after decades of turmoil. The Dual Monarchy, split between Austrian (Cisleithanian) and Hungarian (Transleithanian) halves, enjoyed a renewed sense of order and embarked on a period of economic and social development. Yet, beneath the surface, deep-seated forces simmered. Nationalism continued to grow among the various ethnic groups in the empire, from Czechs and Poles to Croats, Serbs, Romanians, and Italians. Politically, liberalism and conservatism collided in each half, shaping new party systems and debates over suffrage, language rights, and local autonomy.

This chapter explores the empire's transformations between 1867 and the closing years of the 19th century. We look at how Austria-Hungary modernized its economy, constructed railways, and expanded its cities, creating both wealth and social tensions. We also examine the complex interplay of national movements. In the Austrian half, debates over Bohemian or Polish autonomy grew louder, while the Hungarians, newly empowered, pursued a policy of Magyarization that fueled discontent among non-Magyar peoples. Despite these tensions, the monarchy found ways to manage conflict, generally avoiding major upheavals. However, the strains introduced in this era would become key factors in the early 20th century, especially as the empire turned its eyes toward the Balkans.

17.2 Post-Compromise Governance in Austria

17.2.1 The Constitution of 1867 and the Reichsrat

After the Compromise, the Austrian half of the empire was governed by a constitutional framework often called the **December Constitution (1867)**. This legislation recognized certain basic civil rights—freedom of religion, assembly, and press (albeit with restrictions)—and established the **Reichsrat (Imperial Council)** in Vienna. The Reichsrat was bicameral:

1. **Upper House (Herrenhaus)**: Composed of hereditary aristocrats, high clergy, and individuals appointed by the emperor for life.
2. **Lower House (Abgeordnetenhaus)**: Elected by provincial diets at first, then gradually moved toward direct elections with limited suffrage expansions over time.

The emperor retained significant powers: he could dissolve the Reichsrat, appoint and dismiss ministers, and direct foreign and military policy in conjunction with the shared ministries for both halves of the Dual Monarchy. Still, this arrangement represented a more liberal environment than the neoabsolutist rule of the 1850s. Political parties formed, fostering debates on domestic reforms, language laws, and economic policies.

17.2.2 Rise of the German Liberals

Initially, the **German Liberal** faction dominated the Cisleithanian parliament. They believed in free trade, a strong centralized administration, and the cultural primacy of the German language, viewed as the empire's "civilizing" tongue. Their agenda included:

- **Railway Expansion**: Encouraging private enterprise and limited state involvement to link major cities—Vienna, Prague, Linz, Graz, and Trieste—enhancing commerce and integration.
- **Administrative Reform**: Strengthening Austrian bureaucracy with standardized procedures, seeking efficiency and uniformity across diverse provinces.
- **Cultural Policies**: Supporting German-language schools and universities, sometimes ignoring or opposing non-German demands for equal linguistic rights.

While these policies spurred economic growth in Austrian lands, they alienated Slavic peoples, especially Czechs in Bohemia and Poles in Galicia, who desired recognition of their own languages and traditions.

17.3 Bohemia, Moravia, and the Czech Question

17.3.1 Czech Revival and Demands

Czechs had experienced a cultural renaissance since the early 19th century—the **Czech National Revival**—which revitalized the language through literature, journalism, and academic work. After 1867, many Czech intellectuals argued that Bohemia, historically a kingdom under the Bohemian Crown, deserved a status similar to that which Hungary enjoyed. They aimed for:

1. **Autonomy**: A separate Bohemian parliament and government to legislate local affairs.
2. **Equality of Language**: Czech as an official administrative and educational language in Bohemia, on par with German.
3. **Historical Rights**: Reference to Bohemia's medieval constitutional charters, claiming these were never fully rescinded.

17.3.2 Austro-Czech Negotiations and Federal Dreams

At various points in the 1870s, Emperor Franz Joseph and his ministers considered a "trialist" approach—extending something akin to the Ausgleich to Bohemia. However, Hungarian opposition was fierce, fearing that granting a similar arrangement to the Czechs would undermine the Dual Monarchy's delicate structure. Moreover, Austrian German liberals blocked major concessions, insisting that a unified state with German as its leading language was essential for progress.

Repeated attempts at compromise, such as the **Fundamental Articles** of 1871 (which would have recognized some Bohemian autonomy), foundered under pressure from both the Hungarian side and German liberal circles in Vienna. Disillusioned, many Czech politicians adopted a policy of passive resistance—sometimes boycotting the Reichsrat. Bohemia's growing urban centers, like Prague, became hotbeds of Czech cultural and political agitation, forging national societies and cooperatives outside official channels.

17.4 Galicia and Polish Aspirations

17.4.1 Polish Autonomy in Galicia

Galicia, acquired from partitioned Poland in the late 18th century, also possessed a large Polish noble class. After 1867, the monarchy recognized the practicality of co-opting Polish elites, particularly because they could help administer a region known for poverty and peasant unrest. In 1869 and 1873, reforms granted Galicia a measure of local autonomy:

- **Diet in Lemberg (Lviv)**: A provincial assembly dominated by Polish nobles oversaw education, culture, and certain administrative functions.
- **Polish as Official Language**: Replacing German in local offices, although Ruthenian (Ukrainian) populations in eastern Galicia felt marginalized.
- **Political Bargain**: In exchange for loyalty to Vienna, Polish leaders gained high positions in the central government, shaping a "pro-Austrian Polish" faction that would last into the early 20th century.

Despite these concessions to Polish elites, Galicia remained economically depressed, with mostly agricultural production and an impoverished peasantry. Tensions between Poles and Ruthenians persisted, though limited resources hindered large-scale conflict. Overall, Austrian authorities believed a controlled measure of autonomy kept the region stable and loyal.

17.4.2 Socioeconomic Challenges

Galicia's harsh conditions—low industrial development, land fragmentation, and high illiteracy—pushed many peasants to migrate to other parts of the monarchy or even overseas. Some Polish and Ruthenian intellectuals criticized the feudal remnants in local administration. Yet the monarchy and Polish nobility strove to maintain a conservative political order. This uneasy arrangement prevented the radical nationalism seen elsewhere but left many root problems unresolved.

17.5 Economic and Social Developments in Cisleithania

17.5.1 Railway Boom and Industrial Growth

From 1867 to the 1890s, Austria witnessed a surge in railway construction, aided by private capital, foreign investment, and occasional state intervention. Key routes connected Vienna to Prague, Linz, Salzburg, Graz, and Trieste, facilitating the transport of coal, iron, textiles, and agricultural goods. Emerging industrial centers included:

- **Bohemia**: Textile mills around Reichenberg (Liberec) and breweries near Pilsen (Plzeň). Heavy industry grew in northern Moravia (Ostrava region).

- **Lower Austria**: Steel and machinery plants near Vienna.
- **Styria**: Iron and steel production around Leoben and the Mur Valley.

Urban populations soared. Vienna, already a major city, expanded rapidly, integrating suburbs and constructing grand boulevards like the Ringstraße. This modernization wave demanded skilled workers, fueling social changes.

17.5.2 Urbanization, Class Formation, and Social Movements

Urban centers saw the rise of a working class laboring in factories, railways, and construction. Their discontent with low wages, long hours, and unsafe conditions led to the formation of early labor associations and mutual aid societies. Though Austrian law often restricted unions, workers organized discreetly, aligning with emerging socialist or social-democratic ideas from neighboring Germany.

A nascent **Social Democratic Party** started to take shape by the late 1880s, though it faced state repression and had to operate partly underground until more permissive laws emerged in the 1890s. Meanwhile, a new middle class—managers, clerks, professionals—embraced liberal or moderate nationalist politics, forming the backbone of many civic associations that shaped cultural life in the cities.

17.6 Political Shifts and Suffrage Reforms in Cisleithania

17.6.1 Decline of German Liberal Dominance

By the mid-1870s, the German Liberal government faced economic downturn (the **Panic of 1873** ended a speculative bubble in railway stocks) and rising criticisms over corruption. The subsequent depression eroded liberal credibility. Franz Joseph occasionally switched prime ministers, seeking more conservative or Catholic-aligned cabinets that could draw in broader rural support.

In 1879, the emperor appointed **Count Eduard Taaffe** as minister-president. Taaffe built coalitions with conservative German Catholics, Poles from Galicia, and Czech deputies (who had partially re-engaged in the Reichsrat). This "Iron Ring" coalition sidelined pure liberals, preferring moderate reforms and emphasizing support for empire-wide unity. The coalition recognized Polish autonomy in Galicia and allowed some Czech cultural concessions—short of full Bohemian autonomy. While liberals criticized Taaffe for backsliding on modernization, he remained in power for over a decade.

17.6.2 Gradual Suffrage Extensions

Initially, parliamentary suffrage was restricted to wealthy taxpayers. However, public agitation and the monarchy's need for legitimacy spurred incremental expansions:

- **Electoral Reforms of 1882 and 1896**: Lowered tax thresholds, increasing the electorate. Still, the system remained weighted, with "curiae" or categories (nobility, urban dwellers, rural dwellers, etc.) each electing delegates, a structure favoring upper classes.
- **Czech and Polish Inclusion**: As the electorate broadened, more deputies from minority nationalities gained seats, pressing their linguistic and cultural demands within the parliamentary arena instead of resorting to boycott or extralegal methods.

Although these reforms were cautious, they signaled the monarchy's grudging acceptance that modern politics required broader representation. The late 1890s saw further calls for universal male suffrage, though real universal suffrage would only emerge in the early 20th century.

17.7 Hungarian Politics and the Rise of Magyarization

17.7.1 Hungary's Political Landscape After 1867

In the Hungarian half, the **Dual Monarchy** arrangement allowed a Hungarian parliament (Országgyűlés) with considerable autonomy, though the emperor-king still oversaw military and foreign affairs. From 1867 onward, a liberal-conservative aristocratic elite, often labeled the **Deák Party** or later the **Liberal Party**, dominated. They championed:

- **Maintenance of the Ausgleich**: Working cooperatively with Vienna on joint ministries and budget approvals.
- **Economic Modernization**: Encouraging railroad expansion across the Great Hungarian Plain, plus industrial growth in Budapest.
- **Limited Suffrage**: Voting rights were narrow, restricting representation largely to wealthier Magyar men. Non-Magyar peasants had minimal political voice.

While this arrangement provided stability, radical voices within Hungary demanded even more independence, and minority groups felt alienated by policies favoring the Magyar language and culture.

17.7.2 Magyarization Policies

To forge a cohesive Hungarian nation-state within the monarchy, governments pursued "Magyarization":

1. **Language Laws**: Hungarian became the mandatory language in public administration, secondary education, and official signage. Non-compliant local authorities risked losing funding or official recognition.
2. **Resistance from Minorities**: Romanians in Transylvania, Slovaks in Upper Hungary, Croats in Croatia-Slavonia, and Serbs in Vojvodina pushed back, forming cultural societies, newspapers, and schools to preserve their languages.
3. **Tensions in Croatia**: Although Croatia had a separate compromise (Nagodba of 1868), ensuring some autonomy, Hungarian authorities often overruled local institutions. The Croatian Sabor (parliament) found itself overshadowed by Pest.

While many Hungarian liberals saw Magyarization as progressive nation-building, minorities perceived it as cultural oppression. Over time, this policy fueled resentment, sowing seeds of future conflict.

17.8 Economic Progress in Hungary

17.8.1 Agricultural Base and Land Reforms

Hungary remained predominantly agrarian: large estates, often owned by Magyar nobility, produced grains for export—especially wheat and maize. Slower reforms meant peasants struggled with outdated land arrangements, sharecropping, and heavy taxes. However, some improvements occurred:

- **Railroads**: Budapest connected to major towns and to Vienna, boosting exports and drawing investment.
- **Agricultural Innovations**: A small group of progressive landlords introduced mechanized threshers, modern fertilizers, and new crop rotations, increasing yields.

- **Urban Growth**: Budapest underwent a construction boom, culminating in iconic structures like the Parliament building, bridging Buda and Pest into a metropolis rivaling Vienna's cultural and economic standing.

The monarchy's customs union with Austria opened large markets, ensuring Hungarian grain found consumers in the more industrialized Austrian provinces. Meanwhile, a budding Hungarian industrial sector emerged, focusing on milling, brewing, and manufacturing equipment.

17.8.2 Social Transformations

Rural poverty remained widespread, prompting internal migration to cities or emigration abroad. Hungarian cities developed a professional middle class of lawyers, journalists, and civil servants—mostly Magyar by background or assimilation—who supported the liberal ruling party. A working class also formed, with industrial laborers in Budapest's factories, but they were less organized than counterparts in Vienna or Prague.

17.9 The Balkan Dimension

17.9.1 Shifting Focus to Southeastern Europe

Excluded from German affairs after 1866, the monarchy turned its gaze southward. The decaying Ottoman Empire offered opportunities for expansion or at least a sphere of influence. Emperor Franz Joseph and his ministers believed controlling or influencing the Balkans was crucial to preventing Russian dominance there. This policy sometimes found support among Hungarian elites eager to check Serbian or Romanian nationalism on Hungary's borders.

17.9.2 The 1878 Congress of Berlin and Bosnia-Herzegovina

A key moment came in 1878. After a Russian-led war forced the Ottoman Empire to cede territory, a European congress in Berlin rebalanced the settlement. **Austria-Hungary** was authorized to **occupy and administer Bosnia-Herzegovina** (though it remained nominally under Ottoman sovereignty). The monarchy's motivations included:

- **Strategic Gain**: A buffer region preventing Slav or Russian infiltration toward Croatia or Hungary.

- **Economic Aspirations**: Access to new markets and resources, though Bosnia was underdeveloped.
- **Managing South Slavic Tensions**: The monarchy believed it could keep Bosnian Serbs, Croats, and Muslims under stable governance, forestalling the creation of a large Serb-led state.

Despite initial local resistance, Austria-Hungary established an administration that introduced roads, schools, and partial modernization. But it also entangled the monarchy deeper in Balkan politics, stoking suspicion from Serbia, which claimed cultural ties to Bosnia's Serbs.

17.10 Rising National Movements Among South Slavs

17.10.1 Serbia's Growing Influence

Serbia, an independent kingdom since the mid-19th century, saw itself as a champion of South Slavs—particularly Serbs under Habsburg or Ottoman rule. By the 1880s and 1890s, Serbian nationalist societies promoted the idea of a "Greater Serbia," fueling concerns in both Vienna and Budapest.

Hungarian officials worried about Serb agitation in the southern counties of the kingdom, while Austrian administrators in Bosnia confronted clandestine Serbian-backed groups. The monarchy's apprehension mounted as Serbia gained backing from Russia, which saw an Orthodox Slavic ally in the Balkans.

17.10.2 Croat and Slovene Awakening

- **Croatia**: Divided between a loyalty to the Habsburg monarchy and a rising Illyrian movement that championed unification of all South Slavs under a Croatian framework.
- **Slovenes**: Concentrated in Carniola, Styria, and the Littoral, they formed reading clubs and cultural associations, demanding equal status with German Austrians. Tensions arose in bilingual towns as German-liberal local councils resisted Slovene language rights.

Though overshadowed by Hungarian or Austrian power, these groups persisted in building their own institutions and identity. By century's end, some Croat and Slovene politicians allied with Czech or Polish deputies in the Reichsrat, pushing for further language laws and concessions.

17.11 Intellectual, Cultural, and Social Trends

17.11.1 Vienna's Cultural Zenith: The Ringstrasse Era

After the mid-19th century demolition of old fortifications, Vienna underwent a grand redevelopment. The **Ringstrasse** was lined with monumental buildings—parliament, city hall, museums, the opera—reflecting a mix of historicist styles. This era symbolized the monarchy's aspiration to be a modern European power, bridging tradition and progress.

Prominent composers like **Johann Strauss II** enriched the city's musical life with waltzes and operettas. The city boasted coffeehouses that nurtured intellectual debates among journalists, writers, and politicians. While overshadowed by official censorship, these salons introduced progressive ideas that would bloom in the next century.

17.11.2 Budapest's Transformation and Hungarian Cultural Effervescence

Budapest, unified from Buda, Pest, and Óbuda in 1873, blossomed with boulevards like Andrássy Avenue, grand public buildings such as the Hungarian Parliament by the Danube, and a network of public transport including Europe's second-oldest underground railway (1896). Writers and poets (like János Arany and Mór Jókai) celebrated Hungarian history, fueling national pride. The city's coffeehouse culture also provided a platform for journalists and the budding literary scene, paralleling Vienna's environment.

17.11.3 Rise of Modern Sciences and Education

The monarchy supported universities in Vienna, Prague, Graz, and elsewhere, encouraging advancements in medicine, law, and natural sciences. Although overshadowed by German universities in prestige, these institutions produced a growing cadre of professionals. In Hungary, the University of Budapest drew an expanding class of Magyar-speaking intellectuals. Scientific societies, learned journals, and new museums or libraries promoted scholarship in multiple languages, though the empire's linguistic divides often hampered cross-fertilization.

17.12 Growing Social Conflicts

17.12.1 Social Democracy in Austria and Bohemia

By the 1880s, Marxist ideals spread among workers in Vienna, Linz, and Bohemian industrial regions. Initially operating clandestinely, the **Austrian Social Democratic Party** emerged in the early 1890s after laws relaxed. Influential figures like **Victor Adler** mobilized factory workers and artisans, demanding universal male suffrage, improved labor conditions, and social insurance.

Czech-speaking labor organizers formed parallel or allied groups, sometimes cooperating with German-speaking socialists but also pressing for recognition of the Czech language in the party structure. Divisions between German and Czech workers complicated the movement, as national solidarity sometimes clashed with class solidarity.

17.12.2 Socialist and Radical Ideas in Hungary

In Hungary, the aristocratic-liberal government maintained stricter controls, fearful of peasant revolts and minority activism. A small socialist movement grew in Budapest's factories, though official repression delayed its rise. The authorities considered radical workers' gatherings subversive, leading to arrests and censorship. Nonetheless, by the late 1890s, labor strikes and union formations signaled growing discontent with the paternalistic system.

17.13 Attempts at Further Political Reform

17.13.1 Taaffe's Government and Language Laws (Late 1880s–1890s)

Count Eduard Taaffe's long tenure (1879–1893) saw incremental changes intended to reconcile nationalities, or at least manage them. His government introduced limited language ordinances for Bohemia and Moravia, requiring certain local offices to use both German and Czech. German liberals decried these measures as undermining German cultural supremacy. Czech activists felt they were too little, too late. The resulting deadlock revealed the monarchy's inability to please all sides simultaneously.

17.13.2 Electoral Reform Debates

As workers and lower-middle-class citizens gained a political voice, calls for universal male suffrage intensified. Liberal and conservative elites feared empowering uneducated masses who might vote socialist or in favor of radical nationalists. Nonetheless, partial reforms did pass:

- **1896 Badeni Ordinances** in Cisleithania: Provided for a broadening of the voter base, though still not fully universal.
- **Standoffs in Bohemia**: Attempts to enforce bilingual administrative requirements led to German liberal uproar, culminating in fierce parliamentary obstruction. Emperor Franz Joseph sometimes resorted to emergency decrees to keep governance functional.

By century's end, many recognized the need for more comprehensive reforms, but the monarchy's leadership feared losing control if suffrage expanded too rapidly.

17.14 Foreign Policy After the 1870s

17.14.1 The Dual Alliance with Germany (1879)

Following the Franco-Prussian War (1870–1871), Germany, now a unified empire under Bismarck, sought stable borders. Though Austria-Hungary had been a rival in 1866, Bismarck recognized that an alliance with Vienna would prevent Russian encroachment in the Balkans. In 1879, the **Dual Alliance** was signed: both states pledged mutual defense if attacked by Russia. Emperor Franz Joseph, still wary of Russian interference with South Slavs, welcomed the treaty as security.

17.14.2 The Triple Alliance and Balkans Focus

In 1882, **Italy** joined, forming the **Triple Alliance**: Germany, Austria-Hungary, and Italy. Tensions remained between Italy and Austria-Hungary over the "unredeemed" Italian lands (Trentino, Trieste, etc.), but Italy saw the alliance as a buffer against France. Meanwhile, Austria-Hungary continued to keep an eye on the Balkans, worried about rising Serb and Bulgarian states. Russia, championing Pan-Slavism, often clashed with Austrian policy. This rivalry pointed to possible future conflicts in Southeastern Europe.

17.15 End of the Century

As the 19th century drew to a close, Austria-Hungary had undergone significant modernization and maintained relative internal peace compared to the upheavals of 1848. The Dual Monarchy's structure, however, clearly favored German Austrians in Cisleithania and Magyars in Transleithania. Other nationalities found themselves in subordinate positions, fueling calls for increased federalization or local autonomy. Key trends included:

1. **Czech-German Rivalry** in Bohemia escalated, culminating in repeated legislative deadlocks.
2. **Hungarian Domination** overshadowed minority aspirations, prompting resentment in Slovakia, Transylvania, and Croatia.
3. **Rising Social and Radical Movements**: Social democrats, anarchists, and nationalist militants each demanded more radical changes, suspecting the monarchy could not reform from within.
4. **Diplomatic Balancing Act**: The monarchy's alliances with Germany and Italy, and its careful handling of Balkan intrigues, kept major wars at bay—for now.

Franz Joseph, still on the throne after over five decades, served as a unifying symbol, personally respected by many despite their grievances with the imperial system. Yet these accumulating national antagonisms, social unrest, and external tensions (particularly in the Balkans) formed a tinderbox that would define the early 20th century.

CHAPTER 18: THE ROAD TO WORLD WAR I

18.1 Introduction

As the 20th century dawned, Austria-Hungary found itself balancing modernization and the rising demands of its multiple nationalities. Internally, the monarchy wrestled with electoral reforms, labor movements, and enduring linguistic disputes. Externally, it navigated a complex environment dominated by alliance politics, imperial rivalries, and the persistent Balkan question.

In this chapter, we examine the empire's trajectory from about 1900 to 1914. We see how Austria-Hungary, allied with Germany, confronted an increasingly hostile international scene. The monarchy's expansion in the Balkans, particularly the annexation of Bosnia-Herzegovina in 1908, accelerated tensions with Serbia and Russia. Meanwhile, domestic politics were turbulent: universal male suffrage emerged in Cisleithania in 1907, empowering new political forces and intensifying national conflicts in parliament. The monarchy remained strong enough to contain these pressures, but each crisis pushed the empire closer to an eventual breaking point.

We conclude by tracing the final steps before the outbreak of World War I in 1914: the assassination of Archduke Franz Ferdinand in Sarajevo, Austria-Hungary's ultimatum to Serbia, and the unstoppable momentum of alliance obligations. While we stop short of the war's full scope, we show how the monarchy's precarious internal situation and aggressive Balkan policies set the stage for the conflagration that would transform Europe.

18.2 Early 20th Century Politics in Cisleithania

18.2.1 Universal Male Suffrage (1907)

One of the most significant reforms in Austria's political sphere came with the introduction of universal male suffrage in 1907. This step responded to decades of pressure from social democrats, national movements, and progressive liberals who criticized the curiae-based electoral system as elitist. The newly expanded electorate included millions of working-class voters, Slavic communities, and other groups previously excluded.

Key impacts:

1. **Rise of Mass Parties**: The Social Democratic Workers' Party (SDAP) surged in support, becoming a major parliamentary faction. Czech, Polish, and other ethnic parties gained seats, voicing national demands.
2. **Fragmentation of Parliament**: With new parties representing diverse social classes and nationalities, forging stable governing coalitions grew more difficult. The Reichsrat was prone to stalemates and frequent dissolutions.
3. **Continuing Imperial Authority**: Despite electoral reforms, Emperor Franz Joseph maintained the power to appoint governments and issue emergency decrees if parliament deadlocked. This tension between a modern electorate and an old imperial structure defined Austrian politics in the final pre-war years.

18.2.2 National Conflicts Intensify

Bohemia's "language ordinances" remained a flashpoint, with German and Czech deputies clashing over bilingual requirements in local administration. Polish deputies sought further concessions in Galicia, while Ruthenian (Ukrainian) activists demanded their own linguistic rights. Each crisis often led to parliamentary paralysis, as nationalist blocs filibustered or walked out. The monarchy relied on short-lived cabinets and bureaucratic rule to keep governance functioning.

18.3 Hungary's Political Stalemates

18.3.1 Demands for Army Reforms and Hungarian Control

In Hungary, the post-1867 settlement guaranteed local governance but left the common army under joint oversight with Austria. Hungarian politicians, especially from more radical nationalist circles, resented the monarchy's refusal to allow Hungarian as a language of command in the common army. They argued that Hungarian recruits should serve under Hungarian officers, bridging the monarchy's dual arrangement into military affairs.

From 1903 to 1907, bitter debates raged. Prime Minister **István Tisza** (from the Liberal Party) tried to maintain loyalty to the emperor-king while facing demands from nationalists for a "Hungarian national army." Tisza firmly opposed any measure that threatened the monarchy's unity. Tensions soared, culminating in repeated parliament dissolutions and chaotic election campaigns.

18.3.2 Widening the Franchise in Hungary?

Unlike in Austria, universal male suffrage made minimal progress in Hungary. The ruling liberal oligarchy feared empowering non-Magyar majorities in some areas, worried about losing their parliamentary control. Hungary thus retained property-based voting requirements. Critics, including socialists and minority parties, labeled this an "electoral dictatorship" of the Magyar upper class. This disconnect between Austria's expanded democracy and Hungary's narrower system underlined the patchwork nature of the monarchy.

18.4 The Annexation of Bosnia-Herzegovina

18.4.1 Background and Motives

Since 1878, Austria-Hungary had "occupied and administered" Bosnia-Herzegovina, nominally still Ottoman territory. By the early 1900s, with the Ottoman Empire weakening further, foreign minister **Alois Aehrenthal** decided to formalize Austria-Hungary's hold. In October 1908, the monarchy **annexed** Bosnia-Herzegovina outright. Aehrenthal believed this bold move would strengthen the monarchy's position in the Balkans and discourage Serb expansion.

18.4.2 International Repercussions

The annexation set off a diplomatic storm:

- **Serbia** denounced it, viewing Bosnia's Serbs as potential brethren of a larger Serbian state. Russia, though still recovering from the Russo-Japanese War (1904–1905), supported Serbian objections but was too weak militarily to confront Austria-Hungary directly.
- **Germany** backed Austria-Hungary, pressuring Russia to accept the annexation or face isolation.
- **Ottoman Empire** protested, but lacking power, it eventually recognized the annexation in exchange for financial compensation.

This **Bosnian Crisis** nearly sparked a general war. Russia's forced climbdown humiliated Pan-Slavic sentiments there, deepening resentment toward Austria-Hungary. Serbia, embittered, accelerated efforts to foster clandestine networks in Bosnia. The monarchy thus "won" diplomatically in 1908, but the event heightened its vulnerability, creating a long-term rivalry with Serbia and fueling tensions that would explode by 1914.

18.5 Internal Administration of Bosnia-Herzegovina

Now a formal province, Bosnia-Herzegovina was governed by a special "Landesregierung" under the joint authority of Austria and Hungary. The monarchy claimed it would modernize the region:

- **Infrastructure**: Building roads, rail lines, and administrative centers.
- **Legal Reforms**: Introducing Austrian-Hungarian codes, albeit adapted to local traditions.
- **Ethnic Balancing**: The population comprised Bosnian Serbs (Orthodox), Bosnian Croats (Catholic), and Bosnian Muslims, each with distinct identities. The monarchy tried to remain "neutral" among them, but strong Serb and Croat nationalism complicated the task.

Some development did occur, yet many residents viewed Austrian officials as foreign rulers. Local Serb activists formed underground ties to Serbia, while Croat nationalists sought alignment with Croatian movements in the monarchy. The monarchy's presence stabilized the region but also sowed seeds of resentment that clandestine nationalist groups would exploit.

18.6 Diplomatic Alignments and Balkan Tensions

18.6.1 The Balkan Wars (1912–1913)

In 1912, a coalition of Balkan states (Serbia, Montenegro, Bulgaria, and Greece) attacked the Ottoman Empire, hoping to expel it from Europe. Austria-Hungary watched warily, fearing an enlarged Serbia could threaten its southern borders and stir Slavic populations under Habsburg rule. The first Balkan War ended with Ottoman losses and a triumphant Serbia, which doubled in size. A second Balkan War in 1913 pitted Bulgaria against its former allies, leaving Serbia even stronger.

The monarchy tried to block Serbia's access to the Adriatic Sea, backing the creation of Albania. Austria-Hungary's foreign minister, Count Leopold Berchtold, believed containing Serbia was vital to the empire's survival. Russia supported Serbia's ambitions, deepening the Austro-Russian rivalry. Although Europe avoided a wider conflict over these wars, the monarchy's leadership concluded that Serbia represented a growing existential menace, especially after 1908's Bosnian Crisis.

18.6.2 Ties with Germany

Throughout these Balkan crises, Austria-Hungary relied on German support to deter Russian intervention. The **Triple Alliance** (with Italy as well) theoretically guaranteed mutual defense, though Italy's position became increasingly uncertain, as its own ambitions in the Adriatic clashed with Habsburg interests. Nonetheless, Germany stood firmly behind Vienna, urging a strong stance against Serbia. The monarchy's foreign policy pivoted on this reassurance that any conflict with Serbia (and possibly Russia) would find Berlin's backing.

18.7 Domestic Unrest and the Rise of Radical Movements

18.7.1 Greater Serbia Ideology and Secret Societies

In Serbia and among Bosnian Serbs, nationalist societies like **Narodna Odbrana** and **Black Hand** (Ujedinjenje ili Smrt) espoused the unification of all South Slavs under Serbian leadership. These groups gained traction among youth, students, and certain army circles. The monarchy's police tried to suppress arms smuggling and infiltration, but local sympathizers often aided these efforts. By 1912–1913, intelligence reports indicated heightened activity, which Austrian officials viewed as a direct threat.

18.7.2 Assassination Plots and Political Violence

Across the empire, political violence escalated:

- **Czech radicals** occasionally targeted German administration symbols.
- **Hungarian anarchists** or socialists occasionally engaged in sabotage, though limited.
- **Bosnian Serb networks** considered acts of terrorism to force the monarchy out of Bosnia.

Emperor Franz Joseph, aging and still mourning personal tragedies (the suicide of Crown Prince Rudolf in 1889, the assassination of Empress Elisabeth in 1898), relied on harsh policing and loyal aristocratic officials. However, many recognized that frustration among nationalities, especially the younger generation, bred desperation and potential for dramatic attacks.

18.8 The Assassination of Archduke Franz Ferdinand

18.8.1 Archduke Franz Ferdinand's Position

Heir to the Habsburg throne after the death of Crown Prince Rudolf and others in line, **Archduke Franz Ferdinand** embodied a new generation's outlook. Known for his somewhat reformist ideas on reorganizing the empire into a "trialist" or federal structure that might integrate South Slavs, he also harbored distrust of Hungary's privileged position. Some Hungarian politicians disliked him, fearing he would curb their autonomy.

Franz Ferdinand's visit to Sarajevo, Bosnia's capital, on June 28, 1914, symbolized the monarchy's authority in the region. It coincided with a sensitive date for Serbs (the anniversary of the Battle of Kosovo in 1389, a cultural-laden day in Serbian history). Security was deemed sufficient by local officials, though intelligence indicated possible Serb extremist plots.

18.8.2 The Sarajevo Assassination

A group of young Bosnian Serb nationalists, aided by elements of the **Black Hand**, prepared an attack. On June 28, **Gavrilo Princip** shot and killed Archduke Franz Ferdinand and his wife Sophie during their motorcade ride through Sarajevo. This shocking event reverberated worldwide:

- **Monarchy's Outrage**: Vienna saw it as conclusive proof that Serbia fomented terrorism within Habsburg domains.
- **Public Reaction**: Austrians and Hungarians alike grieved the archduke's death, stoking calls for a firm response against Serbia.
- **Diplomatic Uncertainty**: Europe's major powers recognized the danger; if Austria-Hungary moved against Serbia, Russia might intervene, prompting Germany to honor its alliance with Austria. A chain reaction loomed.

While the assassins were quickly caught, the monarchy believed Serbia's government was complicit or at least negligent. Foreign Minister Berchtold resolved that a decisive blow against Serbia was necessary to reassert Habsburg prestige and deter further subversion.

18.9 The July Crisis

18.9.1 German "Blank Check"

Before acting, Austria-Hungary sought Berlin's position. German leaders, including Kaiser Wilhelm II and Chancellor Theobald von Bethmann Hollweg, offered the so-called **"blank check"** in early July 1914, encouraging Vienna to deal with Serbia firmly, pledging Germany's full support if Russia intervened. This emboldened the monarchy to draft an ultimatum designed to be nearly impossible for Serbia to accept.

18.9.2 Crafting the Ultimatum

On July 23, Austria-Hungary presented Serbia with an ultimatum demanding, among other things:

- **Suppression of anti-Habsburg societies and propaganda**
- **Dismissal of certain officials** deemed hostile to the monarchy
- **Allowance for Habsburg police to operate inside Serbia** to investigate the assassination

Though Serbia agreed to most points, it rejected the demand allowing Austrian authorities to conduct investigations on Serbian soil, seeing it as a violation of sovereignty. This partial compliance was dismissed by Vienna. On July 28, Austria-Hungary declared war on Serbia.

18.10 Prelude to World War I

Once Austria-Hungary attacked Serbia, the alliance network triggered escalation. Russia mobilized to protect Serbia. Germany declared war on Russia (and soon on France), while France and Britain, bound by their own treaties, entered the fray.

Within days, nearly all of Europe was drawn into the conflict, marking the start of **World War I** in August 1914.

The monarchy's final steps into war were shaped by decades of tension—national rivalries inside the empire, hostility with Serbia, mistrust with Russia, and a reliance on German backing. Austria-Hungary found itself leading the charge into a massive confrontation that would test every aspect of its internal cohesion and might.

18.11 Assessing the Road to War

Looking back, several key factors explain how Austria-Hungary reached the brink of global conflict:

1. **National Discontent**: Ongoing frictions among Czechs, Poles, South Slavs, Romanians, and others left the monarchy always on edge, seeking to assert authority and deter perceived secessionist threats.
2. **Serbian Rivalry**: The monarchy's annexation of Bosnia in 1908 and Serbia's growing ambitions clashed irreconcilably in the Balkans. Each crisis boosted the other's resolve for eventual confrontation.
3. **Alliance Dependence**: The monarchy counted on German support to balance Russia. This "blank check" emboldened Vienna's warlike approach.
4. **Internal Politics**: The monarchy's attempts at compromise with nationalities were incomplete, fueling radicalism. Leading figures believed external success (like a victory over Serbia) might unify the empire's peoples around the Habsburg throne.

While the monarchy's leaders never envisioned a full-scale European conflagration, their step-by-step approach in July 1914 made a broader war inevitable once alliances activated. The final trigger was the Sarajevo assassination of Archduke Franz Ferdinand, an event orchestrated by youthful Bosnian Serbs but rooted in far deeper resentments.

CHAPTER 19: AUSTRIA DURING WORLD WAR I

19.1 Introduction

When Austria-Hungary declared war on Serbia in July 1914, few Austrians or Europeans anticipated the scale of the conflict that would unfold. Fueled by a dense web of alliances, longstanding rivalries, and new industrial-era capabilities, the war quickly drew in major powers, igniting the **First World War (1914–1918)**. For Austria, this war represented the empire's greatest test since the Napoleonic era—but on an even larger, more devastating scale.

This chapter examines how Austria—technically the Cisleithanian half of the Dual Monarchy—participated in the war under the broader umbrella of **Austria-Hungary**. We will look at the empire's military campaigns, the burdens placed on society by total war, the strains on its multiethnic composition, and the monarchy's final decline under Emperor Karl I (who succeeded the long-reigning Franz Joseph). Despite early enthusiasm, the war's toll—human, economic, and political—ultimately overwhelmed Austria-Hungary. When defeat loomed in 1918, the monarchy fragmented as nationalities proclaimed independence.

We will conclude this chapter by considering how the empire's war effort unraveled, creating the conditions for Austria's postwar transformation. Though we stop short of truly modern times, these war years decisively ended the centuries-old Habsburg realm, setting Austria on a new path entirely.

19.2 Outbreak of War

19.2.1 July Crisis and Mobilization

In the weeks following the assassination of Archduke Franz Ferdinand (June 28, 1914), Austria-Hungary's leaders—particularly Foreign Minister Count Leopold Berchtold and Chief of Staff Franz Conrad von Hötzendorf—pushed for swift military action against Serbia, convinced that a punitive strike was necessary to protect the monarchy's prestige and deter Slavic nationalism. German support (the "blank check") emboldened them, despite concerns that Russia might intervene to defend Serbia.

On July 28, Austria-Hungary declared war on Serbia. By early August, the **Great Powers** were drawn in: Russia mobilized, Germany declared war on Russia and France, and Britain entered to uphold Belgian neutrality. Thus, the conflict became a multi-front war involving the Central Powers (Germany, Austria-Hungary, later the Ottoman Empire and Bulgaria) against the Entente (primarily France, Russia, Britain, Serbia, and later Italy, Romania, the United States, and others).

19.2.2 Early Engagements Against Serbia

The monarchy's first offensive targeted Serbia, with armies crossing the Drina and Sava rivers in August 1914. Expectations of a quick victory soon crumbled. Serbian forces, hardened by the Balkan Wars, inflicted surprising defeats on the Austro-Hungarian army at battles like **Cer** (August) and **Kolubara** (November–December). Poor coordination, inadequate logistics, and underestimation of Serbian resolve led to humiliating setbacks for Austria-Hungary's generals.

These failures dented morale at home. Habsburg leadership found itself diverting more troops to the Balkan front than anticipated. Only in late 1915, with German and Bulgarian help, would the monarchy and its allies finally overrun Serbia. Even then, the protracted fighting had already drained resources that were needed elsewhere.

19.3 The Eastern Front and the Russian Threat

19.3.1 Battles in Galicia (1914–1915)

Simultaneously, Austria-Hungary faced Russia along its **Galician frontier**. In August 1914, Russian armies surged into Galicia, threatening the major city of Lemberg (Lviv). Early Austro-Hungarian offensives faltered at **Gnila Lipa** and **Komarów**, culminating in severe casualties and the Russian capture of Lemberg. By late 1914, the monarchy had lost much of eastern Galicia, including the fortress of Przemyśl (besieged until March 1915).

These defeats shocked the empire. The monarchy looked to Germany for aid, culminating in joint operations that stabilized the front in early 1915. A major counteroffensive, the **Gorlice–Tarnów Offensive** (May–June 1915), led chiefly by German troops but supported by Austro-Hungarian forces, pushed the Russians back from Galicia and Poland. While this success recaptured territory, it left the Austro-Hungarian army heavily reliant on German command and support for major victories.

19.3.2 Impact on the Civilian Population of Galicia

Galicia's multiethnic population—Poles, Ukrainians (Ruthenians), Jews, and others—suffered immense hardship during the back-and-forth battles. Displacement was massive: hundreds of thousands fled eastward or westward, depending on who held control. Food shortages, disease, and forced requisitions by armies ravaged the region. Austrian authorities suspected many Ukrainians of sympathizing with Russia, leading to crackdowns, internments, or deportations. Tensions flared between Poles and Ukrainians over local administration, intensifying ethnic antagonisms in the chaos of war.

19.4 The Italian Front and the Southern Theater

19.4.1 Italy's Entry into the War (1915)

Despite being part of the **Triple Alliance** with Germany and Austria-Hungary, Italy remained neutral in 1914. In secret negotiations (the **Treaty of London**, April 1915), the Entente powers promised Italy territorial gains (Trentino, South Tyrol, Trieste, etc.) at Austria's expense. Thus, Italy declared war on Austria-Hungary in May 1915, opening the **Italian Front**.

This new front stretched across the **Isonzo River** and the mountainous Alpine regions. The monarchy scrambled to fortify positions in the **Trentino** and along the **Carso Plateau**, while Italy aimed to seize Trieste and push deep into Austrian littoral territory. Though less industrially potent than major powers, Italy possessed a sizable army that forced Austria-Hungary to divert resources from the Eastern Front.

19.4.2 The Isonzo Battles

Between 1915 and 1917, Italy launched eleven major offensives along the **Isonzo River**—the so-called **Battles of the Isonzo**. Austrian defenses, perched on higher ground, inflicted massive Italian casualties, but at great cost to themselves as well. The fighting became a grueling siege-like struggle with little strategic movement, reminiscent of trench warfare on the Western Front. Towns like Gorizia changed hands multiple times, each offensive draining men and material.

Austria-Hungary's battered army often relied on German help. A joint offensive at **Caporetto** (October 1917) finally broke the Italian lines, forcing a massive Italian retreat. This brief triumph again highlighted how crucial German support was, as Austria-Hungary alone struggled to sustain large-scale offensives or defenses without logistical and strategic backing from Berlin.

19.5 The Western and Other Fronts

Although Austria-Hungary was less prominent than Germany on the Western Front, small contingents did assist German allies. A minor number of Austro-Hungarian artillery units served in France or the Balkans. Meanwhile, the monarchy engaged in limited naval actions from its Adriatic ports, primarily from **Pola (Pula)** in Istria. The Austro-Hungarian navy, overshadowed by Italy's and the Entente's fleets, mostly conducted coastal defense and submarine warfare.

Additionally, Austria-Hungary participated in the **Macedonian Front** alongside German, Bulgarian, and Ottoman forces, facing Entente armies in Salonika. However, the monarchy's main focus remained the Eastern and Italian fronts, where its survival was most threatened.

19.6 Internal Pressures

19.6.1 Wartime Economy and Shortages

World War I demanded unprecedented mobilization of resources. Factories shifted to arms production, agricultural output was requisitioned for the army, and civilian rationing became the norm. By 1916–1917, serious food shortages afflicted Austrian cities. Bread lines grew, inflation soared, and malnutrition became widespread.

The monarchy struggled with a poor transportation network for distributing goods—particularly from Hungary, which controlled its own grain. While official negotiations mandated certain quotas from Hungary to the Austrian half, inefficiencies and local hoarding complicated deliveries. This deepened resentment among Austrian civilians, who perceived Hungarian foot-dragging. Meanwhile, in mountainous or rural Austrian areas, smaller-scale subsistence farming mitigated hunger somewhat, but urban populations suffered severely.

19.6.2 Strikes and Discontent

Labor strikes erupted in late 1916 and early 1917, as workers demanded better rations and wages. The Austrian Social Democratic Party wavered between patriotic support of the war and sympathy for these grievances. The monarchy's censors suppressed pacifist or antiwar sentiments, but morale steadily eroded under conditions of total war. By 1917–1918, even some middle-class Austrians voiced doubts about the conflict's purpose, discussing the possibility of a negotiated peace.

19.7 Ethnic Tensions and Political Fragmentation

19.7.1 Nationalities Under Suspicion

The war heightened suspicion of potentially "disloyal" minority groups. Slovenes, Czechs, Ukrainians, and others faced accusations of sympathizing with Russia or the Entente. Harsh crackdowns occurred in border zones:

- **Czech Lands**: Intellectuals suspected of Russophilia or Pan-Slavic leanings were arrested. Tomáš G. Masaryk, a prominent Czech professor and politician, fled abroad, organizing Czech and Slovak independence movements.
- **Ruthenians (Ukrainians)**: In Galicia, many were interned or relocated if suspected of pro-Russian sentiments.
- **Italians in Tyrol or along the littoral**: Some were viewed as sympathizers with Italy's cause.

These measures undercut loyalty to the Habsburg monarchy, prompting clandestine contacts between activists inside the empire and exile groups lobbying Entente governments for support.

19.7.2 Czechs, Slovaks, and the Emergence of Independence Movements

Prominent exiled leaders—like **Tomáš G. Masaryk**, **Edvard Beneš**, and **Milan Rastislav Štefánik**—formed the **Czechoslovak National Council** abroad, seeking the defeat of Austria-Hungary to enable a new state of Czechs and Slovaks. They organized volunteer "Czechoslovak Legions" that fought alongside the Entente on Eastern and Western fronts. Their successes gained international recognition, as the French, British, and later Americans grew sympathetic to the idea that the empire's nationalities deserved self-determination.

Inside Bohemia and Moravia, clandestine committees discussed postwar options, sending appeals to foreign embassies. By late 1917, the monarchy's secret police noted an uptick in anti-Habsburg rhetoric among Czech workers and intellectuals. While official Czech politicians in Vienna maintained a cautious line, real support for independence expanded. Similar sentiments spread among Poles, South Slavs, and Romanians, all seeing an Entente victory as a path to freedom from Habsburg rule.

19.8 Leadership Changes and the Death of Emperor Franz Joseph

19.8.1 Franz Joseph's Death (November 1916)

Emperor Franz Joseph, who had ruled since 1848, passed away on November 21, 1916, amid the war's gloom. Although many in Austria revered him as a unifying symbol, his policy decisions contributed to the monarchy's predicament. His death severed a personal bond that had anchored loyalty in some quarters.

19.8.2 Emperor Karl I's Attempts at Reform

Franz Joseph's grandnephew, **Karl I** (known in Hungary as Károly IV), ascended the throne. Young, devoutly Catholic, and less entrenched in the old aristocratic circles, Karl recognized the empire's precarious position. He initiated cautious reforms:

- **Peace Overtures**: Karl secretly contacted the Entente in 1917–1918, hoping to negotiate a separate peace. However, his efforts collapsed once Germany discovered them, and the Entente demanded sweeping concessions.

- **Domestic Liberalization**: Karl considered granting more autonomy to nationalities, but Hungary's elites resisted federalization. Many Czechs, South Slavs, and others believed these late concessions were insufficient and insincere.

Karl's rule thus faced internal factionalism, continuing military crises, and distrust from allies and enemies alike. Unable to extricate Austria-Hungary from the war or quell nationalist drives, he presided over the monarchy's final unraveling.

19.9 The United States Enters the War and Mounting Pressures

In April 1917, the United States declared war—initially on Germany, later extending hostility to Austria-Hungary by December of that year. Though America's main focus was the Western Front, the possibility of American resources tipping the balance heightened the monarchy's desperation for a negotiated peace.

Meanwhile, Russia experienced revolution in 1917. The **February Revolution** toppled the Tsar, replaced by a provisional government. The **October Revolution** brought the Bolsheviks to power, who concluded the separate **Treaty of Brest-Litovsk** (March 1918) with the Central Powers. This ended fighting on the Eastern Front, temporarily relieving Austria-Hungary from Russian pressure. However, the monarchy's armies were by then severely drained, and the newly freed German forces shifted to the Western Front, intensifying that theater rather than rescuing Austria's problems with war-weariness and nationalism.

19.10 Final Year of War and the Collapse

19.10.1 Military Exhaustion and Breaking Morale

The monarchy's final offensives included an attack on the Italian Front in June 1918 (the **Second Battle of the Piave River**). While Austria-Hungary briefly advanced, shortages of ammunition and food, plus plummeting troop morale, led to a decisive defeat. Desertions soared, with soldiers from Czech, Slovak, South Slav, and even some German units questioning the monarchy's cause. On other fronts, minimal action occurred, as the empire lacked resources.

By the autumn of 1918, the Central Powers collapsed in sequence: Bulgaria signed an armistice in September, the Ottoman Empire followed in late October, and Germany faced revolution in November. Austria-Hungary, starving and fracturing from within, could not continue the fight alone.

19.10.2 Declaration of Independent National Councils

As defeat loomed, various national councils within the empire declared independence:

- **Czechoslovakia**: On October 28, 1918, Czech and Slovak leaders in Prague proclaimed the new Czechoslovak Republic.
- **South Slavs**: Slovene, Croat, and Serb representatives formed a "State of Slovenes, Croats, and Serbs," eventually merging with Serbia.
- **Poland**: Poles in Galicia joined with Polish territories from Russia and Germany, restoring Poland's independence after over a century of partition.
- **German Austria**: German-speaking deputies in Vienna discussed forming a "German-Austrian" state separate from the monarchy.

Karl I's attempt to reorganize the empire into a federation on October 16, 1918, came too late. National councils simply brushed aside these belated concessions, forging their new states.

19.11 Armistice and the Empire's Dissolution

19.11.1 The Armistice of Villa Giusti (November 3, 1918)

On the Italian Front, the monarchy's forces collapsed after the Allied victory at **Vittorio Veneto** in late October 1918. Austria-Hungary signed an armistice at **Villa Giusti** near Padua on November 3, 1918, effectively ending hostilities. With this capitulation, the monarchy disintegrated. Troops abandoned the front, rushing home to newly declared national states or to uncertain futures in an empire that no longer existed.

19.11.2 Emperor Karl's Abdication of Power

On November 11, 1918—two days after Kaiser Wilhelm II abdicated in Germany—Karl I "renounced participation" in state affairs. He did not formally abdicate his throne but withdrew from government, hoping a future plebiscite might restore him. However, the empire had already vanished in practice. Various successor states declared themselves republics or monarchies independent of Habsburg rule.

On November 12, the **Republic of German-Austria** was proclaimed in Vienna, severing the last ties to the Habsburg monarchy in Austrian lands. Karl would briefly attempt to reclaim the Hungarian throne in 1921 but failed, eventually dying in exile in 1922. Thus ended nearly seven centuries of Habsburg dominion over Central Europe.

19.12 Consequences of the War for Austria

The war wrought tremendous suffering across Austria:

1. **Casualties**: Austro-Hungarian forces lost around 1.2 million dead from battle, disease, or captivity, with many more wounded. Civilians succumbed to hunger, influenza epidemics, and harsh winters.
2. **Economic Ruin**: Hyperinflation set in, as the monarchy's war finances collapsed. Industrial output fell, farmland was devastated, and infrastructure near frontline regions lay in shambles.
3. **Territorial Disintegration**: The empire's multinational composition dissolved into newly formed states—Czechoslovakia, Yugoslavia, Poland, a truncated "German-Austria," and more. Boundaries would be finalized at the postwar peace conferences.

As we will see in the next (final) chapter, Austria faced an entirely new reality after 1918, forging a small republic from the German-speaking heartlands once encompassed by a vast empire. Though we stop short of modern times, the seeds of interwar challenges were sown in the immediate chaos of the monarchy's collapse.

CHAPTER 20: CONCLUSION AND OVERVIEW OF POST-WAR SHIFTS

20.1 Introduction

World War I's end in November 1918 toppled the Habsburg monarchy, disintegrating the centuries-old empire into multiple successor states. For Austria, this meant the abrupt transition from the core of a vast realm to a small republic of predominantly German-speaking provinces. Bohemia, Moravia, Galicia, Hungary, Croatia, and other former crown lands formed or joined new countries. Although we stop well before modern times, it is necessary to briefly outline how Austria's immediate postwar environment shaped the final stage of our historical narrative.

This chapter provides a concluding overview of how the newly proclaimed **Republic of German-Austria** emerged from the old monarchy's ruins, the initial challenges it faced, and how the final treaties—particularly the **Treaty of Saint-Germain-en-Laye (1919)**—redrew Austria's borders. We also reflect on the broader significance of the Habsburg era, from medieval beginnings to the dramatic transformations after 1918. By stopping here, we leave Austria on the threshold of the 20th century's next tumultuous chapters, well aware that future events lie beyond our historical scope but are deeply influenced by the legacies left behind.

20.2 The Immediate Aftermath of the Empire's Collapse

20.2.1 Proclamation of German-Austria

Even before the armistice with Italy on November 3, 1918, local authorities and national councils assumed power in the monarchy's provinces. On November 12, the German-speaking deputies of the defunct imperial parliament in Vienna declared a provisional government for **German-Austria**, asserting it was now a republic and a part of the German national community. They envisioned uniting with Germany, though the Allied powers strongly opposed such an Anschluss at that point.

Karl Renner became the head of this provisional state council, tasked with maintaining order, feeding the populace, and negotiating with the victorious Allies. Hunger and chaos prevailed in Vienna, with many returning soldiers, rising inflation, and minimal police oversight. Workers formed councils reminiscent of revolutionary models seen elsewhere in Europe, but Austria's socialist leaders opted for parliamentary solutions rather than radical upheaval.

20.2.2 Social and Economic Collapse

The monarchy's currency lost much of its value overnight. Bank reserves were depleted, and the breakdown of imperial trade networks meant that Vienna, previously reliant on grain from Hungary, now struggled to import enough food. Many factories closed, lacking raw materials or markets. Meanwhile, returning soldiers and refugees from lost territories crowded urban centers, further stressing housing and public services.

To combat these crises, the provisional government enacted emergency measures: rationing continued, foreign loans were sought, and negotiations began with ex-crown lands about transitional trade arrangements. Yet nationalist tensions made cooperation challenging. In Bohemia or Hungary, new governments had little interest in sending supplies to Vienna except on their own terms.

20.3 The Treaty of Saint-Germain and the New Austrian Borders

20.3.1 Versailles and the Allied Framework

While Germany negotiated its peace at Versailles (June 1919), Austria's terms were settled separately with the Allies, culminating in the **Treaty of Saint-Germain-en-Laye** (signed September 10, 1919). Austria's delegates had little bargaining power, given the monarchy's defeat and the Allies' principle of dismantling Austria-Hungary.

Key outcomes:

- **Territorial Losses**:
    - **Bohemia, Moravia, Austrian Silesia** joined the new **Czechoslovakia**.
    - **Southern Tyrol (South Tyrol), Trentino, and Trieste** went to **Italy**.

- **Carniola** to the new **Kingdom of Serbs, Croats, and Slovenes** (later Yugoslavia).
- **Galicia** joined a restored **Poland**.
- **Bukovina** was assigned to **Romania** (a direct arrangement with the former crown land of Cisleithania's easternmost region).

- **Population**: The once over 50-million-strong empire was reduced to a German-Austrian remnant of roughly 6 million people.
- **Prohibition of Anschluss**: The treaty explicitly forbade unification with Germany without League of Nations consent, aiming to maintain a stable balance in Central Europe.

20.3.2 Consequences for the Austrian Republic

The new **Republic of Austria** encompassed only the predominantly German-speaking alpine and Danubian provinces: Lower Austria (including Vienna), Upper Austria, Salzburg, Tyrol (northern part), Vorarlberg, Styria, Carinthia (minus some Slovene-inhabited areas), and parts of Carniola or Lower Styria that remained after boundary plebiscites. This drastically reduced territory and population left Austria an economically fragile state. The Allies mandated reparations, though Austria's capacity to pay was minimal.

The treaty also recognized minority rights for Slovene and Croatian communities in southern Carinthia and Styria, though in practice tensions persisted. Carinthia held a plebiscite in 1920, voting to remain part of Austria despite Slovene claims.

20.4 The Fate of Emperor Karl and the End of the Habsburg Dynasty's Rule

20.4.1 Karl's Attempts at Hungarian Restoration

After renouncing political power in November 1918, Karl retreated to Switzerland. Twice in 1921, he tried to reclaim the throne of Hungary, where some royalist factions still supported the Habsburg monarchy. However, Regent Miklós Horthy refused to yield power, fearing Allied reprisals and internal chaos. Karl was thus expelled once more.

Subsequently, the Allied powers insisted that Hungary formally dethrone the Habsburgs. Karl died in exile on the Portuguese island of Madeira in April 1922, sealing the final end of Habsburg rule in both Austria and Hungary. A handful of Habsburg relatives remained, but the monarchy was effectively abolished.

20.4.2 Habsburg Legacy

Centuries of Habsburg reign concluded abruptly. While some Austrians still felt nostalgia for the empire and Emperor Karl's pious persona, the new republic strove to move forward with democratic institutions. Meanwhile, in successor states—Czechoslovakia, Yugoslavia, Poland, etc.—the monarchy's memory was mixed, overshadowed by new national identities.

20.5 Reflection on the Habsburg Multinational Experiment

20.5.1 Historical Significance

For over five centuries, the Habsburg family had been central to the political landscape of Central Europe. By the 19th century, Austria-Hungary represented an attempt—albeit imperfect—to govern a diverse realm of many languages, religions, and cultures under dynastic rule. Despite structural flaws, the empire also promoted cultural exchange, constructed railways linking distant lands, and oversaw significant modernization.

World War I exposed the monarchy's fragility. Its partial reforms failed to reconcile growing national aspirations or effectively organize for total war. The empire's dissolution offered a stark lesson in the limits of a dynastic order in an age of mass politics and nation-states.

20.5.2 Divergent Memories

Austrians and others in the empire's successor states carried distinct memories of Habsburg rule. Some recalled oppression, forced Germanization or Magyarization, and limited political rights. Others revered the monarchy for providing stability, a vibrant cultural scene in Vienna, and relative peace among fractious nationalities for long stretches. This duality of perspectives shaped interwar narratives in Central and Eastern Europe.

20.6 Austria's Postwar Challenges

Though we do not delve into truly modern developments, it is helpful to note the immediate challenges the Austrian Republic faced after 1919:

1. **Economic Hardship**: The rump Austrian state lost industrial regions (such as Bohemia), farmland (Hungary's grain), and key ports (Trieste). The era saw hyperinflation, unemployment, and reliance on foreign loans or aid programs.
2. **Political Polarization**: Parties ranged from Social Democrats—strong in Vienna—to conservative Christian Socials aligned with rural interests, to German nationalist groups advocating union with Germany (despite the treaty ban).
3. **Cultural and Social Shifts**: Vienna's intellectual and artistic scenes continued to flourish in certain respects, exemplified by the likes of Sigmund Freud and the Vienna Circle of philosophers. However, broader societal tensions over nationalism, class conflict, and the memory of war shaped daily life.

Austria thus emerged from the war drastically transformed, still searching for an identity that balanced German cultural affiliation with a new existence as a small, landlocked republic.

20.7 The Broader Legacy of Austria in Historical Perspective

Stepping back to consider the entire sweep of Austrian history we have covered, several key themes stand out:

- **Geographic Crossroads**: From its earliest Celtic and Roman influences, through the medieval formation under the Babenbergs, to the Habsburg ascent, Austria consistently served as a bridge between Western and Eastern Europe. Its terrain, notably the Danube and Alpine passes, shaped trade routes, migrations, and military campaigns.
- **Dynastic Continuity**: The Habsburgs, ruling for centuries, molded Austria into a central European power despite near-constant challenges—Reformation turmoil, Ottoman invasions, Napoleonic wars, and

19th-century revolutions. Their adept marriages and alliances built a multinational realm that thrived on compromise and evolving traditions, if never fully reconciling its diverse subjects' aspirations.

- **Cultural Achievements**: Austria contributed profoundly to European culture—music (Mozart, Haydn, Schubert, Strauss), architecture (Baroque magnificence in Vienna, Melk, and Salzburg), philosophy, and science (Vienna's universities and intellectual salons). Even under imperial censorship or conflict, creativity flourished.
- **Nationalism and Modernity**: The 19th century's wave of liberalism and nationalism fundamentally reshaped Austria. The compromise with Hungary (1867) delayed dissolution but could not quell all national demands. Ultimately, World War I's catastrophic strain and emerging self-determination principles undid the empire.
- **End of an Era**: By 1918, the dissolution of Austria-Hungary closed the chapter on centuries of dynastic empire-building in Central Europe, heralding a new era of nation-states. Austria itself became a small republic grappling with the legacy of imperial grandeur and the challenges of national identity.

20.8 Stopping Short of Modern Times

Our narrative halts here, at the dawn of a new Austrian republic in 1919. Further developments—like the interwar period's turbulence, the economic depression, the political crises of the 1930s, and eventual annexations—lie beyond the scope of this historical overview. But it is clear that the radical transformations set in motion by World War I and the monarchy's collapse would shape the next chapters of Austrian history.

20.9 Concluding Reflections

From prehistoric settlements along the Danube to the creation of a vast medieval duchy under the Babenbergs, from the rise and dominance of the Habsburgs to the forging and downfall of Austria-Hungary, Austria's history is a tapestry of resilience, adaptation, and cultural richness. Over centuries, Austria stood at the center of Continental politics, bridging Latin Christendom with Slavic and Balkan frontiers, forging alliances and dynastic expansions that made it a European powerhouse.

The 19th century introduced new ideologies—liberalism, nationalism, socialism—that eroded the monarchy's feudal pillars. Austria's responses—Metternich's conservative order, partial constitutionalism after 1867, and the eventual war—proved unable to contain these seismic shifts. By the war's end, the old empire had vanished, giving birth to a host of successor states charting their own courses.

Austria, stripped of empire, faced the future as a modest republic, discovering the challenges of forging national identity among a German-speaking populace newly cut off from centuries of imperial dominion. Thus, our story leaves Austria at the crossroads of a tumultuous 20th century. While the monarchy's legacy echoes in architecture, cultural memory, and the historical consciousness of Central Europe, the abrupt changes of 1918–1919 forever altered Austria's place in the world.

With that, we conclude our sweeping history of Austria, stopping just before it navigates the fully modern era. The foundation laid by these centuries—from Celtic tribes and Roman provinces, through medieval duchies, the grand Habsburg monarchy, and its collapse in World War I—remains vital to understanding Austria's identity and its continuing role in European heritage.

Help Us Share Your Thoughts!

Dear reader,

Thank you for spending your time with this book. We hope it brought you enjoyment and a few new ideas to think about. If there was anything that didn't work for you, or if you have suggestions on how we can improve, please let us know at **kontakt@skriuwer.com**. Your feedback means a lot to us and helps us make our books even better.

If you enjoyed this book, we would be very grateful if you left a review on the site where you purchased it. Your review not only helps other readers find our books, but also encourages us to keep creating more stories and materials that you'll love.

By choosing Skriuwer, you're also supporting **Frisian**—a minority language mainly spoken in the northern Netherlands. Although **Frisian** has a rich history, the number of speakers is shrinking, and it's at risk of dying out. Your purchase helps fund resources to preserve and promote this language, such as educational programs and learning tools. If you'd like to learn more about Frisian or even start learning it yourself, please visit **www.learnfrisian.com**.

Thank you for being part of our community. We look forward to sharing more books with you in the future.

Warm regards,
The Skriuwer Team

Printed in Dunstable, United Kingdom

64182513R00125